Mil Mi-8/M

Rotary-Wing Workhorse and Warhorse

Yefim Gordon
and Dmitriy Komissarov

MIDLAND
An imprint of
Ian Allan Publishing

Mil' Mi-8/Mi-17:
Rotary-Wing Workhorse and Warhorse

ISBN 1 85780 161 X

Published by Midland Publishing
4 Watling Drive, Hinckley, LE10 3EY, England
Tel: 01455 254 490 Fax: 01455 254 495
E-mail: midlandbooks@compuserve.com

Midland Publishing is an imprint of
Ian Allan Publishing Ltd

Worldwide distribution (except North America):
Midland Counties Publications
4 Watling Drive, Hinckley, LE10 3EY, England
Telephone: 01455 254 450 Fax: 01455 233 737
E-mail: midlandbooks@compuserve.com
www.midlandcountiessuperstore.com

North American trade distribution:
Specialty Press Publishers & Wholesalers Inc.
39966 Grand Avenue, North Branch, MN 55056, USA
Tel: 651 277 1400 Fax: 651 277 1203
Toll free telephone: 800 895 4585
www.specialtypress.com

Design concept and layout by
Polygon Press Ltd. (Moscow,Russia)
Line drawings by G.F.Petrov and S.D.Komissarov

This book is illustrated with photos by Yefim Gordon, Dmitriy Komissarov, Sergey Komissarov, Dmitriy Petrochenko, Nikolay Ionkin, Lutz Freundt, Thomas Girke, Peter Davison, T. Shia, Simon Watson, Carlo Kuit, Etienne Zammit, Waclaw Holys, ITAR-TASS, as well as from the archives of the Mil' Moscow Helicopter Plant, Kazan' Helicopters, the Ulan-Ude Aircraft Factory, *Aviatsiya* and *Vertolyot* magazines, Yefim Gordon, Sergey and Dmitriy Komissarov, and the Russian Aviation Research Trust

Printed in England by Ian Allan Printing Ltd
Riverdene Business Park, Molesey Road,
Hersham, Surrey, KT12 4RG

Contents

Front cover illustration:
The 'Terminator' – Mi-8AMTSh RA-25755 No.3 (c/n 59489611121) – in original configuration at the MAKS-97 airshow with 'U-UAZ' titles.

Rear cover illustrations:
Top: Bulgarian Air Force Mi-17 '407 Black' (c/n 103M07?) in ex-UNPF colours; bottom: Mi-171Sh '14987' (c/n 59489614987?) at the MAKS-2001.

Title page illustration: A Russian Army Mi-8MT armed with two UPK-23-250 cannon pods and two B-8V20 rocket pods. Note the mounting platform for the Mak-UFM missile warning system (MWS) sensor under the port clamshell cargo door; the sensor itself is missing.

Below: '23 Yellow', a Ukrainian Air Force armed Mi-8T (1968-model Mi-8TV) upgraded by the Aviakon company, at Kiev-Svyatoshino in September 2000 during the Aviasvit-XXI airshow. Note the blade aerial on the tailboom indicative of an upgraded communications suite.

Introduction

There are not very many aircraft types in world aviation history which may be termed classic aircraft – not in the 'vintage and warbird' sense of the phrase but rather as a measure of the impact they had on the air transport or military aviation of their time. Among fighters the true classics are the Supermarine Spitfire and its chief adversary, the Messerschmitt Bf 109; if we look to more recent times, we should mention the North American F-86 Sabre and the Mikoyan MiG-15 (another pair of adversaries), the Dassault Mirage III and the Sukhoi Su-27 family. The classics among airliners and transport aircraft include such famous designs as the Antonov An-2, Douglas DC-3/C-47 Dakota and Boeing 707.

When it comes to rotary-wing aircraft, the subject of this book, the Mi-8 developed by the famous design bureau under Mikhail Leont'yevich Mil', has doubtless earned a place in aviation history's hall of fame. Consider this: the Mi-8 is probably the world's only helicopter to find use in every single type of mission that helicopters are designed to fulfil. These include scheduled passenger services, VIP transportation, cargo carriage, flying crane work, military transport and assault missions, close air support of troops on the battlefield, search and rescue (SAR), firefighting and much more.

First flown more than 40 years ago, the Mi-8 proved to be a uniquely adaptable design with tremendous upgrade and modification potential. New versions are still appearing, as various international airshows in which the Mi-8 participates testify, and the latest variants are much more capable than the progenitor of the family. The helicopter's considerable capabilities and mission flexibility turned it into one of the bestsellers among Soviet/Russian aircraft, which it remains to this day. As of now, the Mi-8/Mi-17 family has been delivered to more than 50 nations worldwide, including some which certainly were not among the traditional operators of Soviet hardware – such as Japan and the USA. Even now, this extremely popular helicopter remains one of Russia's chief high-technology export products, bringing in substantial earnings in hard currency.

The demand for the Mi-8 both on the home market and for export proved to be so high that, as of this writing, the two factories producing the Mi-8/Mi-17 family – the Kazan' Helicopter Plant and the Ulan-Ude Aircraft Production Association – have manufactured more than 11,000 (!) copies of various versions (approximately 7,300 have been built in Kazan' and 3,800 in Ulan-Ude); of these, more than 4,000 have been delivered abroad. This makes the Mi-8 the world's most widespread helicopter in its size/weight class by a substantial margin. In contrast, the famous Sikorsky Aircraft Company and its overseas partners have manufactured only 1,500 S-61/H-3 Sea King/Westland Sea King/Westland Commando helicopters and 2,000-plus S-70 (H-60 Black Hawk/Seahawk) military helicopters. Boeing Vertol and Kawasaki built only 740 V-107 (H-46 Sea Knight)/KV-107 II transport helicopters between them, while production of the Aérospatiale SA 321 Super Frelon in France and China (where it was known as the Changhe Z-8) totalled a mere 105 aircraft.

The Mi-8 was conceived as a replacement for the piston-engined Mi-4. This is CCCP-31537 No.1, an early-production Mi-4P passenger helicopter identifiable by the small rectangular cabin windows (which were enlarged on later Mi-4Ps) and wheel spats. The registration later passed to an Antonov An-2 biplane.

One of the Mi-4's Western contemporaries and counterparts was the Sikorsky S-58 having the same powerplant arrangement. This is Belgian Air Force B4/OT-ZKD at RAF Greenham Common in 1981; the type was retired in October of that year.

The Vertol V-107 twin-turbine helicopter was a contemporary of the original Mi-8 and was comparable in performance, if not in layout. This is a US Navy CH-46D Sea Knight, BuNo 153412/'SA' of the HC-3 transport helicopter squadron.

The larger, three-engined Aérospatiale SA 321 Super frelon (illustrated here by French Navy 32 Flotille SA 321G '118' at the Royal International Air Tattoo 2002) was built in a mere 105 examples.

Consider also that the Mi-8's record figure is not final yet, as the type is still in production after all these years, having entered large-scale production back in 1966. (Nearly 40 years of production – that's a record of longevity in itself.)

In terms of sheer numbers the Mi-8/Mi-17 family ranks second only to the Bell 204/205/212 (UH-1 Huey)/214/412 family of single/twin-engined light utility helicopters used for a host of applications, including CAS and anti-submarine warfare; of these, nearly 14,000 have been built, including licence production in Germany by Dornier, in Italy by Agusta, in Japan by Fuji and in Taiwan by AIDC. However, these aircraft belong in a different class, with an empty weight ranging from 2.75 tons (6,060 lb) for the Bell 204 to 2.93 tons (6,740 lb) for the Bell 212 and a maximum take-off weight of 5.5 tons (12,125 lb) for the Bell 204 to 7.94 tons (17,500 lb) for the Bell 214ST Super Transport. Besides, as far as aggregate airframe weight (ie, single airframe weight multiplied by the number of machines built) and aggregate payload are concerned, the Mi-8 remains unsurpassed in the history of world helicopter construction.

The Mi-8 has seen service from pole to pole. Apart from the abovementioned 50-odd customer nations, there is hardly a country in the world where this helicopter has not been operated in this or that capacity at some time or other. Frequently it served as an instrument of death and destruction, participating in numerous armed conflicts; just as often, however, the Mi-8 served exactly the opposite purpose, operating relief and peacekeeping missions for the United Nations.

The Mi-8 has been described by many as Mikhail L. Mil's greatest achievement and 'a design which is difficult to surpass'. There is reason behind this opinion.

Acknowledgements

The authors would like to say that the *50 Years of the Mil' Moscow Helicopter Plant* book, the four-volume work *Sowjetische Fliegerkräfte in Deutschland* by Lutz Freundt and the book *The Hot Skies of Afghanistan* by Viktor V. Markovskiy were most helpful in making this book. The *Half a Century Soviet Transports* reference book (Peter Hillman, Stuart Jessup, Guus Ottenhof and Tony Morris) and the monthly updates in *Scramble* magazine have also been extremely useful for visualising the geography of Mi-8 deliveries all over the world. Thanks go to the CIS Interstate Aviation Committee for providing access to the official records of civil Mi-8s, which allowed accident causes to be analysed and operational details included. Finally, the authors wish to thank Peter Davison for the colour slides he kindly supplied.

Chapter 1

The Mi-8 is Born

The mid-1950s were characterised, among other things, by the advent of gas turbine engines for helicopters (turboshaft engines), which sparked the development of second-generation rotary-wing aircraft. The Soviet Union was quick to follow the new trend; the first turbine-powered helicopters to be designed on Soviet soil were the mighty Mi-6 'big lifter' developed by OKB-329 under Mikhail Leont'yevich Mil' (first flight, 5th July 1957) and the much smaller and highly specialised Ka-25 anti-submarine warfare (ASW) helicopter brought out by Nikolay Il'yich Kamov's OKB in 1960. (OKB = ***op**ytno-kon**strook**torskoye byu**ro*** – Experimental Design Bureau.) By the end of the decade, however, the need for a different aircraft – a medium-lift transport and passenger helicopter to replace the obsolescent Mi-4 multi-role helicopter – became increasingly acute in the Soviet Union. Hence as early as 1957 the engineers of OKB-329 began drawing up preliminary specifications and design parameters for a new turbine-powered medium-lift helicopter. Importantly, the successor to the Mi-4 was conceived as a twin-engined helicopter from the outset (although, as you will see, it proved impossible to put this concept into practice immediately); this ensured the future helicopter high performance and enhanced flight safety in the event of a single-engine failure.

Mikhail L. Mil', the founder of the Soviet Union's (and now Russia's) most famous helicopter design bureau.

It is a well-known – and unfortunate – fact that the Soviet aircraft industry was underfunded in the late 1950s/early 1960s because the burgeoning space and missile industry enjoyed top priority due to the Soviet leader Nikita S. Khrushchov's famous 'missile itch'. If fixed-wing aircraft design and production had low priority at the time, the helicopter manufacturers were even worse off, having to make do with, figuratively speaking, scraps from the aircraft makers' table. Hence, in order to obtain a government order for the development of a new helicopter (and accordingly secure funding for same), Mikhail L. Mil' had to resort to cunning, passing the project off as a 'massive upgrade of the existing Mi-4'. The 'upgrade' capitalised on substituting the single 1,700-hp Shvetsov ASh-82V nine-cylinder air-cooled radial engine by two turboshafts and incorporating a new forward and centre fuselage. (This alone makes the 'massive upgrade' statement rather tenuous; with design changes on this scale, obviously you get an all-new helicopter! Anyway, the trick worked – and it is just as well that it did, or the world would have been the poorer by the loss of an excellent helicopter.) The other airframe components (ie, the tailboom), as well as the rotor system, most of the power train, the control system, the landing gear and so on would be borrowed from the Mi-4 in almost unchanged form.

The general arrangement of the new helicopter followed that of the Mi-6, with the engines placed side by side above the cabin ahead of the main gearbox; accordingly the flightdeck was relocated to the extreme nose to maximise the pilots' field of view and facilitate access. (On the Mi-4 it was vice versa: the engine was housed in the extreme nose, while the flightdeck was located above and behind it, the drive shaft to the main gearbox passing between the pilots.) The new layout maximised cargo cabin volume, allowing more people and/or new and bulkier military hardware, including vehicles, to be carried. Right from the start the engineers envisaged a whole family of helicopters; the baseline transport/assault version would be supplemented by a passenger 'helibus', an ASW version and a luxuriously appointed VIP version for government use. The latter version was attached high priority because US President Dwight D. Eisenhower was due to visit Moscow shortly.

The Soviet Ministry of Civil Aviation (MGA – *Mini**ster**stvo grazh**dahn**skoy avi**aht**sii*) was the first to show interest in the new helicopter; later it gained support from the top command of the Soviet Air Force (VVS – *Vo**yen**no-voz**doosh**nyye **see**ly*). At the insistence of MGA the Soviet Council of Ministers issued a directive on 20th February 1958 tasking the Mil' OKB with creating a helicopter with a payload of 1.5 to 2.0 tons (3,310-4,410 lb) provisionally designated V-8. The V stood for *verto**lyot*** (helicopter); it was common practice at OKB-329 to designate development aircraft with the letter V, and the Mi designation prefix derived from the Chief

Above: Close-up of the display model on the previous page depicting an early project configuration of the V-8. Note the twin engines, the long fuselage with seven cabin windows, the wings offloading the main rotor, the faired swashplate, the retractable landing gear and the T-tail.

Designer's last name was used if and when the helicopter achieved production status.

According to the said directive the V-8 was to be powered by... a single 1,900-shp Ivchenko AI-24V engine developed by Aleksandr G. Ivchenko's OKB-478 in Zaporozhye, the Ukraine. The AI-24V (*verto**lyot**nyy* – helicopter version) was a derated version of the 2,400-ehp AI-24 turboprop which had been created for the Antonov An-24 short-haul airliner then under development; 1,900 shp was considered to be adequate for the V-8, allowing the transmission of its predecessor to be retained.

Now that the V-8 received 'official status', full-scale development (FSD) of the single-engined version got under way at the Mil' OKB. G. V. Remezov was chief project engineer at first (years later he was succeeded in this capacity by V. A. Nikiforov), with Deputy Chief Designer V. A. Kuznetsov performing overall programme guidance. The advanced development project (ADP) and full-scale mock-up were duly reviewed and approved in 1959, whereupon the detail design stage could begin.

Right from the start the Mil' OKB was unhappy with the clause specifying a single-engine powerplant for the V-8, as the twin-engined version would be more reliable and safer in operation. Besides, the specific fuel consumption (SFC) of the AI-24V left a lot to be desired. Admittedly this involved developing an all-new main gearbox, which was a lengthy process; still, eventually Mikhail L. Mil' succeeded in convincing the chiefs of MGA and the State Committee for Aviation Hardware (GKAT – *Gosoo**dar**stvennyy komi**tet** po aviatsi**on**noy **tekh**nike*) that it would be expedient to concentrate efforts on a twin-engined version to be operated in airline service. This argument was all the more effective because the Soviet government wanted a comfortable VIP helicopter and the safety of the nation's leaders should not be compromised. (Note: In 1957, when the aircraft industry was subordinated to the Ministry of Defence Industry (MOP – *Mini**ster**stvo obo**ron**noy pro**myshlen**nosti*), the Ministry of Aircraft Industry (MAP – *Mini**ster**stvo aviatsi**on**noy pro**myshlen**nosti*) lost its ministerial status together with several other ministries and was 'demoted' to GKAT because of Khruschchov's disdainful attitude to manned aircraft. However, when Khruschchov had been unseated in 1965 and Leonid I. Brezhnev became head of state, the ministry regained its original name and 'rank'.)

The main problem was that no suitable turboshaft engine (ie, combining adequate power with an acceptable SFC) existed for a twin-engined version of the V-8 at the time. Hence the Council of Ministers had to issue a special directive tasking several engine design bureaux with developing a turboshaft rated at 1,250 shp. The Leningrad-based OKB-117 headed by Sergey Petrovich Izotov showed the greatest interest in this job, undertaking to develop not only the engine itself but also the V-8's new two-shaft main gearbox. Now all prerequisites for the development of the new twin-engined medium-lift helicopter offering higher capacity, a greater payload and higher safety were on hand.

OKB-329 proceeded with the design of the twin-engined version designated V-8A in parallel with the development of the original V-8. A Council of Ministers directive to this effect appeared on 30th May 1960 after the preliminary design stage and full-scale mock-up construction had been completed.

MAP factory No.329 in the settlement of Panki a short way south of Moscow, which

Above: The unregistered first prototype V-8 (c/n 0101?) – the only one to fly with this designation – pictured in its maiden flight on 24th June 1961. The real thing has six windows on each side. Note the red cheatline, the L-shaped pitots ahead of the nose gear unit and the L-shaped communications aerial further aft.

Two more shots of the V-8 as it comes in to land. These views illustrate the single engine, the car-type flightdeck doors and the hinged cabin door,. Note also the 'towel rail' aerial running around the fuselage, the radio altimeter dipole aerials under the tailboom, the single landing light and the short tail bumper.

Above and below: In 1965 the V-8 was put on display at the Economic Achievements Exhibition (VDNKh) in Moscow. Note the repositioned pitots, the addition of wheel spats on the mainwheels and the revised colour scheme. The plaque on the guardrail around the chopper carried the type in Cyrillic characters (B-8).

hosted Mil's design team, possessed only limited production facilities and was not in a position to undertake prototype construction. Hence the fuselages and other principal components of five V-8 development aircraft were manufactured by what was then MAP aircraft factory No.23 in Fili on the Western outskirts of Moscow which built the Mi-6. (The plant later fell victim to Khruschchov's 'missilisation' and was transferred to the Ministry of General Machinery responsible for the Soviet space and missile programmes.) From there the airframe components were delivered to plant No.329 for final assembly.

V-8 single-engined passenger helicopter prototype

In the process of ADP and detail design the engineers of OKB-329 modernised not only the Mi-4's power train but also several other components and systems. Among other things, the four-unit landing gear characteristic of the Mi-4 gave way to a tricycle gear with a twin-wheel castoring nose unit and long-stroke pyramidal main units fitted with single wheels. The tail rotor pylon was provided with a fin-like fairing; the friction-type dampers of the main rotor's drag hinges gave way to hydraulic dampers, the hydraulic actuators of all four control circuits were mounted in a single hydraulic package on the main gearbox together with other parts of the hydraulic system. The alcohol de-icing system on the main and tail rotor blades was replaced by electric de-icing, artificial feel units and electric trimming units were incorporated into the control system and so on.

Bearing no registration, the first prototype V-8 (presumably c/n 0101 – ie, Batch 01, first aircraft in the batch) was completed by June 1961. It was powered by a single AI-24V, featuring Mi-4 main and tail rotors (the main rotor was four-bladed, while the three-bladed tail rotor had wooden blades tapering towards the tips). This was a forced measure; the Mi-4's rotor system, the swashplate and many other control system and transmission components, the main landing gear units, the tailboom/tail rotor pylon and the tail bumper were borrowed in 'as-was' condition because the programme was running behind schedule, leaving no time to incorporate all intended improvements.

The forward and centre fuselage (which were of all-metal semi-monocoque construction) were all-new as compared to the Mi-4; among other things, for the first time in Soviet helicopter design practice the fuselage made use of large extruded duralumin parts and utilised bonded/welded joints alongside traditional rivet and bolted joints.

The crew of three (captain, co-pilot/navigator and flight engineer) sat in a spacious flightdeck occupying the forward fuselage; the flight engineer sat between and slightly aft of the pilots on a jump seat in the passage leading to the cabin. The extensively glazed flightdeck was accessed via car-type doors on both sides. The original preliminary design project envisaged a stepped nose similar to that of the Mi-6, but this was abandoned in favour of a characteristic rounded nose profile, with two-tier wraparound glazing.

The centre fuselage accommodated a cargo/passenger cabin measuring 5.34 x 2.34 x 1.8 m (17 ft 6¼ in x 7 ft 8 in x 5 ft 11¾ in), with full-width clamshell cargo doors at the rear; as on the Mi-4, the hinge line was at right angles to the fuselage waterline. There was a forward-hinged, outward-opening entry door to port just aft of the flightdeck, with detachable boarding steps. Additionally, the cargo doors featured a large cutout on the centreline closed by a horizontally split passenger door whose upper portion swung upwards into the roof while the lower portion hinged down to act as airstairs. Like the Mi-4P passenger helicopter, the V-8 featured large rectangular cabin windows.

The engine was mounted above the cabin, breathing through a circular air intake and exhausting via a bifurcated exhaust pipe. Further aft was the main gearbox and service tank enclosed by a common large fairing. Continuing the policy manifested on earlier large helicopters of the Mil' OKB, the engine/gearbox cowling panels were stressed to serve as work platforms for maintenance in the field. Two streamlined external fuel tanks were strapped on low on the fuselage sides. The tailboom featured ground-adjustable stabilisers.

The V-8 could carry cargoes weighing up to 2 tons (4,410 lb) internally. Vehicles and other cargoes could be loaded and unloaded, using detachable loading ramps. To facilitate handling non-self-propelled bulky cargoes the cabin floor incorporated rollers and tie-down cleats, plus a loading winch at the front; provision was made for installing a rescue hoist of 150 kg (330 lb) capacity near the entry door. A hinge-and-pendulum type external sling enabled the carriage of slung loads weighing up to 2.5 tons (5,510 lb).

The first prototype was completed in 'heliliner' configuration with 18 comfortable seats (mostly four-abreast) and had a range of 450 km (280 miles). For shorter routes a 23-seat high-density layout was proposed. The military transport/assault version featured tip-up seats for 14 troops along the cabin walls; in casualty evacuation (CASEVAC) configuration the V-8 could transport 12 stretcher patients and a medical attendant.

The single-engined V-8 successfully performed its maiden flight on 24th June 1961 at the hands of test pilot Boris V. Zemskov. The manufacturer's flight tests went smoothly, but Chief Designer Mikhail L. Mil' was in no hurry to deliver the helicopter for State acceptance trials because he had already placed his bets on the twin-engined V-8A. The first prototype was thus used mostly as a demonstrator. On 9th July 1961, a mere two weeks after the first flight the still unregistered aircraft took part in the annual air fest at Moscow-Tushino airfield, watched by thousands of spectators and the nation's leaders. Later the still unregistered helicopter was put on display at the VDNKh fairground (*__Vy__stavka __d__ostizheniy __n__arodnovo __kh__ozia__y__stva* – National Economy Achievements Exhibition) in Moscow. In December 1961 the V-8 left the VDNKh and was finally submitted for State acceptance trials – which, frankly, were of no real importance for the reason stated earlier; from 1963 onwards the single-engined prototype was used as a ground test rig until finally struck off charge and scrapped. (As a matter of fact, most of the aircraft visiting the fairground's central plaza were destined to fly no more.)

The second single-engined V-8 (c/n 0102?) was the static test airframe. The third airframe (c/n 0201) completed in November 1961 in single-engined configuration probably did not fly at all in this guise, serving initially as a fatigue test airframe.

V-8A twin-engined passenger helicopter prototype

In the summer of 1962 plant No.329 took delivery of the first shipset of two Izotov TV2-117 turboshafts and a VR-8 three-stage planetary main gearbox with a reduction ratio of 1:62.6. The TV2-117 was rated at 1,500 shp for take-off and had an acceptable SFC by the day's standards. Thus, two such engines gave the V-8A a power/weight ratio enabling the helicopter to maintain level flight in the event of a single-engine failure.

By this time the airframe of the V-8A was ready to take the new powerplant – the OKB had decided to convert the second prototype V-8 (c/n 0201) into the V-8A. The higher power to be transmitted to the rotors not only necessitated an all-new main gearbox but required other components of the power train to be reinforced; changes were also made to the upper centre fuselage (primarily in the form of new cowlings) and the main gearbox bearer. Also, the seating capacity of the passenger version was increased to 20.

On 2nd August 1962 the twin-engined prototype – likewise unregistered – made its first hover with test pilot N. V. Lyoshin at the controls, and the first real flight followed on 17th September. A few days later the V-8A, as well as the first prototype of the Mil' V-2 light utility helicopter (the future Mi-2; c/n 0101) was demonstrated to the Soviet leader Nikita S. Khruschchov and the leaders of the Warsaw Pact nations at Moscow's Central Airfield

Above and below: The second prototype, the V-8A (c/n 0201), as originally flown. The new powerplant is clearly visible but the rotor system borrowed from the Mi-4 is the same as on the V-8, as are the door design and the shape of the flightdeck glazing. Note the ventral cabin heater intake under the flightdeck.

Above and below: The V-8A modified by the addition of wheel spats but still with the old rotor system. This static view shows clearly the tapered wooden tail rotor blades. Note also that all flightdeck glazing panels in the upper row are curved.

АЭРОФЛОТ
Ми8

АЭРОФЛОТ
Ми8

Opposite page: The V-8A in further modified form with a five-bladed main rotor meant to reduce vibrations and increase lift, plus a new tail rotor featuring constant-chord metal blades; these features were introduced on the production version. Note also the different colour scheme; interestingly, the type is marked on the nose as 'Mi-8'.

This page, above: The upgraded V-8A ground running at Moscow-Vnukovo during a presentation for Soviet government officials in company with the V-2 first prototype, a Mi-6 transport helicopter and a Tupolev Tu-114 long-haul airliner. This view shows the small clamshell doors and rear airstair door. Note that the c/n is now painted on the tailboom aft of the stabiliser.

Right: Sabre-toothed helicopter. The prototypes lacked a transverse frame member in the lower row of the flightdeck glazing, which gave the V-8 and V-8A a rather hair-raising appearance in a head-on view. Note the household thermometer on the glazing frame and the bulged upper windows in both flightdeck doors.

Above: The V-8AT (c/n 0202), the prototype of the Mi-8T utility version, as first flown in 1963 (in Air Force markings and with hinged entry door).
Below: The same aircraft in 1964 with sliding entry door and faired main gear oleos. Note the redesigned flightdeck glazing featuring a machine-gun mount.

Above and below: Registered CCCP-06181, the V-8AP was built as a luxurious VIP helicopter. It was the prototype of the Mi-8P/Mi-8PS, combining the new flightdeck section with the rear end of the V-8A. Note the KO-50 cabin heater ahead of the starboard fuel tank and the anti-collision light on the tailboom.

The V-8AT in later civilian guise as CCCP-06182; the machine-gun mount has been removed. This was the sole 'first-generation' Mi-8 to be built with large clamshell doors and rectangular windows. Note the modified main rotor head and the window beneath the port sliding flightdeck window (deleted in production).

(better known as Khodynka). Both helicopters earned praise from the high-ranking guests.

Manufacturer's flight tests of the V-8A proceeded until the spring of 1963. Apart from Lyoshin, the second prototype was flown by G. V. Alfyorov, I. N. Dryndin, V. P. Koloshenko, Yu. S. Shvachko and other test pilots; A. Ya. Choolkov and V. A. Izakson-Yelizarov were the engineers in charge of the tests. Concurrently some of the helicopter's systems were put through their paces on a suitably converted Mi-4 systems testbed and installed on the V-8A as they were cleared for operation.

In March 1963 the yellow-painted V-8A wearing Aeroflot titles was submitted for Stage A of the joint State acceptance trials which, on the whole, proceeded smoothly, even though flights were suspended from time to time in order to make improvements and eliminate the faults discovered. For instance, in the summer of 1963 the machine was grounded for as long as two months while the engines and main gearbox were undergoing modifications.

Detail changes were constantly incorporated into the V-8A's design. For instance, the helicopter received an automatic engine control system maintaining constant main rotor speed within the prescribed limits and synchronising engine rpm. If one engine failed, the system automatically took the surviving engine to contingency rating. Soon after the beginning of the trials the original main rotor gave way to a new five-bladed main rotor of identical diameter intended to reduce vibration levels. This was accomplished by simply reducing the angle between the blades from 90° to 72° so as to insert a fifth blade; the basic design of the main rotor head remained unchanged. Concurrently the V-8A received an all-new tail rotor featuring all-metal constant-chord blades and an articulated head; the alcohol de-icing system was replaced by an electric one.

The main gear units were modified to feature twin-chamber shock absorbers and fairings on the oleo struts; the tail bumper was also modified. The flight control system incorporated an AP-34 four-channel autopilot which improved the helicopter's stability and handling considerably.

Unfortunately the trials programme, which generally proceeded smoothly, was marred by a tragic accident in January 1966 when the type had already entered full-scale production and service as the Mi-8. During one of the many test flights a bearing in the tail rotor disintegrated, rendering the V-8A uncontrollable; the helicopter crashed, killing captain N. V. Lyoshin, co-pilot I. N. Dryndin and flight engineer F. I. Novikov.

V-8AT transport/assault helicopter prototype

The third prototype (c/n 0202) was completed at plant No.329 in the summer of 1963 as the prototype of the V-8AT utility transport/assault version (the T stood for ***trahns****portnyy* – transport, used attributively). This helicopter incorporated all the refinements made in the course of the preceding trials.

The V-8AT had a redesigned forward fuselage section. The lateral flightdeck doors were deleted, giving place to aft-sliding trapezoidal windows; these were bulged to assist downward vision and could be jettisoned in an emergency. A small window remained beneath the port side (captain's) blister as a leftover from the window incorporated into the V-8A's flightdeck door. The shape of the flightdeck glazing (notably the lower row) was altered (among other things, the centre window incorporated a machine-gun mount) and the three centre panels in the upper row featured optically flat glass panes intended to reduce annoying view distortion. These panes were electrically de-iced.

The cabin entry door, which originally opened outwards (as on the V-8/V-8A), was soon replaced by an aft-sliding door which could likewise be jettisoned in an emergency. The rear clamshell doors were substantially enlarged, featuring a sloping hinge line and

Two views of the V-8AP with wheel spats fitted on display at the VDNKh in 1967 in company with a Mi-10 heavy-lift helicopter. This red/white/grey colour scheme was originally standard for Aeroflot Mi-8Ps, except for the different location of Mil' OKB logos port and starboard (due to the same small window to port).

cutouts in the bottom portions which were closed by integral vehicle loading ramps (though these were not incorporated on the production helicopter). The starboard half incorporated an emergency exit with a jettisonable cover which could be used for firing a machine-gun to provide self-defence against ground fire. Interestingly, the cabin windows were still rectangular, making a unique combination with the large cargo doors of the utility version. A KO-50 kerosene heater (*kero**sin**ovyy obogre**vah**tel'*) was installed in a fairing ahead of the starboard fuel tank.

The cabin featured tip-up seats along the walls for 20 troops, with provisions for seating four more in high gross weight configuration. It could accommodate a light field gun or a GAZ-69 army jeep, among other things; various payload configurations were tried out on a special cabin mock-up prior to the beginning of the trials. The fuselage sides incorporated attachment points for outriggers with pylons enabling the carriage of unguided weapons (bombs and rocket pods) in a similar way to the Mi-4AV.

Wearing olive green camouflage with pale blue undersides and Soviet Air Force star insignia (but no tactical code), the V-8AT joined the State acceptance trials programme after a brief period of manufacturer's flight tests, replacing the V-8A which was subsequently used as a development aircraft and a fatigue test airframe. In the course of the trials the main gear oleo fairings were removed by February 1964.

In the spring of 1964 the V-8AT was outfitted as a government VIP helicopter with a really posh cabin and special communications equipment, gaining a red/white/grey livery as worn by late-production Mi-4Ps operated by Aeroflot (the Soviet state airline) at the time and receiving the civil registration CCCP-06182. Later, when the custom-built V-8AP VIP helicopter (see next entry) joined the programme, the V-8AT was reconverted to transport configuration but retained its new civil identity.

V-8AP VIP helicopter prototype

In May 1964 the OKB's experimental shop completed the fifth and final development aircraft – the fourth flying prototype (c/n unknown) which was built from the start as the V-8AP VIP helicopter (P = *passa**zheer**skiy* – passenger, used attributively). Registered CCCP-06181 (this registration had apparently been reserved even before the V-8AT was modified as described above), the V-8AP wore the same red/white/grey Aeroflot livery and featured the same airframe changes, save that the rear end matched the V-8/V-8A, incorporating small clamshell doors-cum-airstair door. Thus outwardly CCCP-06181 was almost identical to the future production Mi-8P/Mi-8PS, except for the small window beneath the port side flightdeck blister which was deleted in production.

The V-8AP served as a testbed for the improved AP-34B autopilot and the main rotor speed governor. In September 1964 the helicopter was used in Stage B of the State acceptance trials alongside the reconverted V-8AT (CCCP-06182, see above). The helicopter fully lived up to the expectations, meeting the target performance figures. The payload of the twin-engined V-8 was twice that of the Mi-4, the top speed was 50% higher and economic efficiency was improved by a factor of three. Hence in November 1964 the State commission recommended the V-8 for mass production and the military version for service as the Mi-8.

In the winter of 1964-65 the V-8AP was converted to airline configuration with 20 comfortable seats, a coat closet and heat/soundproofing blankets lining the walls. The cabin was equipped with a new heating and air conditioning system and revised interior trim. In this guise the helicopter was tested by the State Civil Aviation Research Institute (GosNII GA – *Gosoo**dar**stvennyy na**ooch**no-is**sled**ovatel'skiy insti**toot** grazh**dahn**skoy avi**ah**tsii*) at Moscow-Sheremet'yevo; the trials were completed in March 1965 and the airline version was likewise recommended for production, entering service as the Mi-8P. In the spring of 1965 CCCP-06181 was converted again at plant No.329 to a 28-seat configuration which subsequently became standard for the Mi-8P.

All in all the four development aircraft (the V-8, V-8A, V-8AT and V-8AP) made a total of 140 test flights, logging 110 hours flight time between them. There were no major accidents during the manufacturer's test programme and State acceptance trials; this goes to show that the helicopter was carefully designed and well built, illustrating the high professionalism of the people who designed it (as already mentioned, the fatal crash of the second prototype occurred after the completion of the trials).

An in-flight shot of the V-8AP with spatted wheels, showing the open port side flightdeck window.

Chapter 2

The First Generation

Production and Updates

Unlike Western aircraft companies, the Soviet aircraft design bureaux did not have their own production plants (apart from limited prototype manufacturing facilities). When an aircraft was cleared for full-scale production, this took place at one of the production factories within the MAP framework (which, true enough, usually had strong ties to the respective OKB and was well familiar with its design practices). Thus, Mi-8 production was initially assigned to helicopter factory No.387 in Kazan', the capital of the Tatar Autonomous SSR, which was manufacturing the Mi-4 at the time. The Mil' OKB started issuing manufacturing drawings and other documents to the factory even as the Mi-8 was undergoing joint State acceptance trials; this allowed production to be set up very quickly, the first production Mi-8Ps rolling off the assembly line at Kazan'-Osnovnoy airport in late 1965. (The plant was later renamed Kazan' Helicopter Production Association (KVPO – *Kazahn-skoye vertolyotostroitel'noye proizvodstvennoye obyedineniye*); now its called Kazan' Helicopters.) The TV2-117 engine and the VR-8 main gearbox entered production at the Perm' engine factory No.19, MAP's northernmost enterprise, later called Perm' Engine Production Association named after Yakov M. Sverdlov (PPOM – *Permskoye proizvodstvennoye obyedineniye motorostroyeniya*; now the Permskiye Motory Joint-Stock Company).

As was the case with the Mi-4, early-production Kazan'-built Mi-8Ps and Mi-8Ts had construction numbers consisting of the aircraft's number in the batch, followed by the batch number; originally there were ten aircraft per batch, the quantity increasing to 20 from Batch 30 or 31 onwards until Batch 60 inclusive. For instance, Aeroflot Mi-8T CCCP-22514 manufactured on 13th March 1968 is c/n 0321 (the third helicopter in Batch 21, ie, the 203rd production aircraft). In January 1971 the factory switched to a different system with the batch number placed first; inexplicably, the lowest batch number under the new system was 21. From then on there were usually 99 (!) aircraft per batch; for example, Mi-8T CCCP-22359 manufactured on 28th May 1977 is c/n 7220, while Mi-8T CCCP-22395 manufactured on 31st October 1977 is c/n 7297. At least until 1974 the c/n was sometimes stencilled on the tailboom (again as on the Mi-4) but this practice was later discontinued for security reasons. Now the c/n is found on the inside of a maintenance panel on the port side of the fuselage.

1970 marked an important milestone in the Mi-8's career: the demand for the new helicopter proved to be so high that plant No.387 could no longer cope, and a second factory – No.99 in Ulan-Ude, the capital of the Buryat Autonomous SSR – joined in. This factory, now called Ulan-Ude Aircraft Production Association (U-UAPO – *Oolahn-oodenskoye aviatsionnoye proizvodstvennoye obyedineniye*), was unique among Soviet aircraft factories in that it produced both fixed-wing and rotary-wing aircraft at the same time. Interestingly, in Soviet times the Ulan-Ude aircraft factory appeared to produce only utility and assault versions, and most of them were delivered to the domestic market; most export Mi-8s were Kazan'-built. At both factories the Mi-8 was known in-house as *izdeliye* (product) 80 (see various versions below).

Originally the Ulan-Ude c/n system was straightforward; the first digit was always a 9 (the plant's number with the first digit omitted to confuse would-be spies), followed by the last two digits of the year of manufacture, the batch number and the aircraft's number in the batch. For instance, Krechet Airlines Mi-8T RA-93925 manufactured on 24th November 1974 is c/n 9744349.

In July 1981 the factory switched to an inscrutable system devised in 1973 (certainly by the KGB to make life even harder for spies!) and used by most Soviet aircraft factories. The batch number and the aircraft's number in the batch were replaced by five digits which do not signify *anything at all* so that the c/n does not reveal how many have been built. The first two digits of these 'famous last five', as they are often called, change independently from the final three. Such aircraft have four-digit fuselage numbers (f/ns); security is all very well but the manufacturer has to keep track of production, after all. For instance, Aeroflot Mi-8T CCCP-24699 manufactured on 29th September 1981 is c/n 98103227, and the f/n is probably 5809 (ie, it would have been c/n 9815809 if the 'rational' system had continued in use. 'Second-generation' versions had separate c/n systems which are explained separately.

The helicopter was constantly improved and upgraded in the course of production. For example, the capacity of the external fuel tanks was increased from an original 745 litres (163.9 Imp gal) for the port tank and 680 litres (149.6 Imp gal) for the starboard tank to 1,140 and 1,030 litres (250.8 and 226.6 Imp gal) respectively by extending the tanks' rear portions aft and enlarging the cross-section area. New avionics were integrated, a more powerful rescue hoist installed and so on.

As already mentioned, the two plants built more than 11,000 Mi-8s of all versions between them (7,300+ in Kazan', including more than 2,800 'second-generation' aircraft, and 3,800+ in Ulan-Ude). New civil and military versions were developed not only by OKB-329 (renamed the Mil' Moscow Helicopter Plant after the founder's death) but by the design offices of the production plants and by the operators themselves. For example, Finland and India have had some (or all) of their Mi-8s upgraded with Western weather radars; the helicopters in service with the air arms of some former Warsaw Pact nations have been made NATO compatible as these countries joined (or expected to join) the NATO. The total number of versions exceeds 120 (!) and it is utterly impossible to describe them all in a book of this size. Hence only the principal versions and some of the upgrades are described herein.

Mi-8T civil transport/military utility helicopter (*izdeliye* 80T)

The most widespread version (both among the 'first-generation' versions and in general) is the Mi-8T powered by two TV2-117A turboshafts with a take-off rating of 1,500 shp. Derived from the V-8AT prototype, the production version differs mainly in having circular cabin windows, all of which open inwards and upwards; on military examples this enables personnel sitting in the cabin to use their assault rifles, turning a seemingly innocuous transport helicopter into a 'battlebus'. Also, the integral vehicle loading ramps of the prototype proved to be a liability in some situations, precluding direct loading from a truck bed, so they were replaced by detachable ramps stored inside the cabin when not in use; each half of the rear clamshell doors now featured small triangular

Above: '65 Yellow', a production Mi-8T operated by the Russian Naval Air Arm (note the Russian Navy flag on the engine cowling) illustrates the circular cabin windows of the production version. The PKT machine-gun in the nose is noteworthy, as are the radar warning receiver blisters flanking the nose and the tail rotor pylon.

sections at the bottom which folded upwards and inwards manually to avoid encroaching on the cabin width during loading/unloading operations. Most (but not all) Mi-8Ts have a fairly large boxy fairing on the underside of the tailboom housing a DISS-2 Doppler speed/drift sensor (***dop**lerovskiy izme**rit**el' **sko**rosti i **sno**sa*).

The Mi-8T can carry internal loads weighing up to 4 tons (8,820 lb) and slung loads weighing up to 3 tons (6,610 lb). The cargo cabin is 5.34 m (17 ft 6¼ in) long, 2.25 m (7 ft 4½ in) wide and 1.8 m (5 ft 10⅞ in) high. As an alternative to cargo, it accommodates 24 passengers on tip-up seats along the walls or 12 stretcher patients (accompanied by a medical attendant); in the latter case special uprights are installed in the cabin, to which stretchers are fixed by special clamps.

The Mi-8T forms the backbone of the transport/utility helicopter fleet both in the CIS republics' civil aviation and in their armed forces. Kazan' production apparently ended in 1986 (the last confirmed example is

Above left: A 1968-model Mi-8TV with two weapons pylons on each side; the pylon mounting outriggers are supported by two faired struts. Note the arm of the rescue hoist above the entry door (the hoist itself is internal) and the lack of a nose machine-gun. In service this version was known simply as the Mi-8T.

Left: The open clamshell doors of a 1968-model Mi-8TV show the folding lower portions, the tool boxes with seats on top, the escape hatch in the starboard door and the vehicle loading ramps. When positioned as shown here they could be used for loading fuel drums and the like.

CCCP-06175, c/n 8621, manufactured on 16th January 1986 which was retained by the manufacturer). U-UAPO continued building the Mi-8T until at least 1999 (the last known example is RA-27012, c/n 99957729, manufactured on 14th May 1999, although RA-27021 manufactured at an earlier date has a higher c/n, 99757742).

The utility version had its international debut in 1969 when a Mi-8T with the non-standard registration CCCP-69316 and the exhibit code H-834 (the same as would be worn by a Mi-8P two years later!) was displayed at the 27th Paris Air Show. After that it received the NATO reporting name *Hip-C*.

Mi-8TV assault/transport helicopter (1968) (*izdeliye* 80TV)

From the outset the Mil' OKB had envisaged an armed assault/transport role for the V-8. Thus the Mi-8T was adapted to take the proven K-4V unguided weapons system used on the Mi-4AV assault/transport helicopter (ie, Mi-4A – *vo'oroo**zhon**nyy*, armed). The K-4V comprised four UB-16-57U rocket pods, each holding 16 KARS-57 (aka S-5) 57-mm (2.24-in) folding-fin aircraft rockets (FFARs). (K = ***kom**pleks* – in this case, integrated system; UB = *oonifi**tsee**rovannyy blok* – standardised [FFAR] pod; S = *sna**ryad*** – cannon shell or, as in this case, rocket projectile.) The pods were carried on four BD3-57KrV pylons mounted on truss-type outriggers attached to the centre fuselage sides; the pylons also permitted the carriage of bombs up to 500 kg (1,102 lb) calibre. (BD = ***bah**lochnyy der**zhah**tel'* – beam-type rack; Kr = *kryl'ye**voy*** – wing-mounted, V = *verto**lyot**nyy* – helicopter version. Thus, the designation means 'Group 3 weapons rack (ie, capable of carrying ordnance up to 500 kg calibre), 1957 model, adapted for helicopters'.

(Incidentally, all Mi-8Ts were built with attachment fittings for these outriggers, making sure that civil examples could be easily militarised in a war contingency. Later, some nations put this feature to good use, converting second-hand examples acquired on the civil market to armed configuration; for example, Lithuanian Air Force '03 Blue' is ex-RA-25770 No.1 (c/n 99254335; see Mi-8PS section!), while Djibouti Defence Force J2-MAM (c/n 3113) is ex-CCCP-25242.)

The lower centre window in the lower row of the flightdeck glazing was replaced by an NUV-1 gimballed mount (nosovaya oostanovka vertolyotnaya – nose-mounted helicopter [gun] installation) with a 7.62-mm (.30 calibre) Kalashnikov PKT machine-gun. The cargo/troop carrying capability was retained in full.

By analogy with its precursor the first armed version of the Mi-8 was known in-house as the Mi-8TV; however, this designation did not catch on at first, and in service the helicopters

Above: Head-on view of an armed Mi-8T ('1968-standard Mi-8TV') with four UB-16-57 FFAR pods. Note the boarding step under the starboard blister window, a feature of early-production examples.

Above and centre: This Mi-8T ('1968-standard Mi-8TV') features a different design of the weapons outriggers with additional bracing struts for more even load distribution and an external rescue hoist.

Above: The version which was actually referred to as Mi-8TV in Soviet Air Force service is the 'second-generation' Mi-8TV brought out in 1974.

Close-up of the weapons racks on a '1974-standard' Mi-8TV coded '52 Yellow' with three pylons on each side (carrying UB-32A FFAR pods in this case) and 2P32M launch rails for 9M17P Falanga-P ATGMs.

with two weapons pylons on each side were called simply Mi-8T – just like the unarmed utility version. Also, the machine-gun in the nose was not deemed necessary at first, and the four-pylon version retained the standard nose glazing in production form. Surprisingly, the NATO, too, referred to the armed version by the same reporting name as the pure transport version (*Hip-C*). However, there may be method to the madness – this may be based on the realisation that any Mi-8T can be armed if necessary!

For the development of the 'Mi-8TV Mk I' five Mil' OKB engineers – S. A. Kolupayev, V. A. Kuznetsov, Ye. V. Yablonskiy, A. S. Braverman and G. V. Remezov – were awarded the State Prize. The first armed version was supplied both to the Soviet Armed Forces and to the armies of 'friendly nations'.

Mi-8TV assault/transport helicopter (1974) (*izdeliye* 80TV)

In 1974 the Kazan' helicopter factory began production of a new and more heavily armed assault/transport derivative of the Mi-8T which inherited the designation of its predecessor, Mi-8TV. The 'Mi-8TV Mk II' featured three pylons on each side instead of two; not just that, they could carry larger FFAR pods – the 32-round UB-32, giving a total of 192 S-5 rockets versus 64 for the armed Mi-8T!

But that was not all. The new version had provisions for four 9M17P Falanga-P (Solifuge; NATO codename AT-2 *Swatter*) anti-tank guided missiles. The Falanga-P was a fairly big weapon with a semi-automatic command line-of-sight (SACLOS) guidance system (the P stood for ***po**luavtoma**tich**eskoye nave**den**iye* – semi-automatic guidance). The ATGMs were carried on 2P32M launch rails on top of the weapons outriggers and aimed by the co-pilot/weapons systems officer, using a gyrostabilised sight. The nose-mounted machine-gun was reinstated. (Thus the 'Mi-8TV Mk II' is one of the most heavily armed helicopters, which has led some authors to decipher the TV suffix as *tya**zhol**oye vo'oroo**zhe**niye*, heavy armament.)

This time the Mi-8TV designation was recognised by the Soviet Air Force. The West, too, could not ignore the obvious and the 'Mi-8TV Mk II' was allocated a new reporting name, *Hip-E*. It has to be said that the six-pylon Mi-8TV should really be described as an 'assault **or** transport version', since with a full ordnance load the helicopter became overweight and sluggish and could no longer carry troops or cargo in the cabin.

Mi-8TVK export assault/transport helicopter (*izdeliye* 80TVK)

A special version of the six-pylon Mi-8TV was developed for export as the Mi-8TVK, the K standing for *kom**mer**cheskiy* (commercial – ie, 'customer version'). It differed from the domestic version in being armed with six 9M14M Malyutka (Baby; NATO codename AT-3 *Sagger*) wire-guided ATGMs instead of four Falanga-Ps. The export version was supplied to East Germany and other Soviet allies.

Interestingly, in the foreign press (and to a certain extent in the Soviet press as well) the Mi-8TV and Mi-8TVK have often been misidentified as the Mi-8TB and Mi-8TBK respectively, the B purportedly standing for *broni**rov**annyy* (armour-plated) or *boye**voy*** (combat, used attributively). This error is probably explained by the Cyrillic letter V (the third letter of the Russian alphabet) being identical to the Roman letter B; the erroneous designations originating in the military press of the Warsaw Pact nations were then 'borrowed' by the Soviet press. Of course, the Soviet officials (who were past masters at classifying things and pulling the wool over the eyes) had no objections to this misinformation...

Mi-8P passenger helicopter (*izdeliye* 80P)

As already mentioned, in its final configuration the V-8AP (CCCP-06181) became the prototype of the Mi-8P passenger helicopter; the production version differed mainly in having an emergency exit incorporated into the rearmost cabin window on each side and in lacking the small window beneath the captain's sliding blister window. A few examples have the ventral DISS-2 fairing under the tailboom.

The baseline version seated 28 (seven rows of double seats) and was used on feeder routes. Later, more comfortable 20-, 24- and 26-seat versions were brought out. If necessary the helicopter could carry cargo in the cabin (in which case the seats were removed) or on a sling; the payload limits were the same as for the Mi-8T – 4 tons (8,820 lb) internally or 3 tons (6,610 lb) externally.

The Mi-8P made its international debut at the 25th Paris Air Show in June 1965. Two years later a Mi-8P with the non-standard registration CCCP-11052 (the first to have this registration; c/n 0403) was displayed at the 26th Paris Air Show with the exhibit code H-242, wearing a non-standard colour scheme remarkably similar to Aeroflot's later standard livery. (This registration was later reused for an Ulan-Ude built Mi-8T c/n 9732810.) The helicopter attracted considerable interest and earned high praise from Western aviation experts who deemed it to be one of the best medium-lift helicopters. The Mi-8P was demonstrated with equal success at a trade fair in Copenhagen a few months later. In 1971 the static park at the 28th Paris Air Show included another Mi-8P in the same livery with the non-standard registration CCCP-11097 and the exhibit code H-834.

Most Mi-8Ps were Kazan'-built, production continuing until 1993 when the Mi-8T had long since been superseded on the Kazan' production line by the Mi-8MT *et seq.*; the last known example is RA-22512 (c/n 8707). According to some sources the passenger version was powered by TV2-117AT engines rated at 1,700 shp (1,250 kW) for take-off; this probably applies to late-production aircraft.

Above and below: Mi-8P CCCP-11052 No.1 (c/n 0403) was the example that made the type's international debut at Le Bourget in 1965. Note the exhibit code H-242 and the flightdeck boarding step/kick step.

Mi-8P CCCP-11097 in the same colour scheme was displayed at Le Bourget in 1971. It is seen here staging through Copenhagen-Kastrup on the way to Paris.

Mi-8PS executive helicopter (first use of designation – *izdeliye* 80P) (Mi-8PS-7, Mi-8PS-9, Mi-8PS-11)

The Mi-8P became the basis for the Mi-8PS executive version developed for government flights and Soviet Air Force units. The S stood for *salonnaya komponovka* (VIP layout); since a more luxurious VIP version designated Mi-8S also exists, some sources deciphered the PS suffix as ***pol**usa**lon**nyy* – 'semi-VIP'! There is some confusion concerning these versions, as will be seen from the next entry.

The Mi-8PS was manufactured in three subvariants differing in interior layout and seating seven, nine or eleven (designated Mi-8PS-7, Mi-8PS-9 and Mi-8PS-11 respectively). Outwardly the Mi-8PS was virtually identical to the standard Mi-8P – except maybe for the nose titles (one Mi-8PS-11, RA-25770 No.2 (c/n 8709), was duly marked as such on the nose!). This means the forward entry door on the port side is a sliding door with detachable boarding steps, there are six rectangular windows on each side and a KO-50 heater to starboard. Many Mi-8PSs featured additional communications equipment which was constantly updated as production progressed; this could be identified by the extra rod aerial halfway between the oil cooler air outlet (behind the main rotor head) and the upper anti-collision light and by the additional dorsal blade aerial immediately ahead of the ACL. But... see next entry.

An uncoded Soviet Air Force Mi-8PS with a sliding door; this variant is outwardly indistinguishable from the Mi-8P. This photo illustrates well the Mi-8's characteristic nose-up attitude on the ground.

Mi-8S VIP helicopter

The various versions with enhanced passenger comfort envisaged at an early design stage included VIP and VVIP versions intended for transporting high-ranking government officials (including the head of state) and the military top brass. Likewise entering production in 1969, the VIP version of the Mi-8P was designated Mi-8S (for [*verto***lyot**-] *'salon'* – VIP helicopter) or Mi-8 'Salon'. Outwardly it differed from the Mi-8PS executive version mainly in having one window less on the port side, the usual sliding door being replaced by a downward-hinged door doubling as airstairs. This was because an air conditioner was installed in a fairing immediately aft of the door (symmetrically to the cabin heater on the starboard side), leaving no room to slide the door; thus the engineers had made a virtue out of necessity. Additionally, military examples with the airstair door feature an extra cabin window to starboard (immediately ahead of the starboard rear clamshell door).

The cabin features improved heat- and soundproofing and a plush interior with comfortable armchairs, tables and a sofa, a coat closet and a toilet. To further enhance comfort the main rotor head is provided with inertia-type vibration dampers in flattened yellow fairings between the blade sleeves. A capable secure communications system with scramblers/descramblers is provided. Like the Mi-8PS, the Mi-8S was available in 11-, 9- or 7-seat configuration; additionally, an extra-long-range six-seat version offering an extra high level of comfort could be built to order. As per customer demand the cabin could be equipped with a TV set, a refrigerator and so on; the interior trim was also specified by the customer.

Most Mi-8Ss were manufactured with TV2-117F engines delivering 1,700 shp for take-off (F = *for***see***rovannyy* – uprated). Maximum take-off weight is 11,080 kg (24,430 lb) for the 11-seat version, 11,100 kg (24,470 lb) for the 9-seater and 11,300 kg (24,910 lb) for the 7-seater. The fuel capacity is 2,615 litres (575.3 Imp gal) or 2,027 kg (4,468 lb); range with 30-minute fuel reserves is 590-600 km (366-372 miles) and endurance is 3.05-3.1 hours.

However, the picture is far from clear because some VIP helicopters with a sliding port side door are sometimes referred to as Mi-8S, while some examples with an airstair door are referred to as Mi-8PS! Interestingly, some Mi-8Ss and Mi-8PSs with an airstair door (with or without air conditioner) are in fact former Mi-8Ts converted to meet customer demands! One such example is RA-27189 (c/n 99357636) which crashed as a Mi-8T on Mt. Fisht near Sochi on 28th September 1996 while operated by Aero-Taxi but was then rebuilt as a Mi-8PS (without an air conditioner) and is still in service – now with an air conditioner!

Mi-8PA passenger helicopter

In the late 1970s OKB-117 brought out the abovementioned TV2-117F version of the engine uprated to 1,700 shp. The first Mi-8 to be powered by the new engines was a Mi-8PS delivered to the Japanese air services company Aero Asahi and registered JA8549 (c/n 26001; see Chapter 6 for explanation of export aircraft c/ns). Designated Mi-8PA (the A presumably standing for Asahi), the helicopter was unusual in having an airstair door. The helicopter was successfully certificated in Japan in 1980 and used for flying crane work, among other things. To this end the air conditioner and the KO-50 cabin heater were removed to save weight and rear/downward vision mirrors were installed on the nose, enabling the pilots to monitor the slung load.

Mi-8AT civil transport helicopter

In the 1980s the Ulan-Ude aircraft factory began equipping late-production Mi-8Ts with 1,700-shp TV2-117AG turboshafts. This cheaper and more durable model differed from the baseline engine in having graphite seals in the compressor/power turbine bearings (hence the G suffix). The version powered by TV2-117AGs received the designation Mi-8AT and was operated mostly in temperate climatic zones with even terrain. However, there are exceptions; Mi-8T RA-79161 of Ikar Aircompany Ltd. (c/n 9754723), which had been upgraded to Mi-8AT standard by fitting the new engines, operated in the Magadan Region of Russia known for its cold weather and hilly terrain.

Mi-8TM civil transport helicopter

Some Ulan-Ude built Mi-8Ts manufactured in the 1990s introduced other improvements in addition to TV2-117AG engines, including two emergency exits to starboard (in the foremost and rearmost windows) and a Kontur (Contour) weather radar in a bullet-shaped radome replacing the lower centre window in the lower row of the flightdeck glazing. This version is designated Mi-8TM.

Known examples are two U-UAPO demonstrators – RA-25755 No.1 (later reregistered RA-22965, c/n 99357303) displayed at the MAKS-93 airshow in Zhukovskiy on 31st August/5th September 1993 and RA-22964 (c/n 99357706) displayed at the MAKS-95 airshow on 22nd-27th August 1995. The latter aircraft differed from the former in having an additional emergency exit in the rearmost window to port and an optional extra deep port side flightdeck blister window which could be fitted for flying crane operations.

Mi-8AP-2 and Mi-8AP-4 passenger helicopters

The Ulan-Ude built version of the Mi-8P was designated Mi-8AP-2 or Mi-8AP-4, depending on the interior layout. Both versions were powered by TV2-117AG engines.

Mi-8APS executive/VIP helicopter

Similarly, the Ulan-Ude built version of the Mi-8PS (Mi-8S) was designated Mi-8APS (ie, Mi-8AP 'Salon') and powered by TV2-117AG engines. One example belonging to the Russian government flight (Rossiya State Transport Co.), RA-27080, was the presidential helicopter of Russia's first President Boris N. Yel'tsin and then of his successor Vladimir V. Putin, featuring an extra comfortable interior and special communications equipment. Two further examples registered RA-25137 and RA-25187 are used by the Russian Prime Minister and other top-ranking government officials.

Mi-8TP transport/passenger helicopter

A convertible version of the Mi-8T equipped with real passenger seats instead of the standard tip-up version was manufactured in Ulan-Ude as the Mi-8TP (***trahns**portno-passa**zheer**skiy* – transport/passenger, used attributively). Such helicopters are powered by TV2-117AG engines. It is open to speculation if the Mi-8TP designation is also applicable to similarly configured Kazan'-built Mi-8Ts, such as Baltic Airlines RA-22308 (c/n 7126).

A few early-production civil Mi-8s were registered in the CCCP-110xx block, including this Mi-8P, CCCP-11053. Note the flightdeck boarding step to starboard and the rescue hoist above the forward door.

Mi-8TS VIP helicopter

A few Soviet/Russian Air Force and Naval Air Arm Mi-8Ts were built or refitted with a VIP interior and designated Mi-8TS (ie, Mi-8T 'Salon'). This version is very rare indeed.

Mi-8T record-breaking version

An early-production Mi-8T with the non-standard registration CCCP-11067 (c/n unknown) was specially modified in 1967 for setting a world speed record. The mainwheels were fitted with spats, and the cabin heater and external tanks were removed to cut drag (all fuel was carried in the cabin).

Mi-8T – Finnish upgrades

At least four Finnish Air Force Mi-8Ts serialled HS-1 through HS-4 (c/ns 13301 through 13304) were retrofitted with a Western weather radar of an unknown type in an egg-shaped pod under the nose. A further example, HS-11 (c/n 13307), has a radar of a different type in a flat-bottomed circular radome (obviously a 360° search radar) and a Nitesun SX-16 searchlight on the starboard side of the fuselage. These versions did not have any separate designations.

Mi-8T – Indian upgrade

A number of Indian Air Force Mi-8Ts, including Z-2402 and Z-2839, were retrofitted with weather radars; this time the radar was installed in a radome with a hemispherical front end supplanting the port panel in the lower row of the flightdeck glazing. There was no separate designation.

Mi-8PS executive helicopter – Finnish upgrades

Both Mi-8PSs delivered to the Finnish Air Force (HS-5 and HS-6, c/ns 13305 and 13306) were also retrofitted with a Western weather radar; this time the radar was located in a bullet-shaped fairing adhering to the underside of the nose. Again, there is no separate designation.

Mi-8T aerodynamics testbed

A single Soviet Air Force Mi-8T (no tactical code, c/n unknown) delivered to the Flight Research Institute named after Mikhail M. Gromov (LII – ***Lyot**no-is**sled**ovatel'skiy insti**toot***) in the town of Zhukovskiy south of Moscow was modified in an attempt to improve the helicopter's performance and

This Mi-8T, CCCP-11067 (c/n 0101?), was used to set a speed record on 23rd August 1967 when an all-woman crew attained 273.507 km/h (169.88 mph). Note the wheel spats and the removed external tanks/cabin heater; the glossy paint where they used to be make a marked contrast with the rest of the airframe.

Above: Finnish Air Force Mi-8T HS-3 (c/n 13303) with a podded weather radar under the nose. The badge of the Kuljetuslentolauvue (Transport Squadron) is visible below the flightdeck window.

Above: Finnish Air Force Mi-8PS HS-6 (c/n 13306) features a different type of radar. The larger pod adhering directly to the fuselage underside makes an interesting comparison with the Mi-8T above.

reduce fuel consumption. The aircraft incorporated a number of low-drag modifications, the most obvious of these being a new clamshell cargo door design; the doors were lengthened and reshaped to give the rear fuselage a profile similar to that of the Bell 206 JetRanger/LongRanger light helicopter. Two-piece teardrop fairings were fitted around the engine jetpipes, the swashplate was faired, and the external tanks, KO-50 cabin heater and DISS-2 fairing under the tailboom were removed, the fuel being carried in the cabin. The helicopter was probably designated Mi-8LL (*le**ta**yuschchaya labora**to**riya* – lit. 'flying laboratory', a term used indiscriminately for any kind of testbed, research or survey aircraft) but this is unconfirmed.

Mi-8VKP (Mi-8VZPU) tactical airborne command post

In the early 1970s the Mil' OKB brought out a tactical airborne command post (ABCP) derivative of the Mi-8T. Designated Mi-8VKP (*voz**doosh**nyy ko**mahnd**nyy poonkt*) or Mi-8VZPU (*voz**doosh**nyy poonkt oopravle**niya; both of these terms mean ABCP), the helicopter was designed to exercise command and control of troops on the battlefield. (Note: The latter designation has also been spelled Mi-8VzPU, with a lower-case 'z'. Some sources decipher Mi-8VZPU as *voz**doosh**nyy zapas**noy** poonkt oopravle**niya* – 'airborne reserve or back-up command post', but this is doubtful.)

The Mi-8VKP was not built as such, all of these helicopters being converted from standard Mi-8Ts at the Soviet Air Force's aircraft overhaul plants. Outwardly this version (code-named *Hip-D* by the NATO) can be identified by two large outward-canted 'towel rail' aerials mounted dorsally on the tailboom (with twin swept rod aerials in between), two rectangular equipment pods permanently mounted on the standard external stores outriggers instead of pylons and a swept twin aerial with an aft-mounted vertical retaining strut located on the underside of the tailboom where the DISS-2 fairing used to be. In addition to the units based on home ground, the Mi-8VKP saw service with the groups of Soviet forces stationed in Eastern Europe.

The Mi-8VKP is identifiable by the aerials on the tailboom and the pylon-mounted equipment pods. '47 Blue' (c/n 0440) belonged to the 487th Independent Combat Helicopter Regiment at Templin, East Germany.

Mi-9 (Mi-8IV, Mi-8 *Ivolga*) tactical airborne command post (*izdeliye* 80IV)

The first purpose-built ABCP derivative of the *Hip* received a separate designation, Mi-9; it was also known as the Mi-8IV or Mi-8 ***I**volga* (Golden oriole) after the helicopter's mission equipment suite. The Ivolga suite comprised a number of radios and relay stations enabling the helicopter's mission crew to exercise control of troops both in the air and on the ground (in the latter case a system of external aerials was used).

The Mi-9's airframe represented a strange cross-breed between the utility and passenger versions, combining the circular windows of the Mi-8T with the Mi-8P's small clamshell doors-cum-rear airstair door. As on the Mi-8P, the rearmost window to starboard incorporated an emergency exit. Other external recognition features included two large strake aerials running all the way from the nose gear to the main gear anchoring points, two large 'hockey stick' aerials on the port clamshell door and immediately aft of the DISS-2 box under the tailboom, a large swept rod aerial mounted symmetrically on the starboard clamshell door and likewise canted outward, and a small blade aerial immediately ahead of the anti-collision light. A small rounded fairing of unknown purpose was located on the underside offset to starboard (right next to the cabin heater).

The forward part of the cabin housed mission equipment operators' workstations, while the centre portion was a 'war room' with tables and armchairs. The rear part of the cabin accommodated support equipment, including disassembled external aerial masts and a ground power unit consisting of an Ivchenko AI-8 gas turbine (used as an auxiliary power unit on the Beriyev Be-12 Chaika (Seagull) ASW amphibian) and a 24-kilowatt GS-24ADS generator. Since the engines were shut down and could not provide power for the mission equipment in ground mode, the GPU was wheeled out and started up when the aerials had been deployed.

The Mi-9 appeared in prototype form in 1977 and entered production at the Ulan-Ude aircraft factory in 1978. A separate c/n sequence was used, the first example under the 'rational' system presumably being c/n 9788501 (by comparison, the last c/n under the 'rational' system for Ulan-Ude built Mi-8Ts is 9815750; obviously Batch 85 could not have been produced ahead of Batch 57 if they had run in the same sequence!). As with the utility version, the 'damn fool system' with the famous five-digit computer numbers – again using a separate sequence – was introduced in 1981. Cf. Mi-8T CCCP-24416 c/n 986**25272** and Mi-9 '60 Red' c/n 986**56786**; in the civil sequence the 56xxx block was not used at all. Late-production examples featured chaff/flare dispensers on the rear fuselage sides and an active infrared countermeasures (IRCM) jammer aft of the main rotor head for protection against IR-homing missiles.

Apart from the Soviet Army Aviation, the Mi-9 was supplied to the air forces of Czechoslovakia, East Germany, Hungary, Egypt and possibly some other Middle Eastern nations. The NATO reporting name is *Hip-G*.

Above: A late-production Mi-9 with no Doppler box under the tailboom. The small clamshell doors, ventral strake aerials and rear aerials are clearly visible.

Mi-8SMV ECM helicopter (*izdeliye* 80SMV)

In 1971 the Mi-8T evolved into an electronic countermeasures (ECM) version – the first of many – designed to protect friendly aircraft over the battlefield by jamming the enemy's air defence (AD) radars. Designated Mi-8SMV, the aircraft featured the heliborne version of the Smal'ta (Smalt) ECM suite called Smal'ta-V (hence the suffix). Outwardly the Mi-8SMV could be identified by the square dielectric panels replacing the second cabin window on each side (discounting the window in the entry door, that is) and located immediately ahead of the clamshell doors; these housed transceiver antennas. Incidentally, the rear pair was located right where the Soviet star insignia were normally applied, causing these to be moved up. A wire aerial stretched between two short struts was located ventrally on the centre fuselage.

According to some sources, the Mi-8SMV entered production in Ulan-Ude in 1977, the first production aircraft reportedly being c/n 9777101 (ie, again a separate c/n sequence was used; compare this to ordinary Mi-8s built in that year: Mi-8TV '53 Yellow' is c/n 977**5230**). The NATO reporting name is *Hip-J*.

In the course of production the Mi-8SMV was upgraded several times. For instance, some examples had the rearmost cabin window to port replaced by a metal plug with a small square dielectric panel. Another subvariant had the first and fourth windows to starboard faired over with sheet metal and featured a single rod aerial halfway between the main rotor head and the anti-collision light (instead of the usual twin rod aerial) plus a large blade aerial immediately ahead of the ACL, while the ventral wire aerial was absent.

Mi-8PP ECM helicopter (*izdeliye* 80PP)

In 1974 the Mil' OKB brought out the Mi-8PP (*postanovshchik pomekh* – ECM aircraft) derivative of the Mi-8T. Equipped with the Pol'e (Field, pronounced ***pol**-eh*) ECM suite, the aircraft was likewise designed for AD radar suppression but had a secondary signals intelligence (SIGINT) role.

Outwardly the Mi-8PP was characterised by two large rectangular housings on the fuselage sides replacing the second and third windows (discounting the window in the entry door); the outer faces of these 'suitcases' were slightly convex and hinged open for access to the equipment inside. Two large frames made of metal tubes and wire mesh were attached on multiple struts to the sides of the rear fuselage and the root of the tailboom; each of these frames carried three pairs of emitter aerials looking like four-bladed propellers on cylindrical struts (each 'propeller' was strut-braced for rigidity). The installation of these antenna farms caused the rearmost window on each side to be deleted and the insignia to be relocated to the said 'suitcases'. The paired four-round signal flare launchers were likewise moved forward from the port clamshell cargo door to a place above the second remaining (ie, originally the fourth) cabin window to port.

The ECM suite generated a lot of heat which was dissipated by means of six faired heat exchangers installed abreast under the fuselage in line with the entry door; the heat exchanger housings were of oval cross-section. The usual detachable boarding steps gave way to a permanently installed step.

As with the Mi-8SMV, production began at the Ulan-Ude plant in 1977, the first production aircraft reportedly being c/n 9777301. Thus the special mission versions manufactured in Ulan-Ude used the same separate c/n sequence, the batches of ECM and ABCP versions being interspersed with each other. The NATO reporting name was *Hip-K*.

Mi-8PPA ECM helicopter

This was a more refined version of the Mi-8PP featuring the *A**ka**tsiya* (Acacia) ECM suite, hence the A suffix; outwardly it was identical to the previous version. The Mi-8PPA saw service with the groups of Soviet forces in Czechoslovakia (Southern Group of Forces) and East Germany (Western Group of Forces). It was also supplied to Czechoslovakia and Iraq.

Mi-8MB MEDEVAC helicopter

Since it was generally assumed in the 1970s that future wars would be fought with large-scale use of nuclear weapons, in 1973 the Mil' OKB developed a special version for evacuating the victims of a nuclear strike and rendering medical assistance en route to a hospital. Designated Mi-8MB, this derivative of the Mi-8T was the first version of the *Hip* to feature on-board operating facilities.

Mi-8PS SAR helicopter (second use of designation)

1976 saw the first specialised search and rescue version of the *Hip*; based on the Mi-8T, it was intended for overwater operations, picking up people in distress in stormy seas with the help of a powerful hoist and a specially

Top: Starboard side view of Mi-8SMV '30 Blue', showing the square-shaped dielectric panels in the second window and ahead of the cargo doors.

Above: Port side view of the same helicopter. Note the plug in the last-but-one window incorporating a smaller antenna panel.

trained rescue worker. Confusingly, the helicopter was designated Mi-8PS; in this case, however, the suffix stood for *poiskovo-spasahtel'nyy* – SAR, used attributively.

Mi-8SP SAR helicopter

In 1977 two Mi-8Ts (identities unknown) were converted into SAR helicopters for the Soviet Cosmonaut Group. Designated Mi-8SP, they were intended for locating and evacuating the re-entry modules of Soviet spacecraft after these had touched down in the steppes of Kazakhstan.

Mi-8SPA SAR helicopter

An upgraded version of the Mi-8SP bore the designation Mi-8SPA.

Mi-8KP airborne command post

A specialised ABCP version of the Mi-8T equipped with the *Saigak* (Saiga antelope) was developed for the Soviet Cosmonaut Group to co-ordinate the operations of the SAR group after the space capsule touched down. Designated Mi-8KP (*komahndnyy poonkt*), the helicopter underwent trials in 1978.

Mi-8BT mine countermeasures helicopter

In 1974 the Mil' OKB developed a mine countermeasures (MCM) version of the Mi-8T to meet an urgent need for clearing mines in

Below: The Mi-8PP displays the characteristic lateral equipment housings, antena farms and ventral array of heat exchangers. This is '18 Red' (c/n 9797527), a 9th Independent Helicopter Squadron aircraft, approaching its home base at Neuruppin, East Germany, in 1990.

Top: Port side view of Mi-8PPA '24 Yellow'. Note the signal flare launchers relocated to a position above the rearmost cabin window and the position of the star insignia on the lateral 'suitcases'.

Above: This view shows the different window placement port and starboard. Note that the helicopter is obviously recoded: the tactical code is applied over a fresh patch of darker paint where the previous code had been.

Below and below right: These views illustrate the bulged sides of the Mi-8PPA's lateral housings and the angle of the antenna arrays, as well as their mounting and bracing struts.

the Suez Canal. Designated Mi-8BT (*book-si**rov**schchik* [***min**novo*] ***trah**la* – mine-clearing sled tug), the MCM version lacked the rear clamshell doors; a winch and holders for the mine-clearing sled were installed in the cabin, as was and an extra fuel tank to increase endurance.

Five Mi-8Ts (identities unknown) were converted to Mi-8BT configuration. When the job was finished, the helicopters served on as testbeds for various specialised maritime equipment. Experience gained with the Mi-8BT proved most valuable when designing the Mi-14BT MCM helicopter.

Mi-8T in ASW configuration

In the 1970s or 1980s several Soviet Navy Mi-8Ts were used in the anti-submarine warfare (ASW) role, if the caption to a photo displayed in the Maritime Transport (!) pavilion at the VDNKh (Economic Achievements Exhibition) in Moscow is to be believed. The photo showed several Mi-8Ts carrying large externally slung structures which were presumably cassettes for sonobuoys or depth charges. However, no mention of an ASW version of the Mi-8 has been found in available literature, including the 50 Years of the Mil' Moscow Helicopter Plant book.

This poor-quality shot is the only available photo of the ASW version of the Mi-8T. Note the splashes created by some stores – probably depth charges – being dropped from the underslung cassettes.

Mi-8T telephone cable laying version

In 1974 the Mi-8T spawned a version with an external cable drum for laying telephone lines. The helicopter could lay up to 10 km (6.2 miles) of cable at a time.

Mi-8AV (Mi-8VSM) mine-laying helicopter

In 1975 the Mil' OKB adapted the Mi-8T for laying anti-tank mines. Racks for a supply of mines and a mine dispenser were installed in the cabin. Outwardly the mine-laying version designated Mi-8AV or Mi-8VSM (*vozdooshnaya sistema mineerovaniya* – aerial mine-laying system) was identifiable by the slender, curved mine dispensing chute which swung down in operational mode, moving from side to side to distribute the mines in a chequerboard pattern. In cruise mode the chute was raised and locked into position against a V-shaped support attached to the tailboom; thus the rear clamshell doors were always partly open.

Mi-8AD mine-laying helicopter

A similar version designed for laying anti-personnel mines was developed in 1978 as the Mi-8AD, subsequently entering service alongside the Mi-8AV.

Mi-8T communications relay versions

In 1975 the first two communications relay versions based on the Mi-8T were brought out. One of them was intended for relaying real-time TV imagery from observation posts to command and control centres.

Mi-8R (Mi-8GR) tactical reconnaissance helicopter

In the mid-1970s the Mi-8R (Mi-8GR) tactical reconnaissance helicopter entered service with the Soviet armed forces. The R stood for [*vertolyot*-] *razvedchik* – reconnaissance helicopter.

Mi-8TG (first use of designation)/ Mi-8TARK battlefield reconnaissance helicopter

Another version which became operational in the 1970s was the Mi-8TARK (*televizionnyy artillereeyskiy razvedchik-korrektirovschchik* – artillery recce/spotter with a TV system); its mission was battlefield observation and tactical reconnaissance, spotting for artillery and missile units, and aerial photography. In service the helicopter was known as the Mi-8TG (not to be confused with the later civil Mi-8TG, which see); in the Western press it was sometimes misidentified as 'Mi-8T(K)'.

According to some sources the Mi-8TG had several mission equipment fits. One configuration had an AFA-42/100 oblique camera (*aerofotoapparaht* – aircraft camera) with a 1,000-mm focal length shooting through the first window on the starboard side and a darkroom with a work table and a PDN-4 photo negative deciphering apparatus. Another layout featured an A-87P long-range operations (LOROP) camera with a reported focal length of 1,300 mm, an SU-6 exposure meter looking through the second window to starboard, a DEFA EAS-70 rapid film processing unit of East German provenance and a PDN-4.

The Mi-8TG saw service with the Group of Soviet Forces in Germany. Later it was replaced in Soviet Army Aviation service by the Mi-24K photo reconnaissance/artillery spotter helicopter.

Mi-8VD NBC reconnaissance helicopter

Since it was generally assumed that in future wars the ground forces would operate in a nuclear/biological/chemical (NBC) contamination environment, the Mil' OKB developed a tactical NBC reconnaissance version of the *Hip* designated Mi-8VD (the suffix probably stood for *vozdooshnyy dozimetr* – 'flying area monitor'). It was later superseded by the Mi-24R.

Mi-8TZ refuelling tanker

A version designated Mi-8TZ (*toplivozaprahvshchik* – refuelling tanker) was developed and put into production in 1977. This was not a flight refuelling tanker but a 'flying petrol station' designed to refuel other helicopters on the ground – or tanks in the field.

Mi-8TECh-24 mobile helicopter maintenance shop

Also in 1977, the Mi-8T served as the basis for a mobile repair shop designed for servicing and repairing Mi-24 assault helicopters in the field when a helicopter could not be flown from a forward operating location to a stationary overhaul shop (for whatever reason). This version was designated Mi-8TECh-24 (*tekhniko-ekspluatatsionnaya chahst'* [*dlya Mi-*] *dvadtsat' chetyre* = maintenance facility for Mi-24s). However, like its successor, the Mi-24TECh-24, it did not reach production.

Mi-8T – Border Guards version

In 1978 a specially equipped version of the Mi-8T (or rather 'Mi-8TV Mk I') spawned was developed for the Border Guards (which at that time were within the framework of the notorious KGB, not the Soviet Armed Forces). The nature of the modifications is not known.

Mi-8T – MoI troops version

A version of the Mi-8T (with no weapons racks) was developed for the Ministry of the Interior (MoI), which has its own paramilitary units for guarding prison colonies etc. The helicopter was armed with a heavy machine-gun on a gimballed mount attached to the starboard side of the fuselage; this was lowered when airborne, letting the gun traverse to give an unrestricted field of fire. It may be conjectured that the helicopter was intended as a last-resort means of riot control.

Mi-8T experimental flying crane versions

In 1970 an early-production Mi-8T was modified for testing a higher-capacity sling system for carrying external loads which was attached directly to the fuselage mainframes inside the cabin. To this end the cabin floor incorporated a hatch closed by a cover through which the system's main cable passed. This became standard on late-production Mi-8Ts, replacing the earlier W-shaped external attachment.

Five years later another Mi-8T was equipped experimentally with a closed-circuit TV system for monitoring the slung load.

Mi-8ATS agricultural helicopter prototype

In 1975 the Mil' OKB attempted to adapt the Mi-8 to the agricultural role by fitting chemical hoppers and powdered chemical spreaders or spraybars for liquid chemicals to the fuselage sides. Designated Mi-8ATS (the S stood for *sel'skokhoziaystvennyy* – agricultural), a suitably modified Mi-8T (identity unknown) underwent trials.

Mi-8FSKh agricultural helicopter prototype

Another experimental agricultural version of the Mi-8T powered by 1,700-shp TV2-117F engines was designated Mi-8FSKh. Possibly it was CCCP-24600 (c/n unknown) which carried a self-contained spray module on a sling and was fitted with a lattice-like air data boom on the nose. The idea was not pursued further because it was clearly uneconomical to use the heavy Mi-8 as a crop-sprayer.

Mi-8TL firebomber (first use of designation)

In 1977 the Mil' OKB brought out a water bomber derivative of the Mi-8T designed for fighting forest fires. This version entered limited production as the Mi-8TL (*lesopozharnyy*) and was used with considerable success.

Mi-8T psy-war version

A version of the Mi-8T equipped with the ZSVS loudspeaker system appeared in 1982. This was a psychological warfare version whose roots lay in the Great Patriotic War-vintage Polikarpov U-2GN (*golos neba* – 'voice of the sky') psy-war aircraft. It is known that the 'voice of the sky' Mi-8 was used operationally during the Second Chechen War.

Mi-8TG (second use of designation) experimental cryogenic fuel helicopter

On 6th March 1979 the Soviet Council of Ministers' standing committee on defence industry matters (VPK – *Voyenno-promyshlennaya komissiya*) endorsed a multi-aspect research and development plan aimed at exploring the possibility of using cryogenic fuels (liquefied natural gas and liquid hydrogen) in aviation. The principal aim of the programme was to create practicable aircraft operating on LNG and LH_2. The Soviet Union's Academy of Sciences, MAP and a whole range of OKBs and plants were instructed to take on the problem.

LNG was cheaper than liquid hydrogen, so in the early 1980s the Mil' OKB and the industry's R&D establishments busied themselves with the idea of adapting helicopter engines to run on this cheap and readily available fuel. This would alleviate the problems caused by kerosene shortages which were already being experienced at the time while cutting harmful emissions dramatically.

Hence OKB-117 in Leningrad developed the TV2-117G (more often referred to as TV2-117TG), an experimental bi-fuel engine capable of running on kerosene and liquid methane alike (the G stands for *gahzovoye toplivo* – gas fuel). Accordingly in 1987 the Mil' Moscow Helicopter Plant converted a standard Mi-8T (identity unknown) into the Mi-8TG development aircraft. This was created in a joint effort with the Central Aerodynamics & Hydrodynamics Institute named after Nikolay Ye. Zhukovskiy (TsAGI – *Tsentrahl'nyy aero- i ghidrodinamicheskiy institoot*), the Central Institute of Aero Engines (TsIAM – *Tsentrahl'nyy institoot aviatsionnovo motorostroyeniya*), the State Civil Aviation Research Institute (GosNII GA – *Gosoodarstvennyy naoochno-issledovatel'skiy institoot grazhdahnskoy aviahtsii*) and the Research & Design Institute of Natural Gas Processing (NIPIGazpererabotka). The project received state funding under the 'Civil Aviation Development Programme up to the Year 2000' which was part of the new *konversiya* policy (reorienting defence industry enterprises towards civilian needs).

The prototype featured external stores outriggers borrowed from the Mi-8TV, to which were attached four small metal tanks for liquid methane; the cylindrical tanks were installed transversely with the axis horizontally. Only one engine was capable of running on LNG; the other was a standard TV2-117A. The first flight took place on 7th September 1987.

The static park at the MAKS-93 airshow featured what was advertised as the first production Mi-8TG. The aircraft (RA-25364, c/n 98206842) differed considerably from the proof-of-concept helicopter described above, featuring one large cylindrical LNG tank mounted lengthwise on struts on each side of the fuselage and being powered by two TV2-117TGs. The helicopter was bedecked with sponsors' logos, including those of the late Vnukovo Airlines (then one of Russia's largest air carriers) and the Interaviagaz Joint-Stock Co. The latter was a consortium formed by more than 30 Russian aircraft, airline and

Mi-8TL CCCP-25967 (c/n 6311) wearing the blue/white 1973-standard livery makes a practice water drop, using the underslung metal 'barrel'.

Seen on its maiden flight on 7th September 1987, the Mi-8TG prototype shows its liquid methane tanks carried on outriggers from a late-model 'Mi-8TV Mk I' (see lower photo on page 21!) and nose-mounted air data boom.

natural gas industry companies for furthering the development of aircraft operating on cryogenic fuels. Such aircraft would operate primarily in regions rich in oil and natural gas (such as the Tyumen' Region of Russia).

The helicopter underwent trials at the Mil' OKB's flight test facility in Panki near Moscow, showing almost identical performance to the standard Mi-8T. The Mi-8TG could operate with equal success on LNG, jet fuel, or a mixture of both. RA-25364 was demonstrated again at the MAKS-95 airshow, taking part in the flying display. So far, however, no more production Mi-8TGs have been identified.

From a very early stage the Mi-8 was widely used in all sorts of research and development programmes by various government agencies of the Soviet Union and subsequently Russia. This included tests of new avionics and equipment (primarily military) to be used on other types of aircraft or prospective versions of the *Hip*, ecological and geophysical survey etc. The capacious cabin and high payload rendered the helicopter well suited for the test vehicle ('dogship') role; also, the large cargo doors meant the equipment fit could be easily changed if necessary. Some of the test and development aircraft are listed below.

Mi-8 *Makfar* geophysical survey helicopters

In 1981 two Mi-8Ts were specially modified for geophysical survey work in the Yakutian Autonomous SSR. Known as Mi-8 *Makfar*, the helicopters were fitted with the Makfar-11 special measurement suite There is a strong possibility that the helicopters in question are CCCP-22936 and CCCP-22937 (c/ns unknown) operated by GosNII GA at Moscow/Sheremet'yevo-1 and that they operated as a pair, the mission suite being too extensive to be carried by a single Mi-8. Both helicopters featured Mi-8TV-style outriggers on which large equipment boxes were installed, and the boxes were different on both aircraft.

Mi-8RF radiometric survey helicopter

This research aircraft converted in 1989 featured a radiometric/thermal imaging system called RF (hence the designation Mi-8RF). The system created IR-waveband images of the earth's surface.

Mi-8LL laser designator testbed

A Mi-8 (identity unknown) served as a testbed for the first Soviet laser target designator developed for strike aircraft and designated *Prozhektor* (Searchlight). The tests were held in one of the Soviet Union's southern regions (in an area with level steppeland) under the direction of V. G. Filatov; testing took place on the ground and in flight both in the daytime and at night.

Mi-8T (?) night vision systems testbed

A Soviet Air Force Mi-8T (tactical code unknown) was used by LII in 1979-1990 for testing night vision systems developed for ensuring night operations of combat helicopters and for locating people in distress at sea. The c/n has been quoted as 3115; however, it is by no means certain this is a Kazan'-built Mi-8T and the helicopter may have been an Ulan-Ude built example (c/n 9733115). (In fact, it is not even certain this was a 'first-generation' Mi-8 at all – the aircraft may also be Mi-8MT c/n 93115 which was also operated by LII as a test aircraft!)

Mi-8T mine countermeasures systems testbed/ecological survey aircraft

Another Soviet Air Force Mi-8T (tactical code unknown, c/n 3611) was used by LII in 1972-1995 as a testbed for mine and minefield detection systems (not maritime but developed for the ground forces). This time the dates of operation leave no doubt this is a Kazan'-built aircraft – Mi-8T c/n 9733611 (or 9743611?) did not exist yet, to say nothing of Mi-8MT c/n 93611!

Later the same helicopter was used for more peaceful applications (as an ecological monitoring aircraft). (We realise that the section header sounds rather like the Soviet anecdote of Sino-Soviet border conflict vintage about the 'peaceful tractor which returned fire when attacked by Chinese infiltrants', but fact is that only the overall period in service with LII is known and it is not known when the helicopter switched to its new role.)

Mi-8LL EMP measurement aircraft

A 'Mi-8TV Mk I' (identity unknown) delivered to LII was converted into a research vehicle designated Mi-8LL for measuring electromagnetic fields and electromagnetic pulses (EMP). Its range of tasks included determining the patterns of emitter antennas, measuring the intensity of electromagnetic fields and determining dangerous radiation levels, and pinpointing the locations of active jammers (ie, an electronic counter-countermeasures (ECCM) function). External identification features were narrow triangular housings pointing upwards from the tips of the external stores outriggers (the BD3-57KrV pylons were removed) and a sensor array carried on a truss-type frame in front of the flightdeck glazing. Additionally, the standard flightdeck sliding windows were replaced with makeshift angular faceted observation blisters.

Mi-8T FBW control system testbed

In the mid-1980s LII began research on fly-by-wire (FBW) control systems for advanced helicopters. Accordingly in 1986 a Mi-8T (identity unknown) became part of a total in-flight simulator (TIFS) complex which also included a ground-based computing system and a data link system. The helicopter's control system included a VUAP-1 autopilot.

In flight the on-board test equipment measured the main flight parameters, as well as cyclic pitch stick/pedal movements, stick forces and autopilot inputs, transmitting them to the ground control centre via data link. The data was processed in accordance with preset algorithms and monitored by test engineers; the ground control centre would then send corrective commands to the helicopter which were decoded and fed into the autopilot. This method allowed the characteristics of stability augmentation systems and FBW artificial-feel units to be developed and optimised.

Mi-8T side-stick control system testbed

In 1989 the same Mi-8T was further modified for testing the feasibility of using a side-stick controller on a helicopter instead of the usual centrally mounted cyclic pitch stick. Two side-stick controllers (for the left and right hands) were installed at the co-pilot's workstation (on the starboard side). The tests took place in November and December 1990 with LII test pilots V. L. Teben'kov, B. Yu. Barsukov, N. V. Pavlenko and V. M. Mukhametgareyev flying the modified helicopter. These pilots had different skill levels and different experience with helicopters, so one of the objectives was to see how demanding to fly a helicopter with a side-stick is to fly for a pilot of this or that skill. Test flights were made with the helicopter's experimental stability augmentation system (SAS) activated or deactivated.

The tests revealed that the side-stick controllers allowed the pilot to assume a more natural and relaxed posture when controlling the aircraft, as both arms lying on armrests were positioned at the same level. As a result, pilot fatigue was reduced dramatically. Moreover, with the SAS activated, flying the helicopter became much easier, allowing the pilot to concentrate on the mission and pay more attention to relevant inputs.

Mi-8P (?) research/survey aircraft

The Aviation-90 trade fair held at the VDNKh fairground in Moscow in November 1990 featured an intriguing model depicting a Mi-8P with a towed antenna system. The model was presented by the Moscow-based NPO Vzlyot ('Take-off' Scientific & Production Association), one of the leading Soviet avionics houses, and GONTI (presumably *Glahvnyy otdel naoochno-tekhnicheskoy informahtsii* – Main Scientific & Technical Information Department, possibly part of TsAGI). In reality the model very probably did not depict the actual aircraft (ie, the helicopter used to carry the actual system – if it existed in hardware form – was not necessarily a Mi-8P; the registration CCCP-02789 on the model was obviously fictitious).

The system looked like a large cigar-shaped container on wheels (for ground handling) with a stabilising parachute which ensured the required position of the container relative to the helicopter in flight. The parachute had a rather strange shape with fins, looking like the rear end of an airship. According to the accompanying data plate the heliborne flying lab was intended for carrying flexible and inflatable wave guides, and for carrying a flexible dipole antenna system around transmitter or receiver aerials on the ground with a view to determining their characteristics.

Seen here inside one of LII's hangars at Zhukovskiy, this Mi-8T was modified by the institute for measuring electromagnetic pulses. The nose-mounted and lateral sensor arrays are clearly visible, as is the unusual scratchbuilt angular blister window.

Mi-8TL air accident investigation laboratory (second use of designation)

At least one Soviet Air Force Mi-8T coded '45 Yellow' (c/n 4155) was converted into a mobile air accident investigation laboratory designated Mi-8TL which could travel to the airbase where a crash had taken place. As distinct from the civil Mi-8TL water bomber, the L suffix stood for *laboratoriya*. The cabin housed specialised equipment for deciphering the 'black boxes' (flight data recorder and cockpit voice recorder) of the crashed aircraft.

Mi-8s with external long-range fuel tanks

In the early 1990s the Aeroton company based in St. Petersburg devised a way of increasing the range and endurance of civil Mi-8s without sacrificing cabin volume to long-range tanks. Quite simply, cylindrical external tanks holding 475 litres (104.5 Imp gal) each were attached to the fuselage sides on Mi-8TV-style outriggers which were suitably modified to make the hardpoints 'wet'. The number of external tanks depends on the original version (ie, on available engine power). 'First-generation' versions can carry four such tanks giving a total of 1,900 litres (418 Imp gal) or 1,490 kg (3,280 lb) of additional fuel; this increases operational range to 1,100 km (680 miles) and ferry range to 1,600 km (990 miles). An example of this configuration is Mi-8PS RA-27196 (c/n 8434) operated

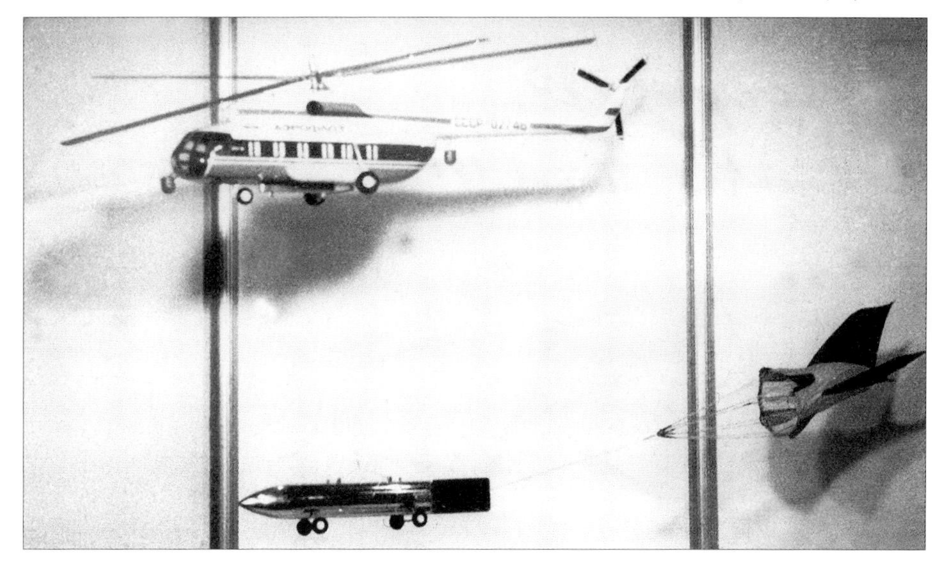

This model of a Mi-8P carrying a towed antenna system with a stabilising parachute was displayed at the Aviation-90 show. Note the antennas mounted in thimble fairings under the nose and tailboom.

Above: Russian Customs Service Mi-17 RA-70896 (c/n 520M21) was displayed at the MAKS-93 airshow to demonstrate the external tank system developed by Aeroton.

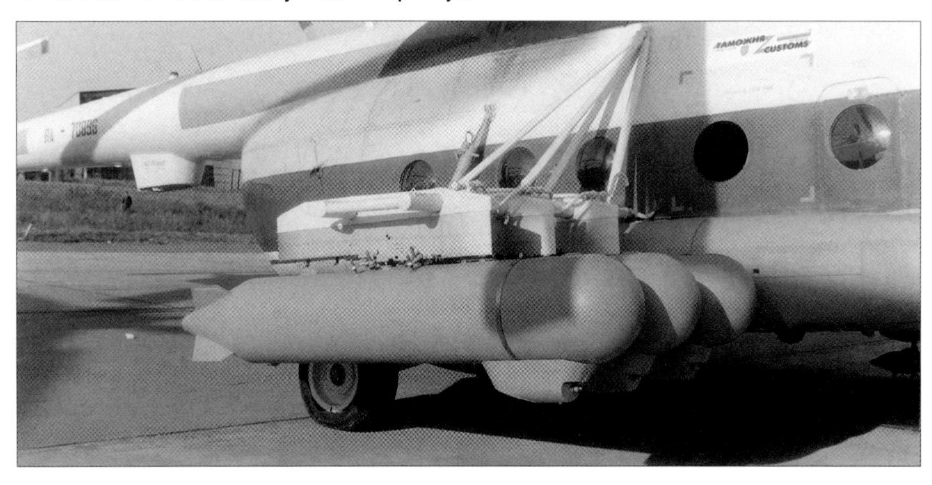

Above: Close-up of the outriggers with three 475-litre tanks on each side on RA-70896; the Mi-8T/Mi-8P can be fitted with four such tanks. The purpose of the fairings under the tanks' front ends is unknown.

RA-27189 (c/n 99357636) of Aero-Taxi started life as a Mi-8T. It crashed on Mt. Fisht near Sochi on 28th September 1996 and was rebuilt as a Mi-8S. It is seen here with two 475-litre tanks on the fuselage sides.

by Urengoygazprom, now a part of Gazpromavia (the flying division of Russia's natural gas industry).

The Mi-8MT *et seq.* featuring more powerful engines can be equipped with six external tanks giving a total of 2,850 litres (627 Imp gal) or 2,220 kg (4,900 lb) of additional fuel; this increases operational range to 1,300 km (807 miles) and ferry range to 1,850 km (1,149 miles). This configuration was illustrated at the MAKS-93 airshow by VIP-configured Mi-8MTV-1 RA-70896 (c/n 520M21); though belonging to the Russian Customs Service, the helicopter was presented by Aeroton.

Of course, the Aeroton system can be used not only on executive helicopters. It is a useful asset for border/maritime patrol or forestry patrol helicopters, reconnaissance helicopters on off-base deployments, helicopters performing supply missions (fuel carriers etc.) and so on.

Lately, another approach to the problem is becoming popular; it involves fitting a single 475-litre tank on each side of the fuselage directly above the windows. Examples include Spetsneftegaz Mi-8S RA-24181 (c/n 98943287) and East Line Mi-8S RA-24282 (c/n 98734415), both of them converted Mi-8Ts, and Yamal Airlines Mi-8T RA-25597 (c/n 99150321).

Mi-8RL CSAR helicopter

The Polish Army developed its own combat search and rescue (CSAR) version of the *Hip* designated Mi-8RL (*ratowniczy, lądowy* – for SAR operations on land). At least one Mi-8T serialled '656 White' (c/n 10656) was converted to this configuration by the Polish Air Force's overhaul plant No.1 (WZL-1) at Łódz-Lublinek.

The Mi-8RL features an avionics suite upgraded by the addition of a Bendix King KLU-709 tactical area navigation (TACAN) system, a Garmin 155XL global positioning system (GPS), Rockwell Collins AN/ARC-210 and Bendix King KHF950 communications radios and a NATO-compatible SC-10D2 identification friend-or-foe (IFF) transponder.

A Nitesun SX-16 search light is installed under the starboard side of the nose and a powerful rescue hoist is fitted above the entry door, augmenting the existing hoist of rather modest capacity. The door itself features an observation blister and permanently installed boarding steps replacing the standard detachable ones. To facilitate loading at the hover both flightdeck blister windows are equipped with rear view mirrors, plus a downward vision mirror for the captain. There is a special device for ejecting signal flags to mark the 'target' area where the rescuees are; in case the rescuees end up in a body of water, the helicopter carries inflatable rafts. The cabin features stretchers and first aid kits.

Mi-8S high-speed experimental helicopter project

In 1964 the Mil' OKB undertook project studies of a high-speed compound helicopter based on the Mi-8. Designated Mi-8S (*skorosnoy* – high-speed), it featured wings and a turbojet engine (or engines?) to be used in cruise flight; thus the Mi-8S bore a certain resemblance to the Sikorsky S-72 experimental helicopter. Design difficulties soon forced the project to be abandoned.

Chapter 3

The Second Generation

Mi-8 Turns Mi-17

The Mi-8MT prototype in armed configuration with six UB-32A FFAR pods. It was some time before the machine-guns, external armour or IRCM equipment were introduced.

Mi-8M upgraded 'heli-liner' project

Also in 1964 the Mil' OKB began development of a thoroughly upgraded high gross weight version of the Mi-8 provisionally designated Mi-8M (*moderni**zee**rovannyy* – updated). Seating capacity in commercial 'helibus' configuration was to be increased to 40 by stretching the fuselage fore and aft of the main rotor axis. (In a similar manner, the military Sikorsky S-61 (H-3 Sea King) was stretched into the commercial S-61N/S-61L.) The Mi-8M would be equipped with more powerful engines, which, besides increasing the payload to more than 4 tons (8,820 lb), was expected to boost the helicopter's hot-and-high performance. This was a crucial parameter in which the baseline Mi-8 was inferior not only to its Western counterparts but even to its Soviet predecessor, the piston-engined Mi-4.

In November 1967 the Communist Party Central Committee and the Council of Ministers issued a joint directive concerning the development of the Mi-8M. The work proceeded quickly and the full-scale mock-up was ready for inspection by the end of the year.

The powerplant consisted of two Izotov TV3-117 turboshafts rated at 1,900 shp for take-off; this new engine had been developed for the Mil' V-14 ASW helicopter which eventually entered production as the Mi-14. Since the TV3-117 was also envisaged for the V-24 attack helicopter then under development (the future Mi-24), the OKB strove for maximum commonality between the three helicopters as regards the powerplant, power train and rotor system.

(Note**:** The Mi-14 is a direct derivative of the Mi-8 – in fact, it was known at the preliminary design stage as the V-8G (***ghid**ro* – 'hydro', ie, amphibious). However, since this is a rather different helicopter both structurally and from a mission standpoint, the Mi-14 lies outside the scope of this book. The need to develop the TV3-117 arose because it was clear that the Mi-14 would be a lot heavier than the Mi-8.)

The advanced development project of the Mi-8M was approved in 1971 but the helicopter was not built in this form, the project serving as a stepping stone towards a more rational design – the Mi-8MT described below – which became the basis of a whole new generation of *Hips*.

Mi-8MT civil utility and military transport/ assault helicopter (*izdeliye* MT)

When the Mi-8M's ADP project had been endorsed, the Mil' OKB and MAP decided to follow TsAGI's recommendation that the modernisation of the Mi-8 be performed as a two-stage programme. Stage A involved development of an intermediate version featuring minimum changes as compared to the production model. The TV2-117A engines and existing power train were replaced by TV3-117MT turboshafts and a reinforced transmission, including the Mi-14's main gearbox designated VR-14.

As distinct from the earlier model, the TV3-117 was started by a low-pressure air starter. Hence an Ivchenko AI-9V auxiliary power unit (APU) was located transversely behind the main gearbox, as on the Mi-14 (the air intake was on the starboard side and the exhaust on the port side).

Outwardly the new engines were identifiable by the 'clean' oval-section jetpipes (in contrast, the TV2-117 has a circular-section jetpipe with several characteristic thin pipes running along the 'leading edge') and a small teardrop bulge in the main gearbox cowling panel on each side aft of the jetpipe. Also, the APU installation changed the shape of the main gearbox cowling, with a pronounced 'hump' aft of the main rotor head instead of the Mi-8T's smoothly curved contour.

Another important change was that the tail rotor was relocated from the starboard side of the tailboom to port, switching from pusher to tractor configuration. The rotor still turned clockwise when seen from the hub so that the forward blade went up, ie, against the main rotor downwash (instead of with it, as on the 'first-generation' versions); this increased tail rotor efficiency dramatically. One more change was the addition of an emergency exit in the first cabin window to starboard.

All government directives notwithstanding, construction of the 'second-generation' prototype – initially still referred to as the Mi-8M – was making slow progress, as the OKB was overburdened with other equally important programmes. Also, MAP was not overjoyed at the idea of disrupting the well-established production of the TV2-117 powered versions of the *Hip*. The jolt that made the ministry change their collective minds came in the early 1970s when retirement en masse of the venerable Mi-4 began – and the Soviet Armed Forces and Aeroflot were left with the Mi-8 (which, as already mentioned, had worse hot-and-high performance than the Mi-4). Consider that it was exactly in areas with hot-and-high conditions where the Mi-4 had spent much of its service career, and the Mi-8 was a poor replacement. Hence the development and service introduction of the upgraded *Hip* became imperative.

Above and below: This armed Mi-8MT incorporates a full range of 'Afghan upgrades' – a flexible Kalashnikov PKT machine-gun in the nose, mounting racks for four more PKTs on the weapons outriggers, internal and external armour protecting the flightdeck, and triple ASO-2V-02 chaff/flare dispenser on the fuselage.

In the summer of 1975 the designation was changed to Mi-8MT (ie, *modernizeerovannyy, **trahns**portnyy* – updated transport version). The prototype was finally completed that year, taking to the air on 17th August. The aircraft was apparently converted from a 'Mi-8TV Mk II', as it was in military configuration with three weapons pylons on each side. Flight tests and State acceptance trials showed that the helicopter's flight performance and tactical potential had improved vastly.

Having passed the complete test cycle, the Mi-8MT entered production at the Kazan' helicopter factory in 1977 as *izdeliye* 80MT and was included into the Soviet Armed Forces inventory. A new construction number system was started for the occasion, Kazan'-built Mi-8MT c/ns running sequentially from 93001 onwards; very probably there are fuselage numbers as well but none have been identified to date. The c/n is normally stencilled on the inside of the emergency exit cover opposite the entry door.

For several years the Mi-8MT shared the production line with the Mi-8T/Mi-8P/Mi-8S because deliveries of the TV3-117MT turboshafts were slow at first. Also, the 'first-generation' Mi-8 had a lot of important specialised versions, and developing equivalent versions based on the new helicopter took time. The Soviet Union's involvement in the Afghan War, where good hot-and-high performance was in demand, changed the situation, causing Mi-8MT production to be stepped up dramatically. By 1986 the 'second-generation' *Hip* and its derivatives had displaced the Mi-8T at Kazan'.

Initially almost all Mi-8MTs were delivered to the Soviet military; civil deliveries did not begin until approximately 1983, by which time close to 400 had been built. The civil version lacked external stores outriggers and some other items (albeit not all military Mi-8MTs had weapons outriggers either).

Of course, the Mi-8MT also underwent upgrades as production progressed. For instance, aircraft built from 1978 onwards were powered by improved TV3-117MT Srs 3 engines.

A host of important changes was brought about by the Afghan War in which the Mi-8 (including the Mi-8MT) was actively used; the Mil' OKB had to take measures to enhance combat survivability and give the helicopter a bigger punch. Among other things, the hatch in the starboard clamshell cargo door was enlarged to facilitate using a machine-gun for self-defence (or egress in an emergency). Operational experience with the Mi-8 and Mi-24 in Afghanistan showed that the big, heavy helicopters inevitably kicked up a local dust storm when operating from dirt pads. To prevent excessive engine wear and foreign object damage (FOD), vortex-type intake filters called PZU (***pyy**leza**shchit**noye **oost**-**roy**stvo* – 'anti-dust device') had to be developed. Several versions were tested; the definitive (so-called mushroom-type) filters resembling partly deflated footballs proved extremely effective; they became standard equipment on the Mi-8MT almost immediately (in 1977) and were retrofitted to some Mi-8Ts as well.

Internal and external flightdeck armour was added to protect the crew. A flexible 7.62-mm (.30 calibre) Kalashnikov PKT machine-gun was installed in the nose, often augmented by two or four more PKT machine-guns with associated ammunition boxes mounted on top of the weapons outriggers. Some aircraft were armed with 12.7-mm (.50 calibre) NSV-12,7 Ootyos (Cliff) heavy machine-guns or 30-mm (1.18 calibre) AGS-17 Plamya (Flame; pronounced ***plah**mya*) automatic grenade launchers in the entry door and rear hatch. The all-time favourite external stores used on the Mi-8MT were the UPK-23-250 pods (*oonifi**tsee**rovannyy **push**echnyy kon**tey**ner* – standardised gun pod) containing a Gryazev/Shipoonov GSh-23L cannon with 250 rounds, the B-8V20 FFAR pods holding 20 80-mm (3.15-in.) S-8 rockets apiece, and the massive GUV gun pod (*gon**dola** ooniver**sahl'**naya verto**lyot**naya* – versatile [gun] pod for helicopters), aka 9A669. The latter could be configured with either a Yakooshev/Borzov YakB-12,7 four-barrel machine-gun flanked by two 7.62-mm (.30 calibre) GShG-7,62 four-barrel Gatling machine-guns or an AG-17A grenade launcher.

The advent of shoulder-launched surface-to-air missiles on the Afghan theatre of operations dictated the need for infra-red countermeasures (IRCM). Triple-lobe air/exhaust mixers called EVU (*ekra**nee**ruyu-shcheye vykhlop**noy**e oo**stroy**stvo* – lit. 'exhaust screening device') could be fitted to

Above: An example of the unarmed commercial configuration of the Mi-8MT. Curiously, this aircraft (CCCP-22367) wears 'Mi-18' nose titles, though it is clearly not a Mi-18 (see below)!

This Hungarian Air Force Mi-8MT (Mi-17) serialled '701 Red' (c/n 104M01) was operated by the United Nations Stabilising Force in Bosnia and Herzegovina (SFOR) in MEDEVAC configuration.

Mi-8MTV-1 RA-27180 (c/n 96182) represents the unarmed commercial configuration. This one, however, is operated by EMERCOM of Russia – the paramilitary civil aid and protection agency.

reduce the helicopter's IR signature. After mixing the exhaust with cool outside air they directed it upwards into the main rotor downwash, reducing exhaust gas temperature by 350-400°C (660-750°F). However, the mixers could only be fitted to aircraft built from approximately 1984 onwards which had vertically cut-off jetpipes.

ASO-2V-02 chaff/flare launchers (*avtomaht sbrosa otrazhahteley* – automatic chaff dispenser) firing 32 26-mm (1-in) flares apiece were mounted under the tailboom for protection against heat-seeking missiles, later giving way to six identical forward-inclined units on the aft fuselage sides. An L-166V-11E active IRCM jammer, aka SOEP-V1A Lipa (Linden, pronounced *leepah*; SOEP = *stahntsiya optiko-elektronnykh pomekh* – lit. 'optoelectronic jammer'), was installed aft of the main rotor head. The jammer was a thimble-shaped fairing enclosing a powerful xenon lamp with a rotating reflector, in the fashion of the flashing light on a police car. It emitted a pulsating IR signal which darted erratically, disappearing and reappearing, causing the missile to lose track of the target.

Incidentally, Soviet ECM equipment habitually received 'horticultural' codenames, but 'lipa' has a double meaning. The word is used colloquially to mean 'fake', which is perfectly applicable since the jammer emits 'fake target' signals!

Some measures were aimed at improving survivability. The fuel tanks were equipped with an inert gas pressurisation system to reduce the danger of explosion if hit by enemy fire. The tail rotor control cables were spaced wider apart to stop them from being shot away by a single round, hydraulic lines were shielded and so on.

Numerous changes were introduced in order to improve maintainability and ease day-to-day operation. As a result, the Mil' OKB succeeded in creating a unique transport/assault helicopter unmatched in combat efficiency and survivability by any other existing helicopter in its class.

Mi-17 export civil/military utility helicopter

In 1981 the Mi-8MT was unveiled at the 33rd Paris Air Show. The Mil' OKB chose to market the export version under a separate designation, Mi-17, and the prototype displayed at Le Bourget with the non-standard registration CCCP-17718 (c/n unknown) and the exhibit code H-350 wore appropriate 'Mi-17' nose titles. After Le Bourget '81 the Mi-8MT/Mi-17 received the NATO reporting name *Hip-H* which was used for both armed and unarmed versions, even though the designation Mi-17 applied only to the unarmed civil/military utility helicopters.

As was the case with the 'first-generation' Mi-8, the Mi-8MT/Mi-17 spawned a large family of more or less specialised versions, both civil and military. These are described below, and the Kazan'-built versions are dealt with first.

Mi-17P passenger helicopter

An export passenger-configured version of the Mi-8MT/Mi-17 similar in cabin layout to the Mi-8P (but featuring circular windows and large rear clamshell doors) was designated Mi-17P.

Mi-17S VIP helicopter

A few Mi-17s were custom-built as VIP aircraft and are still used by the political and military leaders of several foreign countries.

Other Mi-17s (or Mi-8MTV-1s) have been converted to VIP configuration, which involved substituting the normal circular windows with rectangular ones; sometimes a Western air conditioner (the brand varied – Webasto, Sütrak etc.) was installed in a flattened rectangular housing on the fuselage underside.

Known examples are SU-YAF (c/n 202M08) for the Palestinian Administration and 9A-HRH (c/n 95876) for the Croatian Army. Both have been converted from second-hand utility examples.

Mi-8MTV-1/Mi-17 fire-fighting versions

A special version of the Mi-17 was developed for fighting fires in built-up or inaccessible areas and in forests. The helicopter carried an externally slung tank holding 2 m³ (70.6 cu ft) of water or fire retardant; it could also carry up to 20 firefighters who disembarked by rappelling down lines dropped from the helicopter while the latter was hovering at up to 45 m (147 ft).

Similarly, the Mi-8MTV-1s operated by the Russian Ministry for Emergency Control and Civil Protection (EMERCOM of Russia) can be equipped with a VSU-5 rubberised fabric bucket (*vodoslivnoye oostroystvo* – water dropping device) holding 5 m³ (176.5 cu ft) or 5 tons (11,000 lb) of water for fire-fighting operations.

Mi-8MTV-1/Mi-17 Malaysian fire-fighting conversions

Two *Hip-Hs* operated by the Fire and Rescue Department of Malaysia – Mi-17-1V M49-01 (c/n 459M01) and Mi-8MTV-1 M49-02 (c/n 95824) were converted into fire-fighting helicopters by the local company Airod. For fighting fires in high-rise buildings the helicopters were equipped with water cannons which could be set to 'fire' a jet of water straight ahead or at 90° to the direction of flight. The water tank was housed in the cabin and could be refilled in flight by means of a hose dropped down through the hatch for the external sling lock.

Mi-8MT VIP versions

The Mi-8MT served as a basis for a whole series of VIP and executive helicopters built for various Soviet government agencies. These aircraft bore the designations **Mi-8S-1, Mi-8S-2, Mi-8MD, Mi-8MS, Mi-8MSO, Mi-8MSD, Mi-8MO, Mi-8TP (second use of designation)** and so on. Unfortunately no details are known. To be precise, three versions have been identified visually but it is not known which is which. Two of the helicopters were basically equivalent to the 'first-generation' Mi-8S – ie, they are 'a Mi-8MT from the waist up and a Mi-8S from the waist down', combining the former version's TV3-117MT engines, power train and rotor system with the Mi-8S's rectangular windows (five to port and seven to starboard), airstair door, rear entry door and air conditioner. Both aircraft wore Soviet Air Force two-tone green camouflage and star insignia but no tactical codes. One, the helicopter used by the Soviet leader Leonid I. Brezhnev, had two widely spaced rod aerials on the tailboom ahead of the upper anti-collision light and two closely spaced blade aerials aft of it. The other helicopter (used by the Soviet Minister of Defence Marshal Dmitriy F. Ustinov) had one large and one small blade aerial fore and aft of the upper ACL, while the port emergency exit had a solid cover with a circular window.

The third helicopter, CCCP-24101 (c/n unknown), was quasi-civil and was operated by the Soviet Armed Forces General Headquarters in an olive drab colour scheme with Aeroflot titles. The aircraft was a custom-built cross-breed between a Mi-8MT and a Mi-8S, featuring circular windows and one emergency exit to starboard but small clamshell doors/rear entry door and a forward airstair door, plus a weather radar in a hemispherical radome in the nose.

Mi-19 tactical airborne command post

Like father, like son: as the Mi-8 evolved into the Mi-9 airborne command post, so the Mi-8MT served as a basis for the next-generation ABCP designated Mi-19 to underscore the similarity of mission. The design approach was the same: the Mi-19 combined the Mi-9's basic airframe with the Mi-8MT's engines, power train and rotor system. The aircraft, which entered production and service in 1987, was intended for controlling the operations of mechanised infantry and tank divisions. Unlike the Ulan-Ude built Mi-9, no separate c/n sequence was used apparently.

Mi-19R airborne command post

A sub-variant of the Mi-19 ABCP designated Mi-19R was developed for the Strategic Missile Forces (hence the R suffix for *Ra**ket**nyye voy**ska** strate**gich**eskovo nazna**chen**iya* – Strategic Missile Forces).

Mi-19R ambulance conversion

A late-production Mi-19 (c/n 96152) was demilitarised and converted into an ambulance helicopter (possibly it was actually **built** in this guise and never delivered to the military!). Registered RA-25414 and manufactured on 30th July 1993, the aircraft combined the ABCP's Mi-8P-style rear end (with an angular bulge on port clamshell door characteristic of some Mi-9s) and reduced set of circular windows with a Mi-8S-type airstair door and air conditioner, a weather radar and high-set additional external tanks. Delivered to Nadymspetsavia by late 2001, the helicopter carried *Sani**tar**naya avi**ah**tsiya* – ***Mer**iya **Na**dyma* (Ambulance aviation – Nadym City Administration) titles and 'Mi-8MTV-1' nose titles (no separate designation in known).

Mi-8MTI (Mi-13) ECM helicopter

This electronic jamming derivative of the Mi-8MT can be identified by two large rectangular housings on the fuselage sides in the manner of the Mi-8PP (the starboard housing partly obstructs the emergency exit; there are three windows to port and two to starboard). The flat outer faces of these housings are

Above: The Mi-8MTI ECM helicopter (aka Mi-13) is characterised by antenna arrays in rectangular housings flanking the fuselage and tailboom.

Above: Starboard side view of the same Mi-8MTI coded '34 Red'; the starboard forward array appears to partly obstruct the emergency exit but it is still usable (the lower photo shows why).

Front view of the Mi-8MTI, showing how the antenna arrays are mounted on struts a short distance from the fuselage.

Top and above: The Mi-8MTPB (called Mi-17PP or Mi-17TPB in export form) features the same lateral 'suitcases' with bulged sides, the same heat exchanger array and the same placement of the main ECM antenna arrays as the Mi-8PP/Mi-8PPA. These views illustrate the different design of the antenna arrays with 32 individual cells each (eight rows of four), the additional arrays on the tailboom and the quasi-triangular housings replacing the rearmost windows.
Below, left and right: Front and rear views of the Mi-8MTPB. Note how the rear antenna arrays are faired into the tailboom.

composed of 40 square dielectric panels each, accommodating antenna arrays. Two more narrow boxy housings with antenna arrays flank the root of the tailboom (each 'box' has five panels of unequal size). A large blade aerial is installed ahead of the anti-collision light, and the standard Doppler box under the tailboom is retained. There are no ventral heat exchangers; nor is the SOEP-V1A IRCM jammer fitted.

Mi-8MTPB ECM helicopter

This ECM version of the Mi-8MT is very similar to the Mi-8PP, featuring the same 'suitcases' with bulged outer faces on the centre fuselage sides and the six heat exchangers under the fuselage. The *Hip-K*'s antenna farms on the rear fuselage sides are replaced by large arrays, each of which incorporates 32 circular dielectric panels (in eight vertical rows of four); a smaller array incorporating four dielectric panels of the same type is installed on each side of the tailboom in line with the Doppler box, giving a total of 72 emitter antennas.

There are two windows to port and one to starboard, the windows immediately aft of the lateral 'suitcases' being replaced by small housings of quasi-triangular shape with one angle pointing downward; the signal flare launchers are located above the port housing. A large blade aerial is installed ahead of the anti-collision light. The Mi-8MTPB features an SOEP-V1A IRCM jammer and four ASO-2V chaff/flare dispensers under the tailboom.

Mi-8MTSh ECM helicopter

This ECM derivative of the Mi-8MT came in three sub-variants (Mi-8MTSh-1, Mi-8MTSh-2 and Mi-8MTSh-3) differing in equipment fit and external details. While basically similar in appearance to the Mi-8MTPB, the helicopter differs in having the 'suitcases' below the engine jetpipes replaced by smaller but much deeper teardrop housings with flattened outer faces.

Above: The Mi-8MTSh-2 shows its flattened teardrop lateral fairings and the multi-segment rear antenna arrays. Note that the starboard half of the non-functional clamshell doors appears to incorporate an extra APU.
Below ad bottom: These views illustrate how deep the Mi-8MTSh's lateral fairings are and how the rear antenna arrays are attached to the fuselage.

The Mi-8PGE is very similar to the Mi-8MTI (Mi-13), except for the windowless entry door.

The Mi-8MTSh-2 can be identified by the lateral antenna arrays in the form of several vertical boxes of unequal length, some of which incorporate circular apertures; the length of these 'boxes' increases from nose to tail and the rearmost ones are built in two sections. A loop aerial is installed ventrally in line with the main rotor head, and the tailboom carries two identical blade aerials above the Doppler box. The number of heat exchangers is reduced from six to three; the Mi-8MTSh-2 features an IRCM jammer.

The Mi-8MTSh-3 has differently shaped antenna arrays on the rear fuselage sides and lacks the ventral heat exchangers.

Mi-8PGE (Mi-17PG?) export ECM helicopter

An export ECM derivative of the Mi-8MT was announced in 2001 (the E stands for ***eks**port-nyy*); apparently Mi-8PGE is an alternative designation of the Mi-17PG. This version is very similar outwardly to the Mi-8MTI, except that the entry door lacks a window .

Mi-17PP (Mi-17TPB) export ECM helicopter

A version of the Mi-8MTPB was developed for export to the Warsaw Pact nations as the Mi-17PP, although some sources later referred to the same aircraft as Mi-17TPB. The helicopter was designed for jamming the enemy's AD and surface-to-air missile guidance radars, as well as the fire control radars of enemy fighters. A digital signal processing system enabled the mission crew to determine priority threats and select the jamming signal frequency accordingly. Two such helicopters were delivered to the Hungarian Air Force (serialled '706 Red' and '707 Red'), while the Bulgarian Air Force operated at least one Mi-17TPB ('432 White').

Mi-17Z-2 ECM/ELINT helicopter

This ECM version with an additional electronic intelligence (ELINT) capability was developed in Czechoslovakia, the Z standing for *zástavba* (modification or refit). The two helicopters converted to Mi-17Z-2 configuration ('0807 White' and '0808 White', c/ns 108M07 and 108M08) could be easily identified by the upward-inclined racks on the fuselage sides, each of which carried two large dielectric 'drums' positioned vertically in tandem. The mission suite was totally indigenous.

Mi-8MTYa ECM helicopter

This ECM version is identifiable by the huge dipole-like aerials on the fuselage sides installed at a nose-up angle to the fuselage waterline.

Other ECM versions

In addition to the versions described above, the ECM variants of the *Hip-H* include the **Mi-8MTP, Mi-8MTPI, Mi-8MTPSh, Mi-8MTD, Mi-8MTS, Mi-8MTR1, Mi-8MTR2, Mi-8MTU, Mi-8MT-1S** etc. Some of these versions were exported as the Mi-17P (equals Mi-8MTP?), Mi-17PI (equals Mi-8MTPI) and so on. Unfortunately few or no details are known, making a detailed description impossible.

Mi-8RTR SIGINT helicopter

Several Mi-8MTs were converted for signals intelligence (SIGINT). Outwardly these machines designated Mi-8RTR (***rah**diotekh-**nich**eskaya raz**ved**ka* – SIGINT) could be identified by three ventral aerials.

Up-armoured/heavily armed versions

The Mil' OKB developed a number of versions based on the Mi-8MT featuring enhanced armour protection and permanently installed or removable machine-gun, cannon and rocket/missile armament. These included the Mi-8PPV (***push**echno-poole**myot**noye vo'oroo-**zhen**iye* – cannon and machine-gun armament), Mi-8BV, Mi-8MTVO and other versions; unfortunately again no details are known.

Mi-8MTB armoured MEDEVAC helicopter

In 1978 the Mi-8MT evolved into the Mi-8MTB casualty evacuation/flying surgery ward helicopter featuring armour protection for the flightdeck and cabin alike (the B presumably stood for *broni**rov**annyy* – armoured). It was used successfully during the Afghan War.

Mi-8MTM MEDEVAC helicopter

Another 'flying hospital' version of the Mi-8MT was designated Mi-8MTM (*medi**tsin**skiy* – medical). This version saw limited production.

An evacuation crew carries a Soviet cosmonaut on a stretcher from the re-entry capsule to the waiting Mi-8MTN MEDEVAC chopper. The cosmonaut is barely able to move after a lengthy period of zero gravity.

Mi-8MTN SAR helicopter

In 1979 the Mil' OKB brought out the Mi-8MTN, an SAR version for the Soviet Cosmonaut Group designed for evacuating spacemen from the touchdown site and providing medical assistance. The Mi-8MTN could be identified by the full-length Dayglo orange 'lightning bolt' markings applied over the standard two-tone green camouflage and by the FPP-7 landing light/searchlight in a fairing offset to starboard in line with the entry door.

Mi-8MN and Mi-8MTT SAR helicopters

Two further SAR versions of the Mi-8MT for the Soviet Cosmonaut Group, designated Mi-8MN and Mi-8MTT, were intended for locating and evacuating the re-entry modules of Soviet spacecraft and the spacemen themselves.

Mi-17M *Spasatel'* SAR/ambulance helicopter

By mid-1992 the Kazan' Helicopter Plant had converted one of its own Mi-8MTV-1s, CCCP-95448 (c/n 95448) manufactured in 1990, into the prototype of a new SAR/MEDEVAC helicopter designated Mi-17M; the M could be deciphered as *modifi**tsee**rovannyy* or *medi**tsin**skiy* with equal justification.

The standard 1.4 x 0.62 m (55⅛ x 24½ in) entry door was replaced by a double-width sliding door measuring 1.4 x 1.25 m (55⅛ x 49¼ in) and incorporating two windows which was borrowed from the Mi-14PS maritime SAR helicopter; this required the port strap-on fuel tank to be modified. An SLG-300 cargo/rescue hoist (*stre**la**-le**byod**ka groozo**va**ya*) with a lifting capacity of 300 kg (660 lb) was installed near the door, allowing two rescuees to be lifted at a time by means of a special basket. A rack with rescue means was mounted on the inside of the port clamshell cargo door, while the starboard door incorporated an enlarged hatch. An FPP-7 landing light/searchlight was fitted in a fairing offset to starboard, as on the Mi-8MTN, and a ventral anti-collision light was added. Inflatable emergency floats were fitted low on the forward fuselage sides and on the main gear axles for overwater operations; the main floats looked almost like wheel spats when stowed, assuming a doughnut shape in inflated condition.

The helicopter featured a Kontur-Ts weather radar with a colour display (hence the Ts for *tsvet**noy** ek**rahn***). The Doppler box under the tailboom was extended aft, the shallower 'add-on' housing a BUR-1-2Zh flight data recorder, and the forward IFF aerial was moved to a teardrop fairing on the flightdeck roof, as on the Ulan-Ude built Mi-171 (see later). Two unswept blade aerials were installed on the tailboom fore and aft of the upper anti-collision light.

Above: The nose of the Mi-17M demonstrator (CCCP-95448) at the MosAeroShow-92, showing the radar, the forward flotation bag fairings and the faired FPP-7 searchlight under the cabin heater.

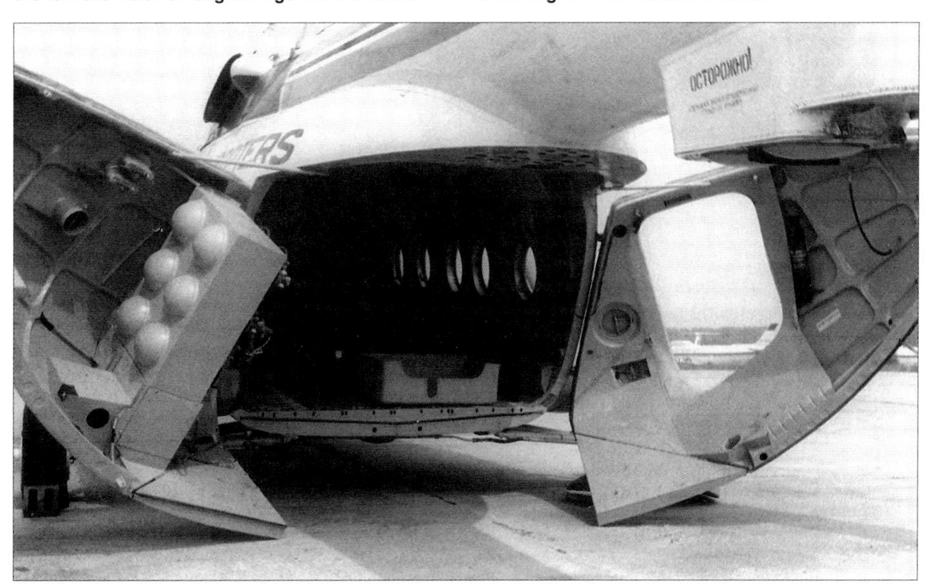

Above: The open clamshell doors of the Mi-17M with the lower portions unfolded and the escape hatch cover removed. Note the rescue equipment rack on the port door.

CCCP-95448 makes a demonstration flight at the MosAeroShow-92 on 14th August 1992 with the flotation gear inflated – much to the joy of the spectators.

In this guise Mi-17M CCCP-95448 was unveiled at MosAeroShow-92, Russia's first real airshow, on 11-16th August 1992 at Zhukovskiy, taking part in the flying display. Later the helicopter was reregistered CCCP-70937 and then RA-70937. With the latter registration the aircraft was displayed at Le Bourget in 1993, wearing a new red/white colour scheme and the exhibit code H-305.

Mi-17G ambulance helicopter

This was the advertised export 'flying hospital' version of the Mi-17 (G = ***gos****pital'* – hospital).

Mi-8MTD 'Navstar' SAR helicopter

In 1979 the Mil' OKB developed an SAR version of the Mi-8MT equipped with the Navstar radio navigation system. Its mission was to locate aircraft in distress (instrumentally and visually) and then rescue the survivors from the crash site in hover mode. Designated Mi-8MTD 'Navstar', the helicopter was tested with the active participation of Soviet Air Force test pilot Col. Anatoliy Andronov.

Mi-8MA SAR helicopter (first use of designation)

A special SAR version of the *Hip-H* optimised for operations in the Arctic regions was designated Mi-8MA (*ark****tich****eskiy* – Arctic, used attributively).

Mi-8MTA tactical reconnaissance helicopter

A tactical reconnaissance derivative of the Mi-8MT designated Mi-8MTA saw production and service with the Soviet Army. No details are available of its design and equipment.

Mi-8MTS and Mi-8MTT radiation reconnaissance helicopters

Two radiation reconnaissance versions based on the *Hip-H* – the Mi-8MTS and Mi-8MTT – were developed in 1986.

Mi-8MTF photo survey helicopter

A photo survey version derivative of the Mi-8MT designated Mi-8MTF (*foto****s'yom****ochnyy*) appeared in 1984. It featured a port for a vertical camera at the rear of the cabin, obtained by removing the lower triangular portions of the cargo doors and fitting a special structure instead.

Mi-8MT paradrop training version

A trainer version of the *Hip-H* designed for training personnel in paradrop techniques was brought out in 1987. No details are known.

Mi-8MT RPV trials support version

In 1988 a Mi-8MT was specially modified for locating and recovering target drones, remotely piloted vehicles (RPVs) and cruise missiles undergoing trials and fitted with test equipment so that the flight data recorders could be deciphered. Quite probably there is a slight error in dates and the aircraft in question is an uncoded early-production Soviet Air Force Mi-8MT (c/n 93115) operated by LII. This aircraft served as a recovery systems testbed in 1984-89; the rear clamshell doors were removed and two long hinged booms painted in black and white stripes were hinged to the aft fuselage near the aperture; these could be swung down to snag the parachute deployed by the RPV as it floated earthwards, its engine cut.

Mi-8MA patrol helicopter (second use of designation)

Confusingly, the Mi-8MA designation was reused in 1990 for a version of the Mi-8MT designed for patrolling the Soviet Union's borders and economic exclusion zone.

Mi-8MTSKh agricultural helicopter

Like the Mi-8T, the Mi-8MT had an experimental agricultural version designated Mi-8MTSKh (***sel'****skokho****ziay****stvennyy* – agricultural).

This bizarre-looking Mi-8MT photographed at Pushkin was extensively modified by LNPO Leninets as a radar systems testbed. Note the 'gun camera' above the entry door.

Mi-8MTL firebomber

In 1983 the Mi-8MTL water bomber designed for fighting forest fires was brought out as a successor to the Mi-8TL. This version was widely used both in the Soviet Union (and subsequently Russia) and abroad at the request of foreign governments. For instance, in the summer of 1997 a Bashkirian Airlines Mi-8MTL (identity unknown) captained by Askhat Kooramshin participated in a massive forest fire control operation in Spain, departing Ufa on 7th July. The operation involved a multi-national rotary task force of 250 helicopters configured as firebombers.

Mi-8MT weather research helicopters

In 1990 12 Mi-8MT helicopters were converted for weather research. Unfortunately none have been identified yet.

Mi-8MT EMP measurement aircraft

An uncoded Soviet Air Force Mi-8MT (c/n unknown) operated by LII was converted into a research vehicle designated Mi-8LL for measuring electromagnetic fields and electromagnetic pulses emitted by ships. The helicopter featured a wide, shallow flat-bottomed antenna housing under the flightdeck and carried a lattice-like air data boom on the nose.

Mi-8MT radar systems testbed

Another uncoded Soviet Air Force Mi-8MT (c/n unknown) was converted for testing new radar systems by the All-Union Electronics Research Institute (VNIIRA – *Vseso****yooz****nyy na****ooch****no-is****sled****ovatel'skiy insti****toot*** ***rah****dioelek****troni****ki*), aka LNPO Leninets (Leninist), in Leningrad. (LNPO = *Lenin****grahd****skoye na****ooch****no-proiz****vod****stvennoye obyedi****nen****iye* – Leningrad Scientific & Production Association.) This establishment, now known as the Leninets Holding Company of St. Petersburg, was one of the Soviet Union's leading avionics houses.

The helicopter's appearance was really bizarre. A rectangular-section adapter occupying the entire width of the fuselage supplanted the lower row of the flightdeck glazing; it carried what appears to be a phased-array radar of unknown type in a truncated, suitcase-like radome, making the machine look uncannily like a hippopotamus. The Mi-8MT was based at Pushkin, an airfield near Leningrad where VNIIRA's flight test facility was, and still is.

Mi-18 transport/assault helicopter prototypes

In 1977 the Kazan' branch office of the Mil' OKB embarked on the long-planned Stage B of the Mi-8 modernisation programme. On 29th June of that year the VPK passed resolution No.168 calling for an in-depth upgrade

Above and below: Upon completion of the initial flight test the first prototype Mi-18 (c/n 93038) was converted into this special mission version of unknown purpose. Note the airstair door, the Mi-8P style rear end, the unusual window arrangement, the large blister to starboard and the dorsal aerial farm.

of the Mi-8MT, and a specific operational requirement (SOR) for the new version was formally approved on 7th April 1978. The Kazan' branch had to do all the work on the programme because the head office in Moscow had its hands full designing and upgrading other helicopter types.

Two Mi-8MTs were earmarked for conversion into the prototypes of the Stage B helicopter which received a new designation, Mi-18. Work on increasing the *Hip-H*'s cabin volume began in mid-1978. On the first prototype (c/n 93038) it was decided to simply stretch the fuselage by inserting two 'plugs' fore and aft of the CG – a 500-mm (1 ft 7⅝ in) section at the manufacturing break between the forward and centre fuselage sections and a 680-mm (2 ft 2¾ in) section at centre fuselage frame 13. This increased seating capacity to 36 passengers versus 28 (nine rows four-abreast), 29 fully equipped troops versus 24 and 18 stretcher patients versus 12 (although the latter case is hardly *seating* capacity!).

The helicopter's flight instrumentation and avionics were updated concurrently. The engines, power train/rotor system and landing gear remained unaltered. There were seven cabin windows to port (including the one in the entry door) and six to starboard; the Doppler box under the tailboom was extended all the way forward to the fuselage and received a more streamlined aft end.

In this guise the unpainted and unmarked 'Mi-18 Mk I' entered flight test in 1979. Early flights were in unarmed configuration, but soon standard external stores outriggers with triple pylons were installed, allowing weapons tests to be performed. However, it soon became clear that the 'quick fix' approach did not work; the stretch had reduced the Mi-18's vibration and structural stiffness characteristics unacceptably.

To explain the situation better it should be noted that two mainframes in the Mi-8's centre fuselage (Nos 7 and 10) absorbed virtually all structural loads. These two huge U-shaped structures, each of which consisted of three milled components, carried the main gearbox bearer truss (ie, the fuselage was effectively suspended from the main rotor by these mainframes). Frame 10 served as the anchoring point for the main landing gear, while frame 7 incorporated the external stores outrigger attachment fittings which, among other things, absorbed the loads created when the rockets were fired. Frames 7 and 10 also served as attachment points for the strap-on fuel tanks and the cabin floor which was manufactured as a separate structure. Given the stretch fore and aft of the all-important structural components, the floor (and the fuselage as a whole) could no longer provide the required rigidity.

In 1980 the Mi-18 was presented to a government commission which voiced a lot of well-argued complaints.

It should be noted that the Mi-18 had been created mainly in the interests of the military. At that time the Soviet Union was sinking deeper and deeper into the morass of the Afghan War; the war claimed thousands of human lives, forcing the aircraft designers to take measures aimed at improving survivability. In the case of the Mi-8MT this meant radically enhancing the armour protection of the flightdeck and introducing an explosion suppression feature in the fuel tanks for higher resistance to ground fire. However, whereas on the Mi-8MT the weight of the extra armour in the nose was counterbalanced by the fuel tanks' inert gas pressurisation system and the extra machine-gun at the rear of the cabin, this did not work for the Mi-18 because the extra flightdeck armour was located much further forward of the CG, causing the latter to shift forward unacceptably.

In May 1981 the Ministry of Defence issued a revised SOR for the Mi-18. By then the design office in Kazan' had devised a way of curing the CG problem; the forward fuselage stretch was eliminated, whereas the length of the rear fuselage 'plug' was increased from 680 mm to 1,020 mm (3 ft 4⅛ in), the resulting rearward CG shift offsetting the weight of the flightdeck armour. At the same time the fuselage was redesigned completely. The engineers developed a new cargo floor design with multi-section frames and one-piece longerons whose height was increased from 180 mm (7 in) to 400 mm (15¾ in). This not only increased structural stiffness and improved vibration characteristics dramatically but also allowed the vulnerable external fuel tanks to be relocated under the cabin floor where they could be protected by armour. Additionally, the reinforced floor increased the helicopter's payload; it incorporated a hatch for the external sling system measuring 350 x 800 mm (1 ft 1¾ in x 2 ft 7½ in).

The stiffer fuselage structure made it possible to utilise a different landing gear design without the Mi-8's characteristically long main gear oleo struts anchored high on the fuselage sides. To improve the helicopter's aerodynamics the engineers decided to use a retractable landing gear on the reworked 'Mi-18 Mk II'. The twin-wheel nose unit retracted aft and the single-wheel levered-suspension main units retracted inwards into small streamlined sponsons on the rear fuselage sides; all wheel wells remained open when the gear was up (as distinct from the Mi-24 which had wheel well doors).

The longer and deeper fuselage, together with the new landing gear design, changed the Mi-18's looks completely; while clearly having more proportional lines than the Mk I, the Mk II had a somewhat cartoon-like appearance, as if someone had taken a stock Mi-8MT and inflated it to the point of bursting. The rear fuselage contours were altered; so was the clamshell cargo door design, the doors appearing rather smaller due to a more sharply sloping hinge line. The stiffer fuselage structure made it possible to incorporate a second entry door symmetrically to starboard, reducing disembarkation time considerably. The Doppler box was deleted, the antennas now being mounted flush with the underside of the tailboom.

Detail design work on the 'Mi-18 Mk II', which received the in-house designation *izdeliye* 184, proceeded at a brisk pace. A large amount of work was performed in 1981-83; among other things, it was decided to utilise new wider-chord tail rotor blades to improve control efficiency. The integral underfloor fuel tanks were filled with explosion suppression polyurethane foam and featured an outer self-sealing layer of latex, which allowed the inert gas pressurisation system to be dispensed with. The all-new landing gear proved to be no heavier than that of the production model and was designed for a gross weight of 14 tons (30,860 lb); it underwent a separate test programme, including crashworthiness tests on a ground rig, and earned the highest praise.

Changes were made to various systems and equipment, including installation of more modern generators with an overload protection system, new alkaline DC batteries and new instrument panels in the flightdeck (the latter also featured a bank of caution/warning lights). Finding a place for the cabin heater proved to be a challenge. The introduction of the starboard entry door made it impossible to keep the KO-50 cabin heater in its usual location low on the starboard side. On the 'Mi-18 Mk I' of 1979 the engineers had tried using the APU for heating and air conditioning, as was the case on the Mi-14, but at normal power the AI-9V could not cope with the larger cabin volume. Running the APU at higher power caused air filters in the system to become clogged and the carbon monoxide content in the cabin air increased to an unacceptable level. Therefore on the Mk II the engineers decided to leave well enough alone and reverted to the KO-50, finding a place for it under the cabin floor (the air intake was located on the forward fuselage underside).

Generally the improved aerodynamics of the redesigned Mi-18 gave good reason to expect an improvement in performance and commercial efficiency. Thus the Mi-18 would have become the progenitor of a family of its own, including heli-liner, combi, VIP and flying hospital versions. The stretched, reinforced fuselage and the proposed new glassfibre main rotor blades offered an increase in payload, while the hermetically sealed integral tanks increased buoyancy in the event of ditching, thereby enhancing safety. The maximum take-off weight was 13,500 kg (29,760 lb).

On 28th April 1984 the 'Mi-18 Mk II' (c/n 93114) successfully made its first flight with Kazan' Helicopter Plant test pilots N. A. Zhen and V. T. Dvoryankin at the controls. Wearing standard two-tone green camouflage and originally no tactical code (it was later coded '84 Red', apparently an allusion to *izdeliye* 184), the second prototype featured a nose machine-gun mount, two pylons on each side (on outriggers of a different type than hitherto) and an SOEP-V1A IRCM jammer. The manufacturer's flight tests revealed a marked improvement of performance over the standard Mi-8MT and it was proposed to launch production at the Kazan' plant as early as 1985. Unfortunately, the onset of *perestroika*, Mikhail S. Gorbachov's new policy, wrecked these plans. The transfer of manufacturing drawings and other documents from the design office to the production plant began in 1987, two years later than intended. For the first time in the Soviet Union the drawings were made on a computer and handed over to the factory on floppy disks (as requested by the factory) – ie, the Mi-18 was the first Soviet aircraft to make use of computer-aided design (CAD).

However, just about then the Soviet government declared it a priority task to develop and produce new types of aviation hardware meeting world standards. This approach suited the factory fine, as the Kazan' Helicopter Plant was not overjoyed at the prospect of building 'just another version of the Mi-8' and was all for building the new-generation Mi-38 medium-lift helicopter which had good sales prospects. (Incidentally, the ADP of the Mi-38 was developed by the Kazan' branch office of the Mil' OKB, using a lot of the design features that had been created for and tested on the Mi-18. What irony!) The Mil' OKB in Moscow, apparently jealous because the Kazan' branch had created the Mi-18 on its own without asking for assistance from the head office, likewise did not insist on having the type put into production (a typical 'not invented here' approach).

These circumstances conspired against the Mi-18 which, for all its high performance, was never even submitted for State acceptance trials. The second example was more fortunate, being preserved for posterity in the base museum of the Soviet Army Aviation's 344th TsBP i PLS (*Tsentr boye***voy** *podgo***tov***ki i pere***oo***chivaniya* **lyot***novo sos***tah***va* – Combat and Conversion Training Centre, = operational conversion unit) in Torzhok. Still, the effort was not in vain: many of the features verified on the Mi-18, such as the extra entry door to starboard, later found use on advanced versions of the Mi-8/Mi-17.

The 'Mi-18 Mk II' had a crew of three; the cabin accommodated 30-36 passengers, 29 troops or 18 stretcher patients. The helicopter was powered by TV3-117MT engines rated at 1,900 shp for take-off. The specifications were as follows: main rotor diameter 21.3 m (69 ft 10½ in), cabin dimensions 6.34 x 2.34 x 1.8 m (20 ft 9⅝ in x 7 ft 8⅛ in x 5 ft 11¾ in); empty weight 7.55 tons (16,640 lb), normal take-off weight 11.5 tons (25,350 lb), maximum TOW 13.5 tons (29,760 lb), normal payload 3 tons (6,610 lb), maximum payload 5 tons (11,020 lb) internally or 4 tons (8,820 lb) externally slung; top speed 250 km/h (155 mph), cruising speed 220 km/h (136 mph), hovering ceiling 3,200 m (10,500 ft), service ceiling 5,000 m (16,400 ft), range 580 km (360 miles).

Later, the first prototype was extensively modified into an obscure special mission version and registered CCCP-22932. It now had a Mi-8S-style airstair door and rear end, a much-reduced complement of rectangular windows, a huge transparent blister over some optical system in the rearmost window to starboard, a standard Doppler box plus large 'hockey stick' aerials atop the tailboom and above the port clamshell door!

Mi-8MTKO night-capable transport/ assault helicopter

Learning from experience gained in the First Chechen War of 1994-96, the Mil' Moscow Helicopter Plant developed a night-capable version of the Mi-8MT to meet an order from the former Russian Army Aviation. (The latter does not exist as a separate service any more, as currently Russia's military rotary-wing assets are under the control of the Air Force.)

Above: One of the prototypes of the night-capable Mi-8MTKO, '29 Yellow' (c/n 94309), at Zhukovskiy in February 2000. It had participated in combat in Chechnya, as revealed by the fact that the tactical code is smeared over with black grease for security reasons. The helicopter carries B-8V20 FFAR pods and UPK-23-250 cannon pods. Note the ground power cable connected to the receptacle on the nose.

The same Mi-8MTKO c/n 94309 in the static park at the MAKS-2001 airshow, now displaying its tactical close for the world to see. The 'ball turret' under the nose is clearly visible.

Above: Close-up of the gyrostabilised optronic system on Mi-8MTKO '67 Yellow' (c/n 94691) displayed at the MAKS-99.

Designated Mi-8MTKO, the helicopter features a gyrostabilised optronic system in a very neat 'ball turret' mounted low on the starboard side of the nose. It is a product of NPO Gheofizika, then an up-and-coming new company on the Russian avionics market. The K in the designation denotes *krooglo**soo**toch-noye prime**nen**iye* (round-the-clock capability), while the O is a reference to the optronic system.

The principal mission of the Mi-8MTKO is to perform tactical reconnaissance in the interests of the ground forces, detecting small groups of the insurgents' personnel and enemy vehicles. 'Free chase' (seek and destroy) missions are also possible.

The Mi-8MTKO was publicly unveiled on 15th August 1999 when the prototype ('67 Yellow', c/n 94691) took part in the open doors day at Chkalovskaya AB near Moscow, seat of the Russian Air Force's 929th State Flight Test Centre where it was undergoing trials at the time. Two days later the aircraft was displayed at the MAKS-99 airshow in Zhukovskiy (17th-22nd August 1999).

The first two operational *Hip-Hs* upgraded to Mi-8MTKO standard arrived on the Chechen theatre of operations (during the Second Chechen War, that is) in late March 2000 for the purpose of evaluation in actual combat. The deployment had been ordered by the then Defence Minister of Russia Marshal Igor' S. Sergeyev. The Mi-8MTKOs were ferried and flown in combat by test crews serving with the 344th TsBP i PLS in Torzhok. The advent of these helicopters stripped the Chechen guerrillas of their cover of darkness. However, just a few days after the deployment, on the night of 27th March 2000, one of the two helicopters was lost in a crash at a mountain test range near Nal'chik, Kabardino-Balkaria. The crew consisting of Test Pilots 1st Class Lt. Col. Nikolay Kolpakov and Lt. Col. Boris Koshkin escaped with minor injuries but the aircraft was a write-off.

Mi-8MTKO '205 Red' (c/n unknown) displayed at the MAKS-2003 airshow appears to be equipped with a different model of optoelectronic package, judging by the different shape of the 'ball turret'.

Above and below: The heavily armoured Mi-172 'Salon' RA-27018 custom-built for the President of Russia lands at Zhukovskiy on 18th August 2003. These views show the smaller-than-usual bulletproof glass windows, the exhaust/air mixers, chaff/flare dispensers, flightdeck armour and extra air conditioner to starboard.

Above: The 'crane operator's' cabin of the sole Mi-8MTV-K flying crane helicopter, seen from behind. Not much rearward visibility, but then it isn't very critical either; downward visibility is far more important.

This view shows the entrance to the rear cabin and illustrates how it fits in place of the clamshell doors.

In late 2000, however, four further night-capable *Hips* arrived on the Chechen TO. Despite being designated Mi-8MTKO, they were rather different, featuring **two** 'ball turrets' (one under each side of the nose) and a large thimble radome replacing the upper centre panel in the lower row of the flightdeck glazing. Their curious looks and the fact that there were four identical 'weirdo Mi-8s' gave rise to the nickname *Tele**poo**ziki* (Teletubbies, after the characters in that horrible children's TV show which ran on Russian TV as well).

The Mi-8MTKO was also in the static park at the MAKS-2001 airshow on 14-19th August 2001 ('29 Yellow', c/n 94309) and the MAKS-2003 airshow on 19-24th August 2002 ('205 Red', c/n unknown). The latter aircraft was apparently equipped with a different optronic system, as the 'ball turret' under the nose had a slightly different shape.

Mi-8MTV transport/assault helicopter

The version which superseded the first representative of the 'second generation' (the Mi-8MT) on the Kazan' production line was the Mi-8MTV. The V suffix stood for *vy**sot**nyy* (high-altitude), since the helicopter was powered by TV3-117MT turboshafts delivering 1,900 shp for take-off, with a 1,700-shp nominal rating, a 1,500-shp cruise rating and a 2,100-shp contingency rating. It took the Mil' OKB two years to create this new baseline model featuring improved hot-and-high performance. The Mi-8MTV could take off and land at altitudes up to 4,000 m (13,120 ft) above sea level and maintain level flight at up to 6,000 m (19,685 ft). In addition to the service ceiling and the hovering ceiling, other performance parameters, such as rate of climb and range, had also improved.

The Mi-8MTV incorporated a number of important improvements based on Afghan War experience. These included additional flightdeck armour which was now a standard fit, fuel tanks filled with explosion suppression polyurethane foam, reinforcement of certain systems components for higher resistance to battle damage and so on. The number of ASO-2V-02 chaff/flare dispensers was increased from four to six and they were moved from the tailboom to the rear fuselage sides, as close as possible to the engine jetpipes. The latter were modified so as to permit installation of EVU exhaust/air mixers. The nose Kalashnikov PKT machine-gun mount replacing the upper centre window in the lower row of the flightdeck glazing and the mounting for the rear PKT near the starboard clamshell door hatch became a standard fit.

Mi-8MTV-1 civil utility helicopter

The civil sub-variant of the Mi-8MTV was designated Mi-8MTV-1. It lacked armament and other military equipment items such as the flightdeck armour, but featured a Kontur weather radar in a bullet-shaped radome replacing the lower centre window in the lower row of the flightdeck glazing. The Kazan' plant launched production of both varieties in 1988.

Mi-8MTV-2 transport/assault helicopter

This is an improved version of the military Mi-8MTV designed for use in transport/assault, MEDEVAC, CSAR and strike configurations. As compared to the baseline model the Mi-8MTV-2 is up-armoured, the number of troops carried is increased from 24 to 30, and the avionics are updated. Among other things, the Mi-8MTV-2 combines the nose-mounted machine-gun with the radar of the civil Mi-8MTV-1 (this is its main external distinguishing feature); it also combines the four ASO-2V-02 chaff/flare dispensers under the tailboom (s on the military Mi-8MT) with the six identical units on the rear fuselage sides to give a total of 320 26-mm PPI-26 magnesium flares (PPI = *peeropa**tron** infra**krahs**nyy* – infra-red [countermeasures] cartridge) to decoy heat-seeking missiles. An SOEP-V1A IRCM jammer is fitted. There are provisions for a long-range radio navigation (LORAN) system.

The Mi-8MTV-2 retains the six BD3-57KrVM pylons of the preceding model. Typical external stores include four B-8V20

FFAR pods with 20 80-mm (3.15-in) S-8 rockets apiece (FFAR launch is controlled by the PUS 36-71 fire control unit), two or four UPK-23-250 cannon pods, up to six bombs of 50-500 kg (110-1,100 lb) calibre and so on. With four UPK-23-250 pods, the Mi-8MTV-2 qualifies as the world's most heavily armed helicopter. In addition to the forward and aft PKT machine-guns, up to eight 7.62-mm machine-guns could be pintle-mounted in the cabin windows and entry doorway.

The Mi-8MTV-2 is equipped with rappelling lines and an increased-capacity rescue hoist for disembarking and picking up troops at the hover in difficult locations.

Mi-8MTV-3 transport/assault helicopter

The Mi-8MTV-3 is a further refined variety of the military Mi-8MTV incorporating much the same improvements as the Mi-8MTV-2. As distinct from the latter it has a weather radar but no nose-mounted machine-gun (!) and features only two pylons on each side instead of three; on the other hand, the number of possible external stores combinations is increased from eight to 24! Besides the twin pylons and radar-only-plus-armour front end treatment, the Mi-8MTV-3 can be recognised by the ventral anti-collision light (which is normally absent on combat versions), the FPP-7 searchlight and the teardrop fairing on the flightdeck roof housing the forward IFF aerial.

Mi-8MTV-GA civil multi-role helicopter

The aforementioned Mi-17M prototype (RA-70937) was redesignated Mi-8MTV-GA (*grazh**dahn**skaya avi**ah**tsiya* – civil aviation) after being refitted with TV3-117VM engines. It was displayed with appropriate nose titles at the ILA'94 airshow at Berlin-Schönefeld shortly before being converted as the prototype of the Mi-8MTV-5.

Mi-8MT/Mi-8MTV 'Arctic version'

In 1986 and 1993 the Kazan' Helicopter Plant built a small number of Mi-8MTs and Mi-8MTVs respectively customised for operating in the High North. The helicopters featured extra thick heat insulation, long-range fuel tanks in the cabin and additional communications equipment.

Mi-8MTV-1 patrol/SAR version

One of Orenburg Airlines' Mi-8MTV-1s, RA-27172 (c/n 96111), was modified for civilian surveillance duties by the Russian company Uniavia. The helicopter featured a Thomson-CSF Chlio S gyrostabilised multi-mode thermal imaging system installed in a neat 'ball turret' in the standard hatch for the external sling system; the operator's workstation was located near the entry door and long-range

Above: Orenburg Airlines Mi-8MTV-1 RA-27172 in the static park at the MAKS-99, outfitted as a patrol/ survey aircraft by Uniavia. The optronic 'ball turret' is just visible. Curiously, RA-27172 has no radar.

The interior of Mi-8MTV-1 RA-27172, showing the operator's workstation with cathode-ray tube display and joystick in the foreground; the two long-range fuel tanks are visible beyond.

Close-up of the 'ball turret' of the Thomson-CSF Chlio S thermal imaging system in the external sling lock hatch of Mi-8MTV-1 RA-27172. This installation does not require changes to the airframe.

Above: '02 Red', a demonstrator of the Mi-17-1V armed export version of the Mi-8MTV, at Kubinka AB during the first open doors day on 11th April 1992. Curiously, this one lacks the nose-mounted machine-gun.

CCCP-95043, the prototype of the Mi-17-1VA ambulance helicopter, in the static park at the 1989 Paris Air Show with the exhibit code H-298 visible on the tailboom. Note the rear boarding ladder on the threshold of the cargo doors.

tanks were installed to increase endurance. Apart from patrolling pipelines and power lines, RA-27172 can be used for locating fires (a useful function when fighting underground peat fires which are hard to extinguish), performing SAR operations and ecological monitoring. The helicopter was on display at the MAKS-99 airshow.

Mi-8MTV-1/Mi-8MTV-3 VIP version

Kazan' Helicopters developed VIP versions of the Mi-8MTV-1 and even the Mi-8MTV-3. The luxuriously appointed cabin featured a galley, a bio-toilet, an in-flight entertainment (IFE) system with a video recorder/TV set and hi-fi audio, an air conditioner and special secure communications equipment. The helicopter had a crew of four and seated nine passengers. At least one such VIP helicopter was delivered to the government of the Republic of Tatarstan.

Mi-8MTV-K flying crane

A single Mi-8MTV-1 (CCCP-25444, c/n 95583) belonging to the Ukrainian Civil Aviation Directorate/Zavodskoye United Air Detachment/252nd Flight and based at Simferopol'-Zavodskoye was converted into the one-off Mi-8MTV-K flying crane (K = *[letayushchiy] krahn*). The conversion involved removal of the rear clamshell doors which were replaced by an extensively glazed cabin with a full set of flying controls connected to the standard control system by push-pull rods. Flying the helicopter from this cabin, the pilot had an unrestricted view of the underslung load and the location where it was to be deposited.

The Mi-8MTV-K was demonstrated at MosAeroShow-92 in August 1992. Later the helicopter was used for some construction work in Moscow's Red Square, installing some heavy equipment on the roof of one of the surrounding buildings.

Mi-8MTVM ambulance helicopter

The Mi-8MTV-1 served as the basis for an ambulance version designated Mi-8MTVM (*meditsinskiy* – medical).

Mi-8MTV-3G MEDEVAC helicopter

Later, the Mi-8MTV-3 was developed into a more modern 'flying hospital' for the army designated Mi-8MTV-3G (*gospital'*).

Mi-8MPS (Mi-8MTVMPS) SAR/ambulance helicopter

The Mi-8MTV-3 was also the starting point for the development of an ambulance/SAR version designated Mi-8MTVMPS (*meditsinskiy, poiskovo-spasahtel'nyy* – ambulance/SAR, used attributively) or simply Mi-8MPS. Its range of missions comprised the following:

- locating the re-entry modules of Soviet spacecraft following touchdown, as well as crashed aircraft or ships in distress (instrumentally and visually);
- locating the re-entry modules of spacecraft (instrumentally and visually) during the parachute descent stage;
- marking the location for larger SAR forces by means of droppable radio beacons;
- delivering teams of rescue workers and first-aid equipment to the area of the accident;
- delivering technical support teams and their equipment to the touchdown area;
- evacuating crews and passengers of crashed aircraft or ships in distress (including physically exhausted persons) or spacemen from the touchdown site, either by picking them up in hover mode or after landing on any suitable pad picked from the air;
- evacuating the re-entry module (weighing up to 3 tons/6,610 lb) to the nearest airfield.

The Mi-8MPS was capable of performing its mission round the clock in all weather conditions and climatic zones, over land or water.

The helicopter's mission necessitated massive changes to both airframe and equipment. The Mi-8MPS featured a double-width sliding door to port, two hatches (emergency exits) to starboard and non-functional clamshell cargo doors which were permanently closed; the starboard door incorporated a recess with an external cover for an inflatable life raft. The helicopter was fitted with the PNKV-8PS integrated flight instrumentation/navigation suite optimised for the SAR role (*pilotahzhno-navigatsionnyy kompleks vertolyotnyy, poiskovo-spasahtel'nyy*), a YuR-40.1 radar system and a TAPAS thermal imaging system for locating vessels in distress (*teplovizionnaya apparatoora poiska avareeynykh soodov*). Appropriate medical equipment was provided for rendering first aid. Finally, the helicopter featured emergency flotation gear allowing it to remain afloat for 30 minutes in the event of ditching, which was enough for the occupants to climb into life rafts.

The PNKV-8PS suite enabled the Mi-8MPS to automatically follow a predesignated route and return to base, automatically move in a shuttle pattern over the area to be investigated (the parameters of the pattern were entered from a keypad in the flightdeck), automatically hover over a chosen location and then continue along the route and so on; it also determined the aircraft's current position in real time. The TAPAS thermal imager made it possible to locate people and heat-radiating objects in the daytime and at night at altitudes up to 1,000 m (3,280 ft). The helicopter carried four radio beacons which it dropped for the main forces to home in on.

The Mi-8MPS was equipped with an LPG-300 hoist with a lifting capacity of 300 kg (660 lb) installed near the door, which allowed two persons to be lifted at a time by means of a special basket. The cabin featured 12 jump seats for the rescuees and could be configured with six stretchers. The ten-man PSN-10 inflatable life raft (*plot spasahtel'nyy nadoovnoy*) could be ejected by the crew, inflating automatically by means of a rip cord, and subsequently lifted by the helicopter.

The design changes described above increased the Mi-8MPS's potential as an SAR aircraft by a factor of two as compared to the standard Mi-8MT. The Mi-8MPS was superior to its US counterpart, the Sikorsky HH-60A, in both operational radius and capacity.

Mi-17-1V export transport/assault helicopter

In armed transport/assault configuration the Mi-8MTV was offered for export as the Mi-17-1V (in this instance the V stood for *vo'oroozhonnyy* – armed, not *vysotnyy*). The helicopter was powered by TV3-117MT engines and had a payload of 4 tons carried in the cabin or 5 tons carried externally; the hovering ceiling was 3,980 m (13,060 ft) with a normal (11.1-ton/24,470-lb) TOW and the maximum TOW was 13 tons (28,660 lb). The cabin accommodated 30 troops in troopship configuration and 12 stretcher patients or 17 walking wounded plus three stretcher cases in CASEVAC configuration. The armament corresponded to that of the domestic version, with nose- and aft-mounted PKT machine-guns and provisions for eight 7.62-mm machine-guns in the cabin windows and entry doorway; the helicopter could be armed with four B-8V20 FFAR pods or UPK-23-250 cannon pods, as well as high-explosive or napalm bombs of up to 500 kg calibre. The IRCM suite corresponded to that of the Mi-8MTV-2. For paradropping operations (or rapid embarkation/disembarkation) the rear clamshell doors could be removed.

The Mi-17-1V entered production in 1982 and was widely exported. Its potential as a transport/assault helicopter is nearly twice that of the Sikorsky UH-60A Black Hawk and 2.5 times greater than that of the Aérospatiale AS 332 Super Puma.

Mi-17-1VA (Mi-171VA) flying hospital

Another version which acquitted itself well is the Mi-17-1VA flying hospital (sometimes referred to as Mi-171VA). It is designed for performing surgery, providing intensive care, childbirth assistance and other forms of medical treatment at remote locations inaccessible for other means of transport, landing at any adequately-sized pad with a surface strong enough to support the helicopter. The Mi-17-1VA is powered by TV3-117MT engines and fully equipped for the medical crew to perform their functions both on the ground and in flight.

Above: The Mi-17MD prototype (ex-RA-70937, c/n 95448) in ultimate configuration with one-piece rear ramp/door, weapons outriggers and exhaust/air mixers. Note the rounded cabin heater housing above the starboard entry door (it is angular on production aircraft) and the 'Night' titles on the external armour plates.

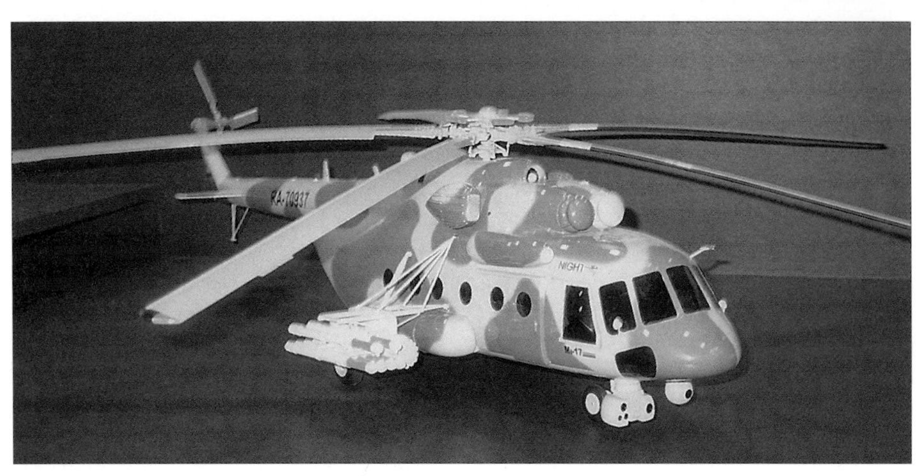

Centre: A Ukrainian-built LuAZ-1302 light jeep in the cabin of the Mi-8MTV-5 (Mi-17MD).
Above: A display model of the Mi-17MD 'Night' with an impressive array of imaging and targeting systems.

According to the manufacturer's documents the Mi-17-1VA is intended for the following missions:

• locating people in distress and providing prompt and qualified medical aid in areas affected by man-made or natural disasters (floods, earthquakes, fires etc.);

• providing on-the-spot medical aid, including surgery, in places inaccessible for ground vehicles;

• transporting accident victims or sick persons (up to four) to a permanent hospital with life support en route;

• performing SAR operations over water, swampland, woodland or other areas where landing is impossible with the help of the on-board rescue hoist;

• transporting patients or new-born babies (in an incubator) between hospitals, transporting women in childbirth and giving childbirth assistance on board if necessary.

The helicopter's mission equipment includes an adjustable operating table, operating lights, a Faza-6IP (Phase-6IP) artificial lung, a DAR-5 portable artificial lung, an MS-3/A portable cardioscope, an EK-51 self-contained electrocardiographic appliance, an SK-OP surgical suction unit, a pulse oxygenometer for monitoring the patient's condition in the process of treatment or transportation, a DKI-N-04 defibrillator with a built-in power unit, emergency kits with all required medical tools and medicines, a vacuum mattress stretcher for transporting persons with spinal injuries, rigid stretchers, a KU-27 all-purpose water boiler and so on. The equipment fit can be tailored to the customer's demands.

The prototype wearing the test registration CCCP-95043 (c/n 95043) was displayed at Le Bourget in 1989, bearing the exhibit code H-298. Reregistered CCCP-70894, the same helicopter was on display at MosAeroShow-92; it is now operated by the Kazan'-based airline Tulpar ('winged steed' in Tatarian) as RA-70894.

The Mi-17-1VA has a normal TOW of 11.3 tons (24,910 lb) with the KO-50 heater installed, a full medical equipment fit and a medical crew of five and three patients on board; maximum TOW is 13 tons. Range at 500 m (1,640 ft) with 30-minute fuel reserves is 610 km (378 miles); top speed at altitudes up to 1,000 m (3,280 ft) is 250 km/h (155 mph) with a normal TOW and 230 km/h (142 mph) with a maximum TOW; the service ceiling in these cases is 6,000 m and 4,800 m (19,685 and 15,750 ft) respectively.

Mi-17MD (Mi-8MTV-5, Mi-17-V5) transport/assault helicopter

The Kazan' Helicopter Plant incessantly worked on perfecting the Mi-8/Mi-17, especially its military versions. This became especially evident in post-Soviet times when the once united nationwide MAP system disintegrated into numerous enterprises which, as the press was wont to put it, had to try their luck in the turbid waters of the Sea of Free Enterprise. Putting its huge experience of Mi-8 operations in armed conflicts to good use, in 1995 the plant brought out a new version jointly with the Mil' Moscow Helicopter Plant. This was destined to be Kazan' Helicopters' baseline military model for the new century – and, in its production form, it looks a lot different from the 'classic' *Hip*.

Designated Mi-17MD for export, the new helicopter combined some proven features of the Mi-8MTV-3 with new avionics and equipment. The prototype was converted in 1995 from the Mi-8MTV-GA demonstrator, RA-70937 (the former Mi-17M, c/n 95448). From the latter model the Mi-17MD inherited the wide port side entry door equipped with an SLG-300 cargo/rescue hoist. A second entry door of normal dimensions was added on the starboard side, as on the Mi-18; unlike the latter, however, the KO-50 cabin heater could not be housed under the floor, so there was no option but to place it above the starboard entry door in a new, much slimmer and more angular fairing.

The most obvious new feature was the redesigned forward fuselage with a full-width streamlined upward-hinged radome which created a totally different nose profile with a stepped windscreen; the lower row of the flightdeck glazing was reduced to a small window on each side. This 'nose job' not only made the helicopter more elegant but also allowed virtually any type of radar to be fitted. On the actual aircraft it was a Model 8A-813Ts Kontur-Ts radar with a colour display.

In its original configuration the Mi-17MD had a cargo door design patterned on that of the larger Mi-26 transport helicopter. There was a short hydraulically powered cargo ramp with manually operable vehicle loading ramps hinged to it; the aperture aft of it was closed by powered clamshell doors. This caused the emergency exit/gunnery hatch in the starboard door to be deleted, but then, the ramp itself could be lowered to provide a much bigger field of fire.

The seating capacity was increased to 36 or 40 troops by installing an extra row of quickly removable seats, facing left, down the centre of the cabin; the two forward doors and rear ramp allowed the 40 troops to board or vacate the helicopter in less than two minutes. An SU-R rappelling line system could be fitted.

Unlike earlier versions, the Mi-8MTV-5 had provisions for installing four auxiliary fuel tanks in the cabin instead of two (ie, two vertical pairs of tanks), giving 1,660 litres (365.2 Imp gal) of extra fuel. Together with the 3,660 litres (805.2 Imp gal) in the main tanks, this gave the helicopter an unrefuelled range of 1,600 km (990 miles); the extra fuel weighed 1,286 kg (2,835 lb). There was provision for a flotation bag system enabling the helicopter to remain afloat for 30 minutes.

The helicopter was equipped with a Koors-MP-70 compass system (*koors* is Russian for 'heading') with an SD-75 distance measuring equipment (DME) kit enabling navigation with the help of VOR/ILS approach and landing systems. An A-723 long-range radio navigation (LORAN) system with a ventral strake aerial was fitted for working with the Omega navaids. Other equipment (some of it optional) included an ARB-PK emergency radio beacon working with the KOSPAS-SARSAT system (*KOsmicheskaya SPAsahtel'naya Sistema* (= space rescue system)/ Search And Rescue SATellite), an R-828 radio for communicating with ground troops, a GPS-600 satellite navigation kit, a BUV-8A control system module, a new DISS-32-90 Doppler speed/drift sensor, AGB-96D and AGB-96D artificial horizons, a TV system with a display near the co-pilot's seat for monitoring slung loads, and a Nitesun SX-16 searchlight. Western avionics could be integrated at customer request. The armament and IRCM suite were identical to those of the Mi-8MTV-3.

Mi-17MD RA-70937 was unveiled at the 36th Paris Air Show in July 1995 with the exhibit code H-346; shortly afterwards it participated in the MAKS-95 airshow (22nd-27th August 1995), fitted with weapons racks.

By mid-1997 the prototype had been further modified, the Mi-26 style cargo doors giving place to a single large ramp/door which closed the aperture completely when raised. This arrangement accepted on the production model resulted in a distinctive flattened rear fuselage underside. In this configuration (dubbed rather unkindly 'flatass' by some observers) the Mi-17MD was displayed again at the MAKS-97 airshow (19-24th August 1997) – now wearing Russian Air Force star insignia but no tactical code *and lacking the weapons racks*! This was the first time when the alternative designation Mi-8MTV-5 for the domestic market was disclosed. The helicopter was on show again at the MAKS-99 – this time with the weapons racks reinstated and EVU exhaust/air mixers fitted.

With TV3-117MT engines the Mi-17MD (Mi-8MTV-5) has a normal TOW of 11.1 tons (24,470 lb) and a maximum TOW of 13 tons (28,660 lb). The maximum internal and external load is 4 tons (8,820 lb); a source, though, quotes a maximum slung load of 5 tons (11,020 lb). The cargo cabin measures 5.34 x 2.34 x 1.8 m; cabin volume is 23 m^3 (812.2 cu.ft).

As with the Mi-17-1VA, top speed at altitudes up to 1,000 m is 250 km/h with a normal TOW and 230 km/h with a maximum TOW; cruising speed being 220-240 km/h (136-149 mph) and 205-215 km/h (127-133 mph) respectively and the service ceiling 6,000 m and 4,800 m. The hovering ceiling with a normal TOW is 4,000 m (13,120 ft).

Export deliveries of the Mi-17MD began in 1999; customers for the military transport/ assault version include the Rwandan Air Force and the Colombian Army. A number of Mi-8MTV-5s has been delivered to the Russian Army; the Russian and Rwandan examples feature external armour on the flightdeck section.

A version differing in equipment was marketed as the Mi-17-V5; the prototype, a Kazan' Helicopters demonstrator registered 96370 (c/n 96370), was demonstrated at the MAKS-2001 airshow (14-19th August 2001) in unarmed configuration. Unfortunately this helicopter crashed near Visviri, Chile, on 4th June 2002 during a demonstration flight – luckily with no fatalities.

Mi-17MD 'Night' transport/assault helicopter

In 1996 the Mi-17MD prototype appeared at the Farnborough International '96 airshow, still with the original rounded rear end, sporting an optronic 'ball turret' under the starboard side of the nose. This configuration was advertised as the Mi-17MD 'Night' (ie, night-capable). The system was removed in the course of conversion to one-piece ramp configuration but the 'Night' titles on the external armour panels remained.

Mi-17MD – South Korean version

A version of the Mi-17MD developed for the South Korean Police is unusual in that it features Mi-8P/Mi-172-style rectangular windows. The double-width port entry door has one centrally positioned window instead of two; thus there are five windows on each side (door+3+exit). The helicopter is unarmed but features a powerful loud-hailer aft of the nose gear unit and is equipped with wire cutters to prevent disastrous damage and a crash in the event of a wirestrike.

Mi-8MTV-1 (mod) – EMERCOM version

At least one Mi-8MTV-1 built for EMERCOM of Russia (RA-25815, c/n unknown) incorporates some features of the Mi-17MD – a double-width port side door *à la* Mi-17M (but with just one window) and an extra door to starboard with the KO-50 cabin heater positioned in a fairing above it. No separate designation is known.

Mi-8MTV-5-1

Another version built for the Indian Air Force and called Mi-8MTV-5-1 is an even more strange hybrid featuring a Mi-17MD-style one-piece ramp/door and starboard entry door/high-set cabin heater (and very probably a double-width port side door as well) but retaining the classic fully glazed nose without even a radar and having three large blade aerials on the tailboom. One example serialled Z-3349 (c/n unknown) has been identified to date.

Mi-172 passenger helicopter

A 26-seat heli-liner derivative of the Mi-8MTV (Mi-17) developed in 1991 was marketed as the Mi-172, featuring a Mi-8P-style fuselage design with rectangular windows and small clamshell doors/rear airstairs. The prototype was possibly RA-95710 (c/n 95710), a Kazan' Helicopters demonstrator which was later sold and reregistered RA-22190. Customers for the passenger-configured Mi-172 included the Service Flight Corporation of Vietnam which used the helicopters on coastal services and offshore oil support missions; hence the Vietnamese Mi-172s were equipped with a flotation bag system.

Like many other versions, the TV3-117VM-powered Mi-172 has a normal TOW of 11.1 tons and a maximum TOW of 13 tons; gross weight with 26 passengers is 12 tons (26,455 lb) and empty weight 7.586 tons (16,724 lb). The speed and hovering/service ceiling figures are identical to those of the Mi-8MTV; range is 620 km (385 miles). The fuel supply amounts to 2,615 litres (575.3 Imp gal) or 2,027 kg (4,468 lb). The helicopter has a crew of three.

In 1994 the Mi-172 was certificated according to US FAR Pt 29 airworthiness regulations by India's Civil Aviation Authority

Mi-172 – VIP versions

The Mi-172 also comes in VIP configuration with a port side airstair door. Interestingly, the aircraft can be completed with a Mi-17MD style stepped nose at the customer's request; one such example is Rwandan Air Force Mi-172 RAF-1909 built for the President of Rwanda in 1999.

One Mi-172 (RA-27018, c/n unknown) completed in 2003 as Vladimir V. Putin's new presidential helicopter is a most unusual machine. For maximum protection against any attempts on the President's life the cabin is heavily armoured – a fact revealed by the bulletproof glass cabin windows which are rather smaller than usual. The flightdeck featured external armour, as on the Mi-8MTV-2; moreover, the helicopter featured EVU exhaust/air mixers and triple ASO-2V-02 IRCM flare dispensers on the rear fuselage sides! In addition to the standard air conditioner to starboard, a second air conditioner in an angular fairing was installed above it, the first cabin window giving place to an air inlet. The helicopter featured a secure HF communications suite with unswept blade aerials on the tailboom.

'False Mi-172' – convertible version

Lately the Mil' design bureau and the two factories building the Mi-8 family have confused the picture a lot by using the same designations for a number of quite different versions. You thought the Mi-172 was, in a manner of speaking, a 'latter-day Mi-8P'? Then try this one! At Farnborough International-2000 Kazan' Helicopters unveiled a variant of the Mi-8 which was so brand new that it did not even have a designation then; soon afterwards it received... 'Mi-172' nose titles.

The story: On 12th August 1998 Mi-8MTV-1 RA-70898 (c/n 95825), a Kazan' Helicopters 'hack', suffered extensive damage during a practice autorotation landing at Kazan'-Osnovnoy, whereupon the Western media promptly listed the helicopter as crashed and dead. Two years later the undead helicopter surfaced at FI'2000 in a new guise, combining the standard clamshell cargo doors with rectangular windows, a Mi-17MD-style radar nose and extra entry door/high-set cabin heater to starboard, and no Doppler box! Moreover, RA-70898 featured a 'glass cockpit' with multi-function displays developed by the Kronshtadt avionics company and a gyrostabilised undernose optronic system developed by the Israeli company Elbit (this 'ball turret' was later removed). Two 475-litre (104.5 Imp gal) external tanks were attached to the fuselage sides directly above the windows.

The cabin could be configured for cargo carriage or in a 28-seat airline configuration. Apparently the latter, plus the rectangular windows, had led someone astray, which accounts for the inappropriate 'Mi-172' titles.

Mi-172A VIP helicopter

A suitably modified version of the Mi-172 passed US FAR Pt 29 certification trials in 1998. Due to the changes required for certification it was known as the Mi-172A (for *ameri**kahn**skiye **nor**my **lyot**noy **god**nosti* – American airworthiness regulations).

Mi-172AG convertible helicopter

A further derivative of the Mi-172A was developed for the powerful Gazprom natural gas industry concern, incorporating changes aimed at enhancing operational reliability and safety. The most important of these were a switch to Klimov VK-2500 (TV3-117VMA-SB3) engines with a 2,000-shp take-off rating and a 2,500-shp contingency rating and the installation of a satellite navigation system. The new version was designated Mi-172AG, the G referring to Gazprom.

Mi-17KF Kittiwake civil utility helicopter

In 1996 the Mil' Moscow Helicopter Plant signed a deal with the Canadian company Kelowna Flightcraft for the development of a 'Westernised' version of the Mi-17 for the purpose of certificating and marketing it in the West. The name of the Canadian partner was reflected in the helicopter's designation, Mi-17KF; the helicopter also received the marketing name Kittiwake (a kind of seagull).

Based on the Mi-8MTV, the Mi-17KF featured Western avionics, namely the Honeywell EDZ-756 electronic flight instrumentation system (EFIS, or 'glass cockpit'), a P-700 weather radar with a colour display, a duplex FZ-706 flight director system, an AA-30 (some sources say M-300) radio altimeter, a Primus II integrated radio system and a VG/DG-14 vertical/directional gyro system, as well as an engine monitoring system supplied by Transicoil Co. and an upgraded electric system. GPS and 'CATS Eyes' night vision goggles could be integrated at customer request. Outwardly the Mi-17KF was identifiable by a Mi-17MD-style stepped nose (the circular windows and rear clamshell doors were retained).

The prototype was converted in 1996-97 from a Mi-17 originally built for Iraq but undelivered due to the UN embargo (c/n 226M205). Registered RA70877 (the registration was actually applied like this, with no dash), the Mi-17KF was unveiled at Air Show Canada 97 which took place at Abbotsford in August 1997. Performance was virtually identical to that of the standard Mi-8MTV, except that range with a normal TOW was quoted as 1,050 km (650 miles) and the maximum slung load as 4.5 tons (9,920 lb).

Above: CCCP-70880, the Mi-17LIZA ecological survey aircraft (c/n 212M144), on display at the MosAeroShow-92. Note the nose-mounted sensor boom and the plug in the second window to port mounting another sensor.

'Pretty Lisa' no more. This is not just a shift to the Russian prefix – RA-70880 has had the equipment fit changed sufficiently to warrant a new designation, Mi-17LL. It is seen here at the MAKS-95 airshow. Note the crude-looking Perspex blister, the blade aerial under the nose boom and the white LII badge.

Above: RA-27182 is an Ulan-Ude built Mi-171TP passenger helicopter (a 'latter-day Mi-8P') operated by Moscow-based Aero-Taxi in this smart three-tone blue/silver livery.

It was planned to certificate the Mi-17KF according to FAR Pt 29 airworthiness regulations. Apparently, however, these plans did not materialise; in 1999 the prototype was reportedly converted into another Mi-17MD demonstrator with the production-standard ramp/door for participation in a Royal Malaysian Air Force tender.

Mi-17V-6 multi-role helicopter

In 2001 the Mi-8MTV-1 was further upgraded, the new version being designated Mi-17V-6. The prototype, 96369 (c/n 96369), is is outwardly identical to the 'false Mi-172' RA-70898 described above (even down to the white colour scheme with green and black trim!), but features a different powerplant comprising VK-2500 engines and a Czech-designed and built SAFIR-5K/G MI APU having higher performance and a longer continuous running time. The helicopter successfully underwent hot-and-high trials in Tibet during September and October 2001.

Mi-8MTV-7 (Mi-17V-7) multi-role helicopter

The Mi-17V-7 is the latest Kazan'-built version as of this writing. It is very similar to the Mi-17V-6, featuring the same powerplant (VK-2500 engines and SAFIR-5K/G MI APU) but has new composite rotor blades. The prototypes have a 1,000 kg (2,200 lb) greater payload and a 20 km/h (12.4 mph) higher cruising speed.

Mi-17LIZA ecological survey aircraft

The fleet of assorted test and development aircraft operated by LII included a Mi-17 from an undelivered foreign order. Painted in orange/blue Aeroflot colours and registered CCCP-70880 (c/n 212M144), the helicopter was fitted out for environmental survey as the Mi-17LIZA, this curious suffix standing for *laboratoriya izmereniya zagryazneniya atmosfery* (atmospheric pollution measurement laboratory). Outwardly 'Pretty Lisa' could be identified by the lattice-like air data boom on

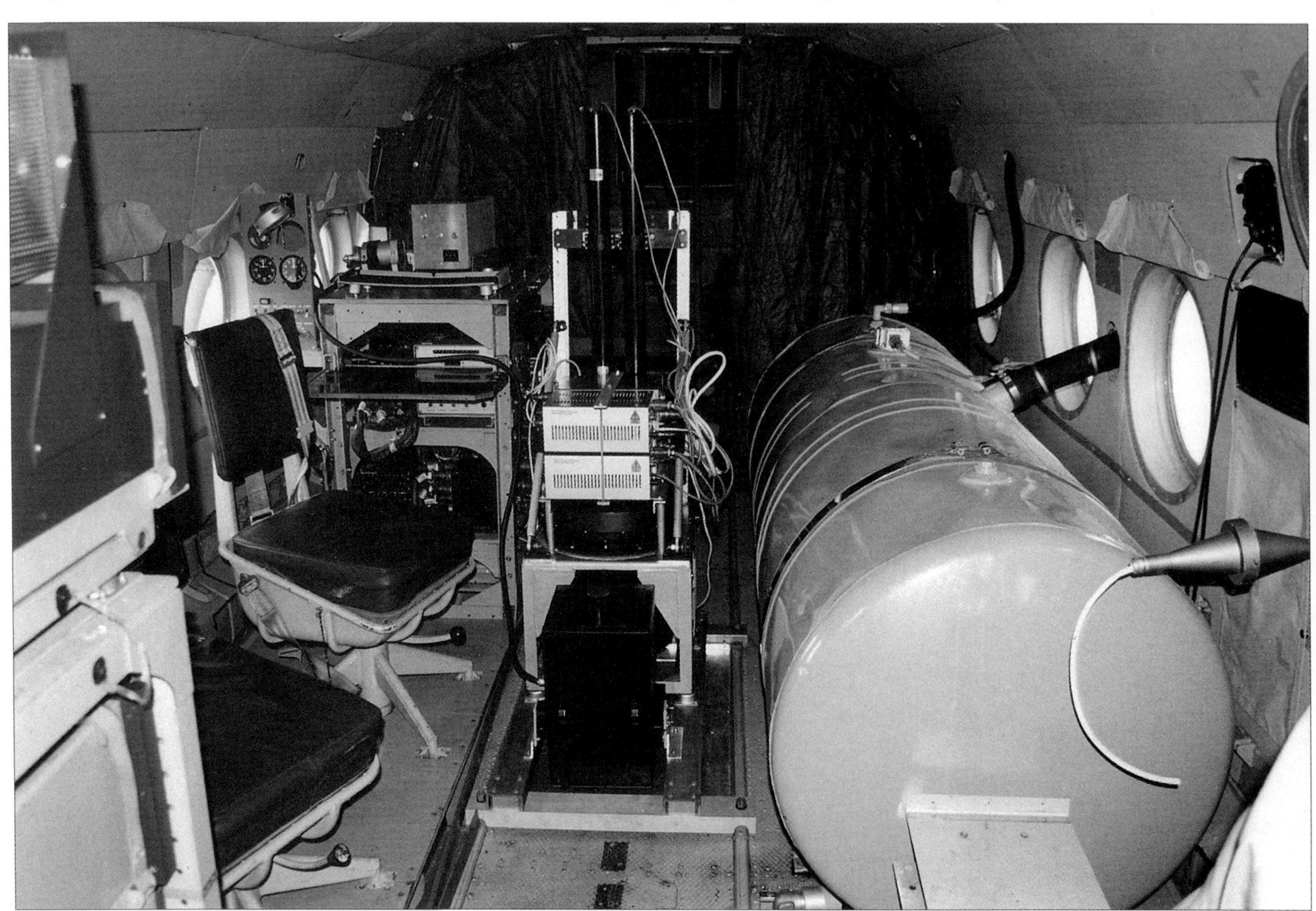

The cabin of the Mi-17LL at the MAKS-95, showing the remote sensing equipment looking downwards through the external sling system hatch, the test equipment rack on the left, the test engineers' workstations and the sensor connected to the probe in the second window to port (just ahead of the auxiliary fuel tank).

96369, the prototype of the re-engined Mi-17V-6, seen during 'hot-and-high' trials in the Tibet. Note the absence of the characteristic teardrop fairing with gills (the intake of the AI-9V APU) – the giveaway that the helicopter has a Czech SAFIR-5KG MI APU. Despite the rectangular windows, it has large clamshell doors.

the nose (the same kind as fitted to several other Mi-8s operated by the institute); the cabin accommodated test equipment racks along the starboard side and an auxiliary fuel tank to port. The Mi-17LIZA was in the static park at MosAeroShow-92.

Mi-17LL research aircraft

Reregistered RA-70880, the former Mi-17LIZA found use in several other test and research programmes in the 1990s; some of them had unspecified military applications. This brought about a change of designation to Mi-17LL and resulted in the addition of a rather crude cylindrical Perspex blister for some kind of sensor in the second window to starboard, plus a blade aerial on the underside of the air data boom. The Mi-17LL has been a regular participant of Moscow airshows, and the equipment fit has been updated periodically.

Mi-17 ecological survey aircraft

A Mi-17 – apparently not the Mi-17LIZA – was modified for determining the range and quantity of pollutants in industrial areas. The mission suite included spectrozonal mapping equipment, radiation metering equipment and a system for remote sampling of the atmosphere and the soil, using different wavebands. Additionally, the helicopter could be configured for photo mapping (vertical and strip photography) which was performed at altitudes of 50 to 6,000 m (164 to 19,685 ft) and speeds up to 250 km/h (155 mph).

Mi-8AMT civil transport/military utility helicopter

In 1991 the Ulan-Ude Aircraft Production Association (U-UAPO) likewise launched production of the Mi-8MTV-1 – and from then on development of the 'second generation' Mi-8 at Kazan' and Ulan-Ude went along separate lines, the two factories being *bitter friends* and competitors.

To begin with, the Ulan-Ude built Mi-8MTV-1 received a separate designation, Mi-8AMT, to distinguish us from them. True, the Mi-8AMT had subtle differences in equipment from its Kazan'-built counterpart. External differences included a small teardrop blister on the flightdeck roof housing an IFF antenna (although some Kazan'-built aircraft have it, too) and a 'notched' DISS-32-90 Doppler box, the excrescence at the end housing a flight data recorder. Also, most examples have the ventral faired searchlight.

The Mi-8AMT introduced a new c/n system at U-UAPO. For instance, Mi-8AMT RA-25748 manufactured on 15th June 1993 is c/n 59489607784. Here, 594 is a code for the factory, 896 is a product code for the Mi-8AMT et seq, and the other digits are the 'famous last five'. The c/n is sometimes found on a plate to the left of the doorway leading to the flightdeck.

Like the Mi-8MTV-1, the Mi-8AMT is powered by 1,900-shp TV3-117VM engines with improved hot-and-high performance and features upgraded equipment. The cabin dimensions are identical (unsurprisingly), and the capacity is similar – 27 passengers on jump seats (or 26 passengers on airline-type seats), 12 stretcher cases or 4 tons of cargo internally or externally. Vibration dampers on the main rotor head are a standard fit; incidentally, the reduced vibration levels and hence fatigue loads have made it possible to increase the Mi-8AMT's designated service life to 20,000 hours.

The basic specifications are as follows. Fuselage length (including radome) is 18.219 m (59 ft 9¼ in), height on ground 4.747 m (15 ft 6⅞ in), main rotor diameter 21.294 m (69 ft 10¼ in), tail rotor diameter 3.908 m (12 ft 9⅞ in), wheel track 4.51 m (14 ft 9¾ in). Dry weight is 7.055 tons (15,550 lb), normal TOW 11.1 tons and maximum TOW 13 tons. Top speed at altitudes up to 1,000 m is 250 km/h with a normal TOW and 230 km/h with a maximum TOW. Range on internal fuel (2,170 litres/477.4 Imp gal in the main tanks and 445 litres/97.9 Imp gal in the service tank) is 570 km (miles), increasing to 1,065 km (miles) with two 915-litre (201.3 Imp gal) auxiliary tanks.

Mi-171 export civil utility and military transport/assault helicopter

The export version of the Mi-8AMT is marketed as the Mi-171. The helicopter is capable of operation in all climatic zones; it is equipped with Baklan-20 and Yadro-1 communications radios, ARK-15M and ARK-UD ADFs, a

Above: Slovak Police Mi-171 B-1786 (c/n 59489617286?), still waring the test and delivery registration 17286, in the static park of the MAKS-2003 airshow. This machine is Ulan-Ude's counterpart of the Kazan'-built Mi-8MTV-5-1, featuring a 'normal' rounded nose but a one-piece ramp/door; note the emergency exit.

A look inside the cabin of Mi-171 B-1786 through the open ramp. Note the markings on the floor to assist vehicle loading.

Above: Confusingly, this Ulan-Ude Aircraft Factory demonstrator registered 17415 (c/n 59489617415?) is also referred to simply as a Mi-171. Note that the nose profile is not identical to that of the Kazan'built Mi-17MD (Mi-8MTV-5), being somewhat more pointed; the shape of the lower windows is different, too.

A model of the Mi-172 in patrol configuration with rectangular windows as supplied to the South Korean Police.

Above: Mi-171Sh '14987' (c/n 59489614987?) at the MAKS-2001. Note the guidance antenna 'egg' under the port side of the nose and the one-piece protective door on the LLLTV/FLIR pod to starboard. The helicopter wears both versions of the U-UAPO logo – the Cyrillic 'U-U' badge and the 'angry bear' motif.

A full frontal of Mi-171Sh '14987', showing to advantage its armament and guidance systems.

DISS-32-90 Doppler speed/drift sensor, AGK-77 and AGR-74V artificial horizons, an F-037 radio altimeter, an A-723 LORAN and an 8A-813 Ts weather radar with a colour display.

An armed transport/assault version of the Mi-171 with four external stores pylons was also produced; customers for this version include the Sri Lankan Air Force.

Mi-171TP passenger/convertible helicopter

A version of the Mi-171 featuring rectangular windows, small clamshell doors and forward/rear airstair doors *à la* Mi-8APS was developed by mid-1995 as the Mi-171TP (***trahns**portno-passa**zheer**skiy* – transport/passenger, used attributively). An example registered RA-25755 (c/n 59489611156) was displayed at the MAKS-95 airshow; curiously, it had inherited the registration from the Mi-8TM mentioned in the previous chapter and even wore the same U-UAPO demonstrator colour scheme, puzzling the visitors mightily. This helicopter was later sold to Gazpromavia as RA-27158 (see also Mi-8AMTSh on this page!).

Mi-171A convertible helicopter

As in the case of the Mi-172A, a suitably modified version of the Mi-171 achieved FAR Pt 29 certification in 1998 as the Mi-171A.

Mi-171AG convertible helicopter

By analogy with the Mi-172AG, the Mi-171AG was a version of the Mi-171A with VK-2500 (TV3-117VMA-SB3) engines and satellite navigation gear developed for Gazprom.

Mi-171 (mod) transport/assault helicopter

In the late 1990s U-UAPO undertook an upgrade of the baseline Mi-171, making it better suited for general military duties. In so doing the engineers in Ulan-Ude borrowed a few sound ideas from their colleagues in Kazan', although the actual design work was doubtless performed in-house because Kazan' Helicopters surely was not going to transfer its technology to the competitor!

The result could be seen at the MAKS-2001 airshow when U-UAPO presented an upgraded Mi-171 registered 17344 (c/n 59489617347). The helicopter combined a 'classic' flightdeck section with a Mi-17MD-type one-piece ramp/door and two entry doors at the front, with the cabin heater repositioned above the starboard door (ie, the result was equivalent to the Mi-8MTV-5-1). However, careful inspection showed that the ramp actuators had a different design; moreover, the entry door arrangement mirrored the Mi-17MD, with a normal-width door to port and a double-width door to starboard! Also, 17344 had two emergency exits/gunner's stations at the rear of the cabin, which the Mi-17MD (Mi-17-V5) does not have. Curiously, these serious design changes did not affect the designation in any way.

The front end treatment was similar to the 'Afghanised' Mi-8MT, with external armour but no machine-gun or radar; there were two weapons pylons on each side. The flightdeck featured two multi-functional liquid crystal displays. A common intake dust/debris filter of Western manufacture could be fitted instead of the standard vortex-type filters, as was demonstrated during the show.

Mi-171 (mod II) utility helicopter

The static park at the MAKS-2003 airshow included a very similar 'flatass' three-door Mi-171 – again with the same designation – built for the Slovak Police. This one was completed in unarmed utility configuration and fitted with a weather radar in the usual thimble radome; the instrument panels were also different. The helicopter wore the test and delivery registration 17286, suggesting that the c/n was 59489617286, and the serial B-1786 was discernible through the paint.

Mi-171 (mod III) military utility helicopter

The Ulan-Ude plant presented one more version of the Mi-171 which, despite the identical designation (again!), was rather different. Registered 17415 (c/n 59489617415?) and painted a dark graphite grey, the helicopter featured a rear ramp/door, two entry doors and a stepped nose similar – but not identical – to that of the Mi-17MD (the profile was more pointed). There was no armament – but, unlike all helicopters seen previously, the cargo ramp incorporated a special hatch closed by double doors through which a machine-gun could be fired even when the ramp was closed!

Mi-171V02 transport/assault helicopter

Currently U-UAPO is offering a three-door military derivative of the Mi-171 designated Mi-171V02. Like the Mi-171AG, the aircraft is powered by Klimov VK-2500 turboshafts. In accordance with the customer's demands it can be completed with either a 'classic' fully-glazed nose or a stepped 'radar nose'; the same applies to the rear fuselage which may incorporate either normal clamshell doors or a one-piece ramp/door.

Range at 500 m (1,640 ft) with 30-minute fuel reserves is quoted as 1,105 km (686 miles). Incidentally, the relocation of the cabin heater due to the provision of the starboard entry door has made it possible to increase the capacity of the starboard fuel tank by 80 litres (17.6 Imp gal).

Mi-8AMTSh (Mi-171Sh) transport/attack helicopter

In the mid-1990s the design office of the Ulan-Ude aircraft factory developed a new heavily armed version of the Mi-8AMT having a good sales potential. Designated Mi-8AMTSh (*shtoormo**voy*** – attack, used attributively) for the home market and Mi-171Sh for export, this helicopter was the best of both worlds, combining the proven airframe and 1,900-shp TV3-117VM engines of the *Hip-H* with the latest guided weapons developed for the Mi-28 attack helicopter. This increased the Mi-8AMTSh's punch appreciably while minimising technical risks and cutting costs.

The Mi-8AMTSh had three pylons on each side enabling the carriage of more potent weapons. These included 9M114 Shtoorm-V (Assault) supersonic anti-tank guided missiles in neat packs of four on the outer pylons, the more modern 9M120 Ataka (Attack) ATGMs in two-packs on the centre pylons, and 9M39 Igla-V IR homing air-to-air missiles, also in twin tubular launcher/containers. The anti-tank missiles employed SACLOS guidance; hence low light-level television (LLLTV) and forward-looking infra-red (FLIR) sensors were installed in a slab-sided housing offset to starboard ahead of the nose gear, with twin protective doors covering the sensor window, and a command link antenna 'egg' was mounted symmetrically to port. Of course, the *Hip-H's* usual unguided weapons (B-8V20 FFAR pods, UPK-23-250 cannon pods and so on) were usable, too.

Kalashnikov PKT machine-guns were installed in the nose and the clamshell door hatch, with provisions for six machine-guns firing through the cabin windows. The crew and tail gunner were protected by armour panels from the front and from below. EVU exhaust/air mixers and twin ASO-2V-02 chaff/flare dispensers on the aft fuselage sides afforded protection against heat-seeking missiles.

Registered as RA-25755 No.3 (c/n 59489611121), the Mi-8AMTSh (Mi-171Sh) prototype had its public debut at Farnborough in September 1996. Interestingly, it featured two emergency exits to starboard (in the foremost and rearmost windows) instead of the usual single exit at the front. A year later the same aircraft was displayed at the MAKS-97 airshow; the sinister-looking, black-painted helicopter immediately earned the nickname 'Terminator'! Later the missile guidance antenna was moved to the usual location of the nose-mounted PKT machine-gun, the the LLLTV/FLIR pod being relocated to the centreline, and the helicopter was repainted grey.

A different Mi-171Sh registered 14987 (c/n 59489614987?) was displayed at the MAKS-2001 airshow, wearing tan/brown

Above: The Mi-8MT upgraded by IAI/Tamam makes a demonstration flight at Le Bourget in 1999.

desert camouflage. This helicopter differed in having three emergency exits – one at the front (opposite the entry door) and two at the rear – and two hardpoints on each side instead of three, with four-packs of Shtoorm ATGMs on the outer pylons and B-8V20 FFAR pods inboard.

The missile guidance antenna 'egg' was slightly larger and the LLLTV/FLIR pod had a one-piece protective door replacing the twin doors on RA-25755 No.3.

Mi-17 – Israeli upgrade

A single Mi-17 of unknown origin was upgraded by Tamam, an avionics division of Israel Aircraft Industries (IAI), in 1999, making its public debut at that year's Paris Air Show with the symbolic 'serial' IAI 817. The helicopter featured a night vision goggles compatible 'glass cockpit', an LLLTV/FLIR 'ball turret' under the nose, Israeli ATGMs and ECM/IRCM equipment. The upgrade was targeted mainly at the Indian Air Force, a major operator of the type.

Mi-8GM upgrade project

The latest in the line of Mi-8 versions is the projected Mi-8GM (*gloo**bok**aya moderni**zah**tsiya* – massive upgrade) which is scheduled to enter production in 2008. The helicopter will feature a two-man flightdeck with four 150 x 200 mm (6 x 8 in) liquid crystal displays and two control display units, plus a new navigation system.

Summing up this chapter, we should mention that a three-stage modular upgrade programme for the Mi-8/Mi-17 concerning both existing and new-production aircraft is currently under way in Russia. Under this programme the good old Mi-8 is to benefit as much as possible from the development of the as-yet unflown Mi-38 – the type originally intended to replace it.

In particular, the *Hip* is to receive new composite main rotor blades, a new bearingless main rotor hub with self-lubricating elastomeric joints, a standardised flotation bag system, a new fuel system, two-chamber hydraulic control actuators, a new sling system with built-in weighing and oscillation damping features capable of handling loads up to 5 tons (11,020 lb), and state-of-the-art avionics. This will enable the Mi-8 to hold the fort until the Mi-38 finally comes up.

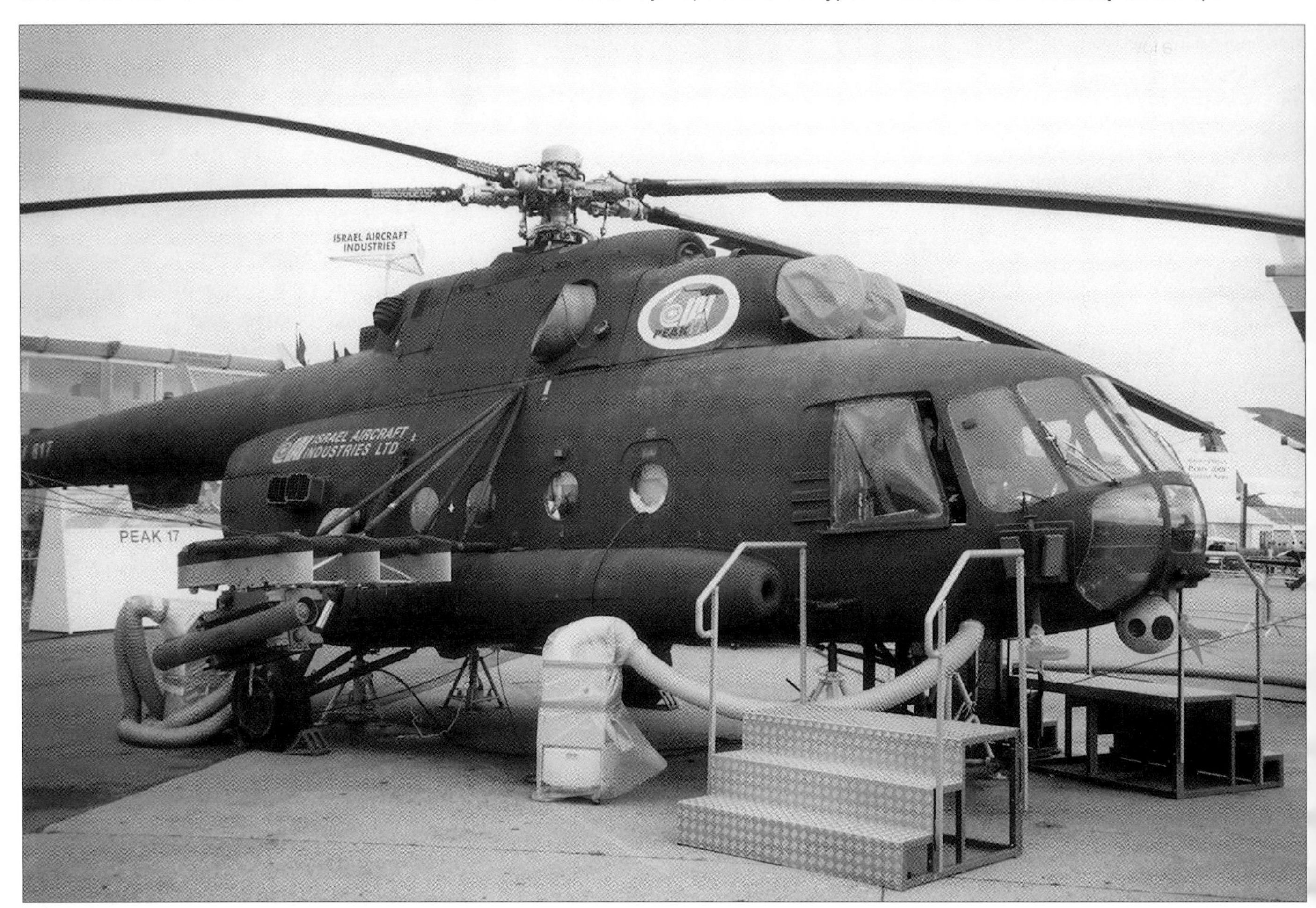

Close-up of the Mi-8MTV modified by IAI/Tamam, showing the centrally mounted LLLTV/FLIR 'ball turret', ECM antennas on the sides on the nose, Israeli ATGMs and new chaff/flare dispenser packs. A mobile air conditioner is connected to the flightdeck by a hose.

Chapter 4

The Mi-8 in Detail

The following structural description applies to the basic 'first-generation' Mi-8T. Details of other versions are indicated as appropriate.

Type: Multi-purpose helicopter designed for day/night operation in visual meteorological conditions (VMC).

Fuselage: Conventional all-metal semi-monocoque structure of riveted construction with frames, longerons and stringers. Structurally the fuselage consists of four sections: forward fuselage, centre fuselage, tailboom and tail rotor pylon. The tailboom is detachable for heavy maintenance or transportation by road/rail.

The ***forward fuselage*** is the extensively glazed flightdeck configured for two or three (two pilots and a flight engineer). It features five windscreen panels in the upper row, four windows in the lower row (with the two centre windows arranged above one another) and two side windows. The three centrally positioned windscreen panels are made of optically-flat glass to avoid view distortion and electrically de-iced, the port and starboard panels directly in front of the pilots being equipped with individual wipers; all other windows are made of Perspex. The lower centre window in the lower row may be replaced with a weather radar in a bullet-shaped radome or, on the Mi-8TV and Mi-8TB, with a flexible mount for a machine-gun; on the Mi-8MT/Mi-8MTV the machine-gun mount sometimes replaces the upper centre window in the lower row. The side windows are sliding direct vision windows; they are bulged for better downward visibility and can be jettisoned in an emergency. On the Mi-8MT/Mi-8MTV, provision is made for external armour plates to protect the crew.

The flightdeck roof incorporates a forward-hinged hatch opening outwards for access to the engines and main rotor head on the ground. The flightdeck features dual controls, three main instrument panels installed in such a way as to maximise the field of view, lateral and centre overhead circuit breaker panels, and more circuit breaker/fuse panels on the rear bulkhead. It is separated from the main cabin by an inward-opening door; there is a jump seat for the flight engineer in the doorway.

Above: The forward fuselage of a Ukrainian AF Mi-8MT, showing the external armour and the machine-gun mount. Curiously, the window in the entry door is faired over; note also the leopard's head nose art.

Two battery bays with external covers are incorporated on each side immediately aft of the flightdeck, one above the other.

The ***centre fuselage*** incorporates the troop/cargo cabin (Mi-8T/Mi-8TV and Mi-8MT/Mi-171) or passenger cabin (Mi-8P/Mi-8PS and Mi-172). The troop/cargo cabin is 5.34 m (17 ft 6¼ in) long, 2.25 m (7 ft 4½ in) wide and 1.8 m (5 ft 10¾ in) high. It is accessed via an aft-sliding jettisonable door on the port side

A Lada 1600 (VAZ-2106) sedan is driven out of a Mi-8T; the last letters on the Soviet-style private vehicle licence plate k 8067 BU indicate Buryatia. Oddly, there is no escape hatch in the starboard clamshell door!

Above: Most versions, like this Mi-8MT, have a single sliding entry door to port. Note the twin DC battery bays immediately ahead of the door and the LPG-150 hoist above it.

VIP helicopters like this Mi-8AMT feature a downward-hinged airstair door closed from within by pulling the retaining cables/handrails. This aircraft appears to have an extra long port side tank but no air conditioner.

measuring 1.4 x 0.62 m (55⅛ x 24½ in), with detachable boarding steps. The rear end of the cabin incorporates detachable clam-shell cargo doors whose lower sections hinge upwards and inwards to avoid encroaching on the cabin width; when closed they increase the floor length to 7.28 m (23 ft 10 in). The starboard half incorporates a smaller door used as an emergency exit or a gunner's station for protecting the rear hemisphere.

The Mi-8T/Mi-8TV has six circular cabin windows to port (the foremost window is incorporated in the entry door) and five to starboard. The windows open inwards and upwards; on military helicopters they feature flexible mounts for the troops' assault rifles. The Mi-8MT/Mi-171 features an emergency exit in the first cabin window to starboard (opposite the entry door).

The cabin is designed to take loads weighing up to 4,000 kg (8,820 lb); the floor features cargo tie-down lugs. Two detachable ramps can be hooked up to the door sill for loading wheeled vehicles.

The passenger cabin of the Mi-8P/Mi-8PS and Mi-172 is 6.36 m (20 ft 10⅜ in) long, 2.05 m (6 ft 8¾ in) wide and 1.7 m (5 ft 7 in) high; the marginally smaller width and height are due to thicker soundproofing panels (according to other sources, the width and height are the same as for the Mi-8T). The rear clamshell doors are smaller and feature a cutout on the centreline closed by rear airstairs and an upward-hinged door segment. There are six rectangular cabin windows on each side (the foremost window to port is incorporated in the entry door); the rearmost window on each side features an emergency exit. Mi-8S VIP helicopters have a downward-hinged windowless airstair door of identical dimensions, with five windows to port; additionally, some examples have seven windows to starboard.

The centre fuselage sides incorporate attachment points for the fuel tanks, the cabin heater and/or air conditioner and, on military examples, weapons pylon outriggers.

A large fairing housing the powerplant, the main gearbox and their oil cooler/cooling fan assembly is provided above the cabin; it incorporates longitudinal and transverse firewalls. The engine and main gearbox cowling panels hinge downwards and are stressed to double as work platforms during maintenance.

The ***tailboom*** is a stressed-skin structure of circular cross-section tapering gently towards the end; it accommodates the tail rotor drive shaft and control cables and carries communications and radio navigation aerials and, on some versions, the flight data recorder. The tailboom terminates in the tail rotor pylon, a separate structure swept back 45° with a fin-like fairing at the rear placing the tail rotor's axis in the main rotor's plane of rotation; this houses the tail rotor's intermediate and final drive gearboxes.

All-moving horizontal stabilisers with a NACA 0012 symmetrical airfoil are installed on the tailboom. Each stabiliser is a single-spar structure with metal skin ahead of the spar and fabric skin aft of the spar. Stabiliser incidence is normally 6° (3° on the Mi-8MTV) but is ground-adjustable from +9° to –9° to suit different payload combinations and hence different CG positions; stabiliser span 2.7 m (8 ft 10¼ in), stabiliser area 2 m² (21.5 sq. ft).

Landing gear: Non-retractable tricycle type; wheel track 4.5 m (14 ft 9 in), wheelbase 4.26 m (13 ft 11¾ in). The pyramidal main units have single 865 x 280 mm (34.0 x 11.0 in) wheels equipped with pneumatic brakes. The levered-suspension nose unit has twin 535 x 185 mm (21.0 x 7.28 in) non-braking wheels. It is fully castoring and centers automatically in no-load condition; steering on the ground is by differential braking. All three landing gear struts have oleo-pneumatic shock absorbers.

A non-retractable tail bumper is provided to protect the tailboom and tail rotor in a tail-down landing. It consists of two struts, a shock absorber and a spring-loaded steel bumper plate.

Powerplant: The Mi-8T/Mi-8P were initially powered by two Izotov (NPP Klimov) TV2-117A turboshafts with a nominal rating of 1,500 shp (1,118 kW); late-production aircraft (for instance, the Mi-8AT) have TV2-117AG engines rated at 1,700 shp (1,267 kW).

The TV2-117A is a single-spool turboshaft with a ten-stage axial compressor, an annular combustion chamber with eight flame tubes, a two-stage axial power turbine, a two-stage axial free turbine and an angled jetpipe through which the power output shaft passes. The first three compressor stages feature variable inlet guide vanes to increase efficiency and facilitate engine starting. The turbines are cooled by air bled from the eighth and tenth compressor stages.

The engine has a dorsally-mounted accessory gearbox for driving fuel, oil and hydraulic pumps and electrical equipment. Starting is by means of a GS-18TP starter-generator; time from start to take-off power is 5 minutes, in-flight restart time 1 minute. Length overall 2.835 m (9 ft 3⅝ in), width 0.547 m (1 ft 9½ in), height 0.745 m (2 ft 5⅜ in); dry weight 330 kg (727.5 lb).

The Mi-8MT and Mi-8AMT/Mi-171 have two Izotov (NPP Klimov) TV3-117MT turboshafts with a nominal rating of 1,900 shp (1,398 kW) and a takeoff/contingency rating of 2,200 shp (1,640 kW); if one engine fails the other automatically goes to full takeoff power.

Above: The Mi-8T/Mi-8P was built with two types of fuel tanks. This is an early-model 'short' 745-litre port tank with three attachment straps on Soviet Air Force Mi-8T '05 Red' (c/n 9755017) at Moscow-Tushino.

Above: The later variety is represented by the 1,140-litre port tank with four straps on Soviet Air Force Mi-8PS '08 Yellow' (c/n 8168), likewise based at Moscow-Tushino. Note the recess for the main gear oleo.

The PZU air intake dust/debris filters on a Mi-8MT. Note the downward-angled tubes through which the separated dust is ejected overboard.

Above: The oval-section jetpipe of the port engine on Mi-8MT '42 Red' (possibly c/n 93344 or 93360). Note also the mounting racks for the exhaust/air mixer below it and the characteristic teardrop bulge aft of it.

Above: The starboard EVU exhaust/air mixer on Mi-8AMTSh RA-25755 No.3.

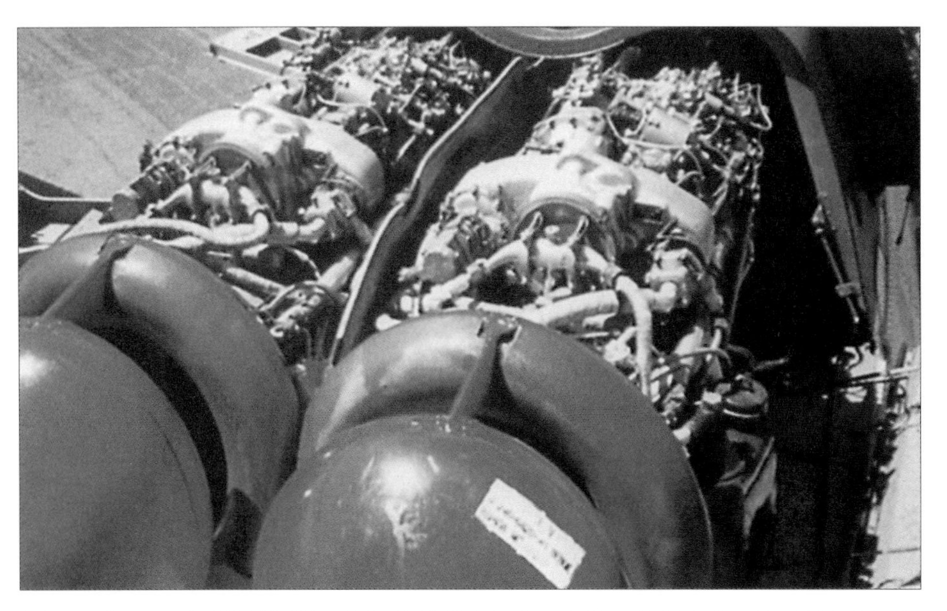

A view of the uncowled TV3-117VM engines of a Mi-8MTV, showing the separating firewall and the dorsal accessory gearboxes.

The Mi-8MTV *et seq*. has TV3-117VM engines flat-rated at 2,500 shp (1,864 kW).

The TV3-117 is a single-spool turboshaft with a 12-stage axial compressor, an annular combustion chamber with 12 flame tubes, a two-stage axial turbine, a two-stage free turbine and an angled jetpipe through which the power output shaft passes. The first five compressor stages feature variable inlet guide vanes; two anti-surge bleed valves are installed aft of the seventh compressor stage.

The engine has a dorsally-mounted accessory gearbox. Starting is by means of an S8-78B air starter connected to the gearbox. The engine has its own oil system using grade B-3V synthetic oil which permits starting at ambient temperatures right down to –40°C (–40°F).

The engines' oil coolers are cooled by a dorsally-mounted powered fan which also serves the main gearbox oil cooler (see below).

The engines are installed side by side on top of the centre fuselage (ahead of the main gearbox), parallel to the fuselage axis. The port and starboard engines are interchangeable, except for the detachable jetpipes which have to be replaced. The Mi-8MTV has provisions for EVU triple-lobe air/exhaust mixers which reduce the helicopter's IR signature and hence vulnerability to IR-homing anti-aircraft missiles. The Mi-8MT *et seq*. are equipped with vortex-type dust/debris extractors on the engine air intakes with an extraction rate of 70-75%; these are sometimes fitted to the Mi-8T by means of special adapters.

The Mi-8MT et seq. features an Ivchenko AI-9V auxiliary power unit (APU) installed aft of the main gearbox. This is a very compact turboshaft engine with an STG-3 starter/DC generator which provides ground power (or backup power if one of the engine-driven generators fails) and compressed air for engine starting. The APU is mounted at 90° to the fuselage axis; the intake louvres are on the starboard side and the exhaust on the port side. The APU is started electrically, using onboard DC batteries or ground power. Dry weight 70 kg (154 lb).

Power train: Engine torque is fed via overrunning clutches into the VR-8A three-stage main gearbox mounted on a truss-type bearer. The first stage has helical gears, the second stage has hypoid gears and the third stage has planetary gears. The main gearbox conveys torque to the main rotor, the accessories gearbox/tail rotor drive shaft and the fan serving the engine oil coolers and main gearbox oil cooler.

The accessories gearbox has a dual role. Besides driving the main generators and hydraulic pumps, it reduces tail rotor drive shaft speed. A long drive shaft passing inside the tailboom connects the accessories gearbox with an intermediate gearbox at the base of the tail rotor pylon turning the axis of the shaft up through 45°; finally, a short shaft links it with the final drive gearbox which turns the shaft through 90° to starboard.

The engine output shafts' maximum speed of 12,000 rpm is reduced to a maximum of 192 rpm for the main rotor, 1,124 rpm for the tail rotor and 6,021 rpm for the oil cooler fan. A shoe-type rotor brake is provided to minimise rundown time after engine shutdown and to lock the rotors during parking or maintenance.

The Mi-8MT *et seq*. features a VR-14 main gearbox designed for an engine speed of 15,000 rpm. Another major difference is that the final drive gearbox turns the shaft to port.

Rotor system: Five-bladed main rotor, turning clockwise when seen from above. The fully articulated rotor head has flapping and drag hinges with adjustable stops and is equipped with dampers. The main rotor axis is inclined forward 4°30'.

The interchangeable blades have a constant chord of 520 mm (1 ft 8½ in) and utilise NACA 230 airfoil. Thickness/chord ratio varies from 12% to 11.38%; camber –5°, tip speed 217 m/sec (712 ft/sec). Each blade has an extruded box spar of partial airfoil section made of AVT-1 aluminium alloy, 21 blade pockets with limiting ribs, a steel leading-edge sheath and a tip fairing; the duralumin skin and aluminium honeycomb filler are bonded to the spar. A balance tab is fitted along the trailing edges of pockets Nos 13 and 14. A compressed-air spar failure warning system is provided.

The three-bladed tail rotor of 3.9 m (12 ft 9½ in) diameter likewise turns clockwise when seen from the hub. The interchangeable blades of constant 260 mm (10¼ in) chord utilise NACA 230M airfoil and are structurally similar to the main rotor blades. The Mi-8T/ Mi-8P and Mi-9 have a pusher-type tail rotor installed on the starboard side, whereas the Mi-8MT *et seq*. have a port side tractor-type tail rotor with wider-chord blades.

Control system: The Mi-8 has full dual controls and a conventional mechanical flight control system, mostly with push-pull rods; cables are used for controlling the tail rotor and rotor brake. Pitch and roll control, as well as climb/descent, are effected by the swashplate; directional control is effected by changing the tail rotor blade pitch.

The control system features an AP-34B four-channel autopilot providing autostabilisation in pitch, yaw, bank, speed and barometric altitude in level flight and in hovering flight.

Above: The 28-seat cabin of Mi-8P CCCP-10459 (c/n 10459) at the MosAeroShow-92; the open rear entry door is visible beyond. Note the illuminated signs above the lateral emergency exits.

Above: The cabin of a Mi-8S, looking forward. This is an early aircraft built in the late 1960s.

The cabin of a Mi-8MTV, looking forward. Most of the tip-up seats along the walls have been removed altogether.

Above: The cabin of a Mi-8MTV-5, looking towards the open one-piece ramp/door. An extra row of troop seats is fitted to maximise seating capacity, the seat backs being formed by straps.

Above: The rear end of Mi-171 17415 (c/n 59489617415?), showing the loading ramp with built-in doors for a tail gunner's station (the latter feature was introduced on this particular machine).

The port weapons outrigger of Mi-8 MT '42 Red' with triple pylons and mounting boxes for two PKT machine-guns. Note the 'short' 745-litre port fuel tank.

Fuel system: Fuel is carried in two cylindrical metal tanks attached to the centre fuselage sides by metal straps. The capacity was originally 745 litres (163.9 Imp gal) for the port tank and 680 litres (149.6 Imp gal) for the starboard tank; late-production Mi-8Ts feature enlarged fuel tanks holding 1,140 litres (250.8 Imp gal) and 1,030 litres (226.6 Imp gal) respectively. On the Mi-8MTV the capacity of the external tanks is further increased. A 445-litre (97.9 Imp gal) service tank is located in the upper part of the centre fuselage aft of the main gearbox. On the Mi-8MTV-2 the tanks are filled with explosion-suppression polyurethane foam for higher combat survivability. Additionally, one or two 915-litre (201.3 Imp gal) cylindrical tanks may be installed in the troop/cargo cabin for ferry or long-endurance missions.

The Mi-8 uses T-1, TS-1 or T-7P jet fuel (T = ***top****livo*) or Western equivalents (JP-1 or JP-4). Refuelling is by gravity via a filler cap on the starboard side of the centre fuselage; the service tank is filled by means of fuel transfer pumps. The TV2-117 engine features an NR-UOV regulator pump.

Hydraulics: Two independent hydraulic systems (main and backup), with hydraulic pumps driven by the accessories gearbox. The main system with a nominal pressure of 45 kg/cm^2 (642 psi) works all hydraulic equipment. The backup system with a nominal pressure of 65 kg/cm^2 (928 psi) takes over automatically in the event of pressure loss in the main system, operating only the control system actuators.

Electrics: 12V/48V DC main electric system with two 18-kW GS-18TP engine-driven starter-generators (TV2-117 powered versions). Six 12SAM-28 lead-acid batteries (12V/55 A·h) in bays in the forward fuselage.

De-icing system: The main and tail rotor blade leading edges, windscreens and pitot/static heads are electrically de-iced. The rotor blade de-icers are activated automatically by an RIO-3 radioactive icing detector (***rah****dioizo****top****nyy indi****kah****tor oblede****nen****iya*) installed in a protective housing on the port side of the oil cooler air intake; the other items are activated manually. The engines have their own automatic de-icing system, with hot air de-icing for the inlets, hot oil de-icing for the front compressor bearing struts (TV3-117) and electric de-icing for the PZU intake filters, if any.

Heating and ventilation/air conditioning system: To ensure comfortable conditions for the occupants the flightdeck and cabin are air-ventilated by outside air or heated air from a KO-50 kerosene heater mounted externally ahead of the starboard fuel tank. In hot climatic zones the heater may be replaced by two compact air conditioners installed in the same fairing; aircraft featuring an airstair door to port have an air conditioner installed ahead of the port fuel tank as standard. The ventilation system demists the windscreen and side windows of the flightdeck.

Avionics and equipment:

a) navigation equipment: ARK-9 automatic direction finder (*avtomaticheskiy rahdiokompas* – ADF) with omnidirectional wire aerial under cabin and faired loop aerial or ARK-U2 ADF with flush antenna, RV-3 radio altimeter with two dipole antennas under the tailboom, GMK-1A combined compass system allowing radio navigation by means of ground beacons, DISS-15D Doppler speed/drift sensor with tandem antennas installed in a ventral fairing or cutout on the tailboom on early aircraft (replaced by a DISS-30 or DISS-32-90 in a larger fairing on late-production aircraft) etc. The Mi-171 features ARK-15M and ARK-UD ADF, an F-037 radio altimeter, a DISS-32-90 Doppler speed/drift sensor, an A-723 long-range navigation (LORAN) system with a ventral strake aerial and an 8A-813 Kontoor weather radar with a monochrome display which is also fitted to many Mi-8MTVs (alternatively, a Kontoor-Ts radar with a colour display can be fitted).

b) communications equipment: R-860-1 two-way UHF command radio with rod aerial on tailboom early versions, replaced by an R-863 UHF radio with a blade aerial in the same location on late versions; military versions also have an R-828 *Evkalipt* (Eucalyptus) UHF command radio with a 'towel rail' aerial under the fuselage for communicating with ground forces and armoured vehicle crews. Karat VHF communications radio with wire aerials; the Mi-171 features *Baklan*-20 (Cormorant) and *Yadro*-1 (Core) communications radios. The flightdeck and cabin are equipped with an SPU-7 intercom (*samolyotnoye peregovornoye oostroystvo*).

c) flight instrumentation: The instruments include duplex ARB-3K artificial horizons, duplex rotor speed indicators etc.; the Mi-171 features AGK-77 and AGP-74V artificial horizons. Air data is provided by pitch and yaw vanes and two pitot heads mounted the forward fuselage. An RI-65 audio warning system (*rechevoy informahtor*) warns the pilot of critical failures (fire etc.) or dangerous flight modes lying outside the helicopter's designated flight envelope.

d) IFF equipment: SRO-2M Khrom (Chromium/*izdeliye* 023) IFF transponder with triple rod aerials on early versions, replaced by the SRO-1P Parol' (Password/*izdeliye* 62-01) transponder with triangular

Above: This front view of the port weapons outrigger on a Mi-8MT shows the bracing struts between the three BD3-57KrVM pylons and the retaining clamps on the latter which prevent the stores from rocking.

Above: The nose-mounted Kalashnikov PKT machine-gun on Mi-8AMTSh RA-25755 No.3, showing the simple mechanical sight.

The Mi-8AMTSh (Mi-171Sh) can carry neat four-packs of 9M114 Shtoorm-V supersonic ATGMs in disposable launch containers.

Above: A typical ordnance load for the Mi-8AMTSh comprises eight Shtoorm ATGMs and two B-8V20 FFAR pods.

Above: The radome of the Mi-8MTV-1's Kontoor weather radar replacing the lower half of the centre glazing panel in the lower row. The inscription in Russian reads 'Danger, UHF [radiation]'.

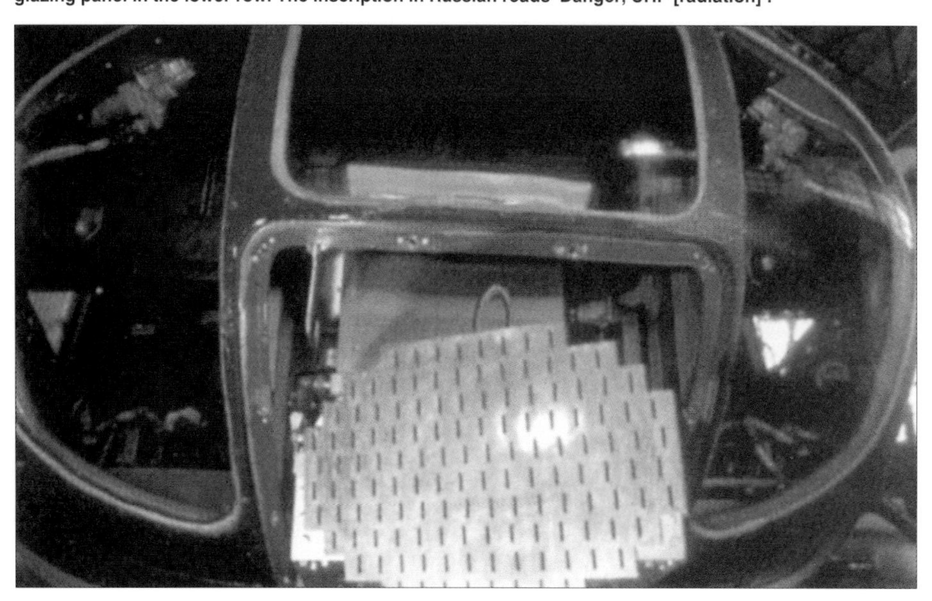

With the radome removed, this view shows the flat-plate scanner of the Kontoor radar.

blade aerials on the Mi-8MTV. The IFF aerials are located under the forward fuselage and under the base of the tail rotor pylon.

e) electronic support measures (ESM) equipment: S-3M Sirena (SPO-15) radar homing and warning system (RHAWS) on some military examples. The Mi-8TV/Mi-8MT has four sideways-firing 32-round ASO-2V chaff/flare dispensers (two on each side) for protection against IR-homing missiles strapped on under the rear portion of the tailboom. Military Mi-8MTVs have a different arrangement with three angled ASO-2V dispensers (faired or exposed) mounted on each side of the aft fuselage, plus an optional L-166V-11E (SOEP-V1A Lipa) active IRCM jammer installed aft of the APU bay.

f) data recording equipment: SARPP-12DM flight data recorder (*sis**tema** avtoma**tich**eskoy reghistr**ah**tsii pa**rah**metrov po**lyo**ta* – automatic flight parameter recording system) or, on some versions, BUR-1-2Zh flight data recorder installed in a ventral fairing on the tailboom to facilitate accident investigation.

g) exterior lighting: BANO-45 port (red) and starboard (green) navigation lights on the sides of the flightdeck section, KhS-39 white navigation light at bottom of tail rotor pylon. The Mi-8T, Mi-8MT and Mi-171 have a single red MSL-3 rotating anti-collision beacon mounted dorsally on the tailboom; the Mi-8P/Mi-8PS and Mi-172 feature a second anti-collision beacon under the flightdeck section. Orange OPS-57 formation lights (*o**gon'** pozitsi**on**nyy stroye**voy***) on the upper surface of the tailboom (military examples only), plus five main rotor blade tip lights which help avoid collisions during night operations.

Two retractable MPRF-1A landing/taxi lights are installed ahead of the nose gear unit. The Mi-8AMT/Mi-171 has an optional FPP-7 landing light/searchlight in a fairing offset to port in line with the entry door. Many aircraft have faired FR-100 lights on the underside of the main gear struts to assist operations with slung loads. Two EKSP-39 electric flare launchers (*elek**tri**cheskaya kas**se**ta sig**nahl'**nykh pat**ro**nov*) are built into the port clamshell cargo door for friend/foe identification (eg, in the event of communications equipment failure). Each launcher fires four 39-mm (1½-in) signal flares (red, green, yellow and white).

Accommodation/cargo handling equipment: The Mi-8T/Mi-8TV and Mi-8MT/Mi-171 have lightweight tip-up seats for 24 mounted along the cabin walls. There are two double and two triple seats to port, one double seat and three triple seats to starboard, and a seat for one on the housing enclosing control runs; additionally, the covers of two tool boxes mounted on the insides of the clamshell cargo doors double as single seats.

In medevac configuration the cabin accommodates 12 stretchers.

An LPG-150 electric hoist with a lifting capacity of 150 kg (330 lb) is located under the floor on the Mi-8T, with an external jib on the port side just ahead of the entry door. A DG-64 electromagnetically actuated cargo hook can be installed under the fuselage on all versions for carrying externally slung loads. It works with a hinge-and-pendulum sling system permitting the carriage of loads weighing up to 2.5 tons (5,510 lb) or a simpler cable suspension system with a lifting capacity of 3 tons (6,610 lb).

The Mi-8P has 28 seats (14 double units) installed four-abreast at 74 cm (29⅛ in) pitch with an aisle 30 cm (11⅞ in) wide. A coat closet is located at the rear of the cabin to starboard, with luggage space symmetrically to port.

The Mi-8PS has a cabin configured for eleven, nine or seven passengers (the versions are designated Mi-8PS-11, Mi-8PS-9 and Mi-8PS-7 respectively). The latter two versions feature an airstair door and a port side air conditioner pack.

Armament:

a) built-in armament: The Mi-8T (in armed configuration)/Mi-8TV/Mi-8TB and military Mi-8MTVs have an NUV-1 gimballed mount with a 7.62-mm (.30 calibre) Kalashnikov PKT machine-gun. There are provisions for installing an identical machine-gun or an AGS-17 Plamya (Flame) 30-mm (1.18 calibre) heavy automatic grenade launcher in the entry doorway and another PKT in the hatch of the starboard clamshell cargo door. Some Mi-8TVs and Mi-8MTVs have one or two PKT machine-guns mounted on each external store outrigger.

b) anti-tank missiles: The Mi-8TV has the K-4U weapons system with four manually-guided 9M17P Falanga-P subsonic anti-tank guided missiles on launch rails mounted dorsally on the external store outriggers. The export Mi-8TVK can carry up to six 9M14P Malyutka subsonic ATGMs in similar fashion.

c) other armament: Truss-type outriggers can be installed on the fuselage sides, mounting four (Mi-8T) or six (Mi-8TV/Mi-8TB/Mi-8MT/Mi-8MTV) BD3-57KrVM pylons. These permit the carriage of various unguided weapons.

The 1968-model Mi-8TV had the following payload options: four bombs of 50-250 kg (110-551 lb) calibre; two bombs of 50-500 kg (110-1,102 lb) calibre on the inboard pylons; two bombs of 50-250 kg calibre plus two UB-16-57 pods with 16 57-mm (2.24-in) S-5KO, S-5KP or S-5MO folding-fin aircraft rockets (FFARs) apiece; two RBK-500 cluster bombs (***rah****zovaya* ***bom****bovaya kas****set****a*); and four RBK-250 cluster bombs or RBS-100 bomb clusters (***rah****zovaya* ***bom****bovaya* ***svyaz****ka*).

Above: The flightdeck of a Mi-8AMT; note the centrally mounted cathode-ray tube (CRT) radar display suspended from the ceiling.

Above: The flightdeck of Mi-171 17415, showing the full-width instrument panel with built-in liquid-crystal display (LCD) radar screen.

The flightdeck of Mi-171 RA-95189.

The flightdeck of the Mi-171V02, showing two displays and a much-redesigned overhead panel.

The Mi-8MT/Mi-8MTV have a much-enhanced offensive capability against area or group targets. They carry up to six B-8V20 pods with 20 80-mm (3.15-in) S-8A, S-8B, S-8M or S-8MKO FFARs apiece. The FFARs are launched in ripples of four or eight from each pod (five or three salvos respectively) as selected by the pilot; the launch is controlled by a PUS 36-71 fire control unit (*pribor oopravleniya strel'boy*). The 'second-generation' versions can also carry two 500-kg ZB-500 incendiary bombs.

Alternatively, the Mi-8MT/Mi-8MTV can carry up to four UPK-23-250 gun pods (each containing a Gryazev/Shipoonov GSh-23 cannon with 250 rounds) for use against ground or aerial targets. Furthermore, as already noted, up to eight persons in the cabin can fire their assault rifles through the windows. The forwards and (if installed) rear PKT machine-guns are remote-controlled and have independently energised electric controls.

Mi-8 family specifications

	Mi-8T*	Mi-8P	Mi-8MT (Mi-17)	Mi-8AMT/Mi-171
Crew	2 or 3	2 or 3	2 or 3	2 or 3
Powerplant	2 x TV2-117A	2 x TV2-117A	2 x TV3-117MT	2 x TV3-117VM
Take-off power, shp (kW)	2 x 1,500 (2 x 1,104)	2 x 1,500 (2 x 1,104)	2 x 1,900 (2 x 1,398)	2 x 2,000 (2 x 1,472)†
Main rotor diameter	21.294 m (69 ft 10⅜ in)	21.294 m (69 ft 10⅜ in)	21.294 m (69 ft 10⅜ in)	21.294 m (69 ft 10⅜ in)
Tail rotor diameter	3.908 m (12 ft 9½ in)	3.908 m (12 ft 9½ in)	3.908 m (12 ft 9½ in)	3.908 m (12 ft 9½ in)
Length, rotors turning	25.24 m (82 ft 9¾ in)	25.24 m (82 ft 9¾ in)	25.24 m (82 ft 9¾ in)	25.24 m (82 ft 9¾ in)
Fuselage length	18.17 m (59 ft 7⅜ in)‡	18.17 m (59 ft 7⅜ in)‡	18.17 m (59 ft 7⅜ in)‡	18.17 m(59 ft 7⅜ in)‡
Fuselage width	2.5 m (8 ft 2½ in)	2.5 m (8 ft 2½ in)	2.5 m (8 ft 2½ in)	2.5 m (8 ft 2½ in)
Height on ground:				
top of main rotor head	4.38 m (14 ft 4½ in)‡	4.38 m (14 ft 4½ in)‡	4.38 m (14 ft 4½ in)‡	4.38 m (14 ft 4½ in)‡
rotors turning	5.65 m (18 ft 6½ in)	5.65 m (18 ft 6½ in)	5.65 m (18 ft 6½ in)	5.65 m (18 ft 6½ in)
Cabin volume, m³ (cu. ft)	23 (812.2)	n.a.	23 (812.2)	23 (812.2)
Operating empty weight, kg (lb)	6,934 (15,286)	7,000 (15,430)	7,200 (15,870)	6,913 (15,240)
Normal TOW, kg (lb)	11,100 (24,470)	11,570 (25,510)	11,100 (24,470)	11,100 (24,470)
MTOW, kg (lb)	12,000 (26,455)	12,000 (26,455)	13,000 (28,660)	13,000 (28,660)
Maximum internal load, kg (lb)	4,000 (8,820)	4,000 (8,820)	4,000 (8,820)	4,000 (8,820)
Externally slung load, kg (lb)	3,000 (6,610)	3,000 (6,610)	3,000 (6,610)	4,000 (8,820)
Top speed at sea level				
at normal TOW, km/h (mph)	250 (155) §	250 (155)	250 (155)	250 (155)
Cruising speed, km/h (mph)	225 (140)	225 (140)	220 (136)	230 (142)
Hovering ceiling OGE, m (ft)	850 (2,790)	60 (200)	1,760 (5,770)	3,980 (13,060)
Hovering ceiling IGE, m (ft)	1,800 (5,900)	1,300 (4,260)	3,500 (11,480)	n.a.
Service ceiling, m (ft)	4,500 (14,760)	4,200 (13,780)	5,000 (16,400)	6,000 (19,685)
Operational range at normal TOW				
with 5% fuel reserves, km (miles)	480 (298) ¶	425 (264) ‖	580 (360)	570/637 (354/395) **

* Unarmed civil version

† The TV3-117VM retains a take-off rating of 1,950 shp (1,435 kW) up to 3,600 m (11,800 ft) ASL in ISA conditions.

‡ Some sources quote the Mi-8T's fuselage length as 18.219 m (59 ft 9¼ in) and the height on ground as 4.747 m (15 ft 6⅞ in)

§ 230 km/h (142 mph) at maximum TOW.

¶ 460 km (285 miles) at maximum TOW.

‖ With 28 passengers and 20-minute fuel reserves.

** At maximum TOW with maximum fuel and a 3,400-kg (7,500-lb) payload.

Chapter 5

The Universal Soldier

The multi-role Mi-8 quickly earned recognition as one of the world's best combat helicopters ever. The Soviet Armed Forces started taking delivery of the Mi-8 in 1965, foreign military sales commencing shortly afterwards. As a result, from the second half of the 1960s onwards the type was involved in virtually every single armed conflict waged in the world. These included the Soviet invasion of Czechoslovakia in 1968, the Indo-Pakistani border conflict which broke out on 3rd December 1971 (and ended in a complete victory for India), the war between the Sandinista government and the Contras guerrillas in Nicaragua, the civil wars in Angola, Mozambique and Ethiopia, drug busting operations in South America, the Iran-Iraq war of 1980-88 and the First Gulf War. But, of course, the most famous conflicts in which the Mi-8 participated are undoubtedly the Afghan War (1979-89) and the First and Second Chechen Wars (1994-96 and 1999-2001). Combat experience accumulated by Mi-8 crews proved instrumental in enhancing the helicopter's operational reliability, survivability and combat efficiency, leading to the development of steadily more heavily armed versions, airborne command posts, mine-laying and mine clearing helicopters, ECM helicopters, flying hospitals and so on.

The 344th TsBP i PLS (*Tsentr boye**voy** podgo**tov**ki i pere**oo**chivaniya **lyot**novo so**stah**va* – Combat and Conversion Training Centre, = operational conversion unit) in Torzhok was the first to master the new helicopter. It was soon followed by other units of the Soviet Air Force (VVS – *Voy**en**no-voz**doosh**nyye **see**ly*) and the Soviet Naval Air Arm (AVMF – *Avi**ah**tshiya vo**yen**no-mor**sko**vo **flo**ta*). Known colloquially as *vos'**myor**ka* (The Eight), the helicopter soon became a true workhorse, serving in all Defence Districts of the Soviet Union – the Baltic DD, Belorussian DD, Carpathian DD, Central Asian DD, Far Eastern DD, Kiev DD, Leningrad DD, Moscow DD, North Caucasian DD, Red Banner Odessa DD, Transbaikalian DD, Urals DD etc.

In the mid-1970s the rotary-wing element of the VVS was reorganised into the Soviet Army Aviation, or ASV (*Avi**ah**tsiya sookho**put**nykh voysk* – ground forces aviation). By the early 1980s the new service had about 15 independent combat helicopter regiments reporting to the headquarters of various mechanised infantry or tank armies, each unit consisting of two Mi-24 squadrons and a single Mi-8TV squadron with 20 helicopters per squadron. Additionally, Mi-8s served with independent combat control squadrons assigned to mechanised infantry or armour divisions.

In addition to the numerous bases in the USSR, Soviet Air Force/Soviet Army Mi-8s were permanently stationed in some of the Warsaw Pact nations, namely Czechoslovakia (TsGV – *Tsen**trahl'**naya **groop**pa voysk*, Central Group of Forces), East Germany (ZGV – ***Zah**padnaya **groop**pa voysk*, Western Group of Forces; called GSVG (***Groop**pa so**vet**skikh **voy**sk v Gher**mah**nii* – Group of Soviet Forces in Germany) until 1989), Hungary (YuGV – ***Yoozh**naya **groop**pa voysk*, Southern Group of Forces) and Poland (SGV – ***Se**vernaya **groop**pa voysk*, Northern Group of Forces).

The ones deployed in Poland served with the 4th VA (*voz**doosh**naya **ar**miya* – air army); the only units identified to date are 55th Sevastopol'skiy OBVP (*ot**del'**nyy boye**voy** ver**tolyot**nyy polk* – independent, ie, direct reporting combat helicopter regiment) based at Bagicz AB and the 245th OSAP (*ot**del'**nyy **smesh**annyy avia**polk*** – independent composite air regiment) at Legnica AB. In East Germany the type was operated by the 16th VA

Above: A detail of Soviet Border Guards soldiers sprint towards Mi-8TV '51 Yellow', ready to intercept an intruder. Note the white stripe on the clamshell doors, the identification markings of Border Guards choppers.

This Border Guards Mi-8TV disgorging a seek-and-detain group complete with a German shepherd is unusual in featuring ATGM launch rails. Wonder if the dog disembarked by rappelling down the line too?

Table 1. Mi-8 units stationed in (East) Germany until 1994

Formation	HQ location	Units	Bases	Versions operated
GSVG HQ		113th OVE	Sperenberg	Mi-8T, Mi-8MTV, Mi-8TL, Mi-9
(direct reporting units)		226th OSAP	Sperenberg	Mi-8T, Mi-8S
		239th GvOVP	Oranienburg	Mi-8T, Mi-8MT, Mi-8MTV
		292nd OVE REB	Cochstedt	Mi-8T, Mi-8PPA, Mi-8SMV, Mi-9
1st GvTA	Dresden	225th OBVP	Allstedt	Mi-8T, Mi-9
		485th OBVP	Brandis, Merseburg	Mi-8MT, Mi-8MTV, Mi-8VKP, Mi-9
		6th OVE	Dresden-Hellerau	Mi-8T, Mi-8PPA (C³I and ECM squadron)
2nd GvTA	Fürstenberg	172nd OBVP	Parchim	Mi-8T, Mi-8MTV
		439th OBVP	Parchim, Lärz	Mi-8T, Mi-8MTV, Mi-8VKP, Mi-9
		9th OVE	Neuruppin	Mi-8PPA, Mi-8VKP, Mi-9 (C³I and ECM squadron)
3rd OA	Magdeburg	440th OBVP	Stendal (Borstel)	Mi-8T, Mi-8MT, Mi-8MTV, Mi-8VKP, Mi-9
8th GvOA	Weimar-Nohra	336th OBVP	Weimar-Nohra	Mi-8T
		486th OBVP	Jüterbog-Altes Lager	Mi-8T, Mi-8MTV, Mi-9
20th GvOA	Finow	337th OBVP	Mahlwinkel	Mi-8T, Mi-8TV, Mi-8MT, Mi-8MTV, Mi-8VKP
		487th OBVP	Templin (Gross Dölln)	Mi-8MT, Mi-8MTV, Mi-8VKP, Mi-9
		41st OVE	Finow, Werneuchen	Mi-8T (C³I squadron)

Notes: GvTA = *Gvardeyskaya tahnkovaya armiya* – Guards tank army; OA = *obshchevoyskovaya armiya* – mechanised infantry army; GvOA = *Gvardeyskaya obshchevoyskovaya armiya* – Guards mechanised infantry army; OVE = *otdel'naya vertolyotnaya eskadril'ya* – independent helicopter squadron; OVE REB = *otdel'naya vertolyotnaya eskadril'ya rahdioelektronnoy bor'by* – independent ECM helicopter squadron; C³I = command, control, communications and intelligence.

until the final Russian withdrawal in 1994 after German reunification. The Soviet Army formations to which ZGV Mi-8 units reported are listed in the table above.

The *Hip* at war: the Afghan experience

The Mi-8's moment of glory – and its ultimate test at the same time – was the Afghan War in which the type was actively involved from beginning to end. Originally, since the Soviet Union was not formally involved, the Soviet Air Force Mi-8s operating into Afghanistan in December 1979 wore Afghan Air Force roundels and three-digit serials – a fact confirmed by Russian sources; however, this masquerade was soon given up.

The sporadic character of the war and the ambush and hit-and-run tactics favoured by the Mujahideen guerrillas of Burhanuddin Rabbani and Gulbuddin Hekmatyar – 'the irreconcilable opposition' (to the Kabul government, that is), as they were referred to in the Soviet press – demanded quick and accurate response to enemy action. Thus, air support was of prime importance – all the more so because, in Afghanistan's rugged mountainous terrain, he who had the high ground was in control of the situation. This, together with the dusty, hot-and-high conditions of Afghanistan, placed high demands on the helicopters' reliability and performance; it was clear from the start this was going to be a 'chopper war' – and the Mi-8 was to prove its worth in it, bearing the brunt of the rotary-wing operations in the war.

The range of missions performed by the *Hip* in Afghanistan is truly amazing. It included vertical envelopment (ie, insertion of troops in the vicinity of villages, roads and other points of importance held by the rebels), CSAR (locating and evacuating downed Soviet pilots who faced a horrible death at the hands of the Mujahideen if they were not rescued in time), casualty evacuation, close air support (CAS), bombing strikes, aerial reconnaissance, command and control, escorting vehicle convoys, communications relay and so on. Thanks to the sturdiness of the helicopters, which soon became legendary, and the dedication of their crews most of the objectives were accomplished and countless lives of Soviet servicemen – many of whom were 18- to 20-year-old kids doing their two-year term of army service – were saved.

Originally the rotary-wing element of the 40th Army, as the Soviet contingent in Afghanistan was called, included just a single Mi-24 attack helicopter; the rest consisted of Mi-6 and Mi-8 transport helicopters. (Incidentally, the 40th Army was then the only one in the Soviet Army to have an aviation element – before the Army Aviation was formed, that is.) By the end of the year the helicopter force had been doubled to 200 aircraft (and the proportion of Mi-24s increased considerably). In early 1981 it included six squadrons of Mi-8s, three squadrons of Mi-6s and four squadrons of Mi-24s.

At first the *Hips* were tasked mostly with moving personnel and materiel; however, two months into the war the share of strike missions started growing steadily. At this stage of the conflict the Mi-8s were mostly armed with either four UB-16-57UMP FFAR pods giving a total of 64 57-mm S-5 rockets or four free-fall bombs of up to 250 kg (551 lb) calibre (alternatively, two 500-kg (1,102-lb) bombs could be carried). The 'first-generation' Mi-8T/Mi-8TV could only carry early-model short-body bombs, whereas the Mi-8MT/ Mi-8MTV featured upgraded pylons compatible with FAB-500M62 low-drag bombs and UB-32 FFAR pods. In the course of the war the Mi-8's armament changed considerably, reflecting the changing situation. For instance, while all cabin windows opened, only five of them could be used by troops for firing their weapons (the third and fourth pairs were not used for fear of damaging the helicopter's weapons pylons). The entry door and the foremost window to starboard (the emergency exit on the Mi-8MT/Mi-8MTV) could be used for firing the more potent Kalashnikov RPK machine-gun; the Mi-8MT/Mi-8MTV introduced modified fixtures in the rearmost pair of windows allowing RPKs to be fired through these as well. In practice, however, the fixtures were rarely used and were often removed, as with a hand-held weapon it was easier to shift fire to new targets and load fresh clips.

If well planned and executed, the 'gunbus' technique could be quite effective – especially in the early days of the war when the helicopter crews lacked experience with bombs and FFARs. For instance, the very first operation of the war in which The Eight was involved – the suppression of a mutiny in the Afghan Army's 4th Artillery Regiment in Nakhrin – succeeded in no small degree due to the participation of the helicopters, a flight of Mi-8s carrying marksmen. En route to Nakhrin the helicopters attacked and dispersed a group of mounted rebels, subsequently discovering and wiping out an ambush with three artillery pieces. With air cover available, the barracks of the rebellious unit were captured in one swipe; the operation lasted less than 24 hours and cost the rebels about 100 men, seven guns and five vehicles for the loss of only two Soviet soldiers. (This kill-to-loss ratio suggests the Soviet troops had been ordered to take no prisoners...)

Even the sight and sound of the roaring, sinister-looking helicopter was sometimes enough to scare the Afghans – friends as well as enemies – out of their wits. The commander of an Afghan Army unit stationed at Kunduz even asked the Soviet helicopter pilots not to fly over their barracks because it took a lot of time and effort to catch and return the recruits who had fled in panic!

The helicopters made both planned sorties and extra sorties as requested by the ground forces if a pocket of resistance was encountered. The Army Aviation (read: helos) accounted for 33% of the planned strike missions; by contrast, its share in real CAS was a whopping 75%. By then there were three levels of ground force operations – army ops, unit ops and the so-called implementation (performed at division, brigade and battalion level respectively). Each type invariably involved helicopter support, and the Mi-8 with its comprehensive weapons range was used alongside the Mi-24 as the proverbial armoured fist (*gepanzerte Faust*).

However, the enemy fought back, and combat experience was bought at a high price. On 23rd February 1980 (for the record, in the Soviet Union 23rd February was a public holiday, Soviet Army Day, and is still celebrated in modern Russia as Homeland Defenders Day) a pair of 280th OVP Mi-8s flown by Capt. Lyamtsev and Capt. Vakoolenko took off from Kandahar to intercept a suspicious vehicle convoy reported by army intelligence. Following the tracks in the sand, the crews quickly located the Toyota Hilux pick-ups (one of the favourite vehicles with the Mujahideen rebels) hidden among the dunes and decided to try 'tickling' them with machine-gun fire. However, no sooner had the co-pilot on one of the helicopters slid open his blister window and poked out his Kalashnikov AKS assault rifle than the canvas cover on the nearest pick-up was flung wide open, revealing a beardee with a Degtyaryov/Shpagin DShK HMG who opened fire immediately. Although the Mujahideen fired at almost point-blank range, miraculously the Soviet airmen suffered nothing more than a few bullet holes in the airframe – and returned fire at once, blasting the convoy with rockets. Immediately afterwards, however, the damaged helicopter had to make a forced landing when one of the engines started losing oil. Having nothing else to repair the punctured oil tank with, the crew temporarily stopped the leak with a piece of modelling clay (which they carted around on the off-chance that it might come in handy) – and made it back to base.

Escorting supply convoys was a singularly important mission. The 40th Army's daily needs amounted to hundreds of tons of fuel, ammunition, food and so on and the convoys delivering them were perpetually ambushed by the rebels. To provide protection the lorries were escorted by tanks and other armoured vehicles; some lorries had rapid-firing 23-mm anti-aircraft cannons mounted on the flatbed which could fire almost vertically at Mujahideen positions on overhanging cliffs.

Air cover, however, proved far more effective. Several pairs of helicopters took turns patrolling above the convoy, zigzagging at 150-170 km/h (93-105 mph). The crews checked the surroundings 2-3 km (1.24-1.86 miles) to each side of the road – this was the rebels' usual attack range – and 5-8 km (3-5 miles) ahead of the convoy. Having detected a Mujahideen ambush, the helicopters made a flank attack if possible, coming in along the road to avoid red-on-red incidents. (A Western author would have said 'blue-on-blue', but it's *them* who are the 'blues'; *we* are the 'reds'. In NATO exercises, Blue Force is the 'good guys' and Red Force is the 'bad guys'; in Soviet (Russian) exercises, it's vice versa.) *Ad hoc* helipads were constructed along the roads for refuelling and 'changing of the guard', as providing constant escort to convoys crawling along at 15-20 km/h (9-12 mph) would otherwise have been impossible.

Sometimes Mi-8s acted as fire director helicopters with a spotter on board, accompanying Mi-24 strike groups. The spotter was usually a local from the Afghan secret service who helped tell friend from foe in the vegetation below and identify the right house in a village – ie, the one in which the enemy had holed up. (Speaking of locals, intelligence came from prisoners, friendly villagers, 'undercover agents' in Mujahideen gangs or paid informers. The latter source was the least reliable; all too often, having sold information on enemy positions, the informer immediately went to the Mujahideen to warn of an impending air raid and get paid by them as well!)

The Mi-8 also proved invaluable for the 40th Army's recovery and repair service, bringing recovery teams to spots where damaged helicopters had force-landed. After that, repairable helicopters were patched up on the spot if possible and flown out of 'Indian country'. If the damage was too serious to repair in situ, non-flyable helicopters were extracted by *Hip-Hs* after being stripped down as much as possible.

Early operational experience showed that the armament of the Mi-8T (or 'Mi-8TV Mk I') was inadequate for Afghanistan. Not waiting for the OKB to remedy this, the helicopter crews tried various field modifications. For instance, the regiment at Kandahar tried fitting the GSh-23L twin-barrel 23-mm cannon – the version used on fighters – to the Mi-8. Squadron commander V. Sidorov even went so far as to suggest installing a 73-mm (2.87-in) 2A28 Grom (Thunder) semi-automatic cannon borrowed from the BMP-1 infantry fighting vehicle (*boye**va**ya ma**shin**a pe**khot**y* – IFV) under the belly of a Mi-8 and volunteered to test this installation. Fortunately the unit's maintenance department had the sense not to try this installation – the helicopter's fuselage structure clearly would not have withstood the recoil. (Incidentally, on the Mi-24P armed with a GSh-30 twin-barrel 30-mm (1.18 calibre) cannon, fatigue cracks caused by the recoil were a serious problem until reinforcing plates and stiffening ribs were fitted.)

In April 1980 General Designer Marat N. Tishchenko, who had become head of the Mil' OKB after the founder's death, visited several Mi-8 units in Afghanistan in company with a group of test pilots. His gaining firsthand acquaintance with the service pilots and the conditions they operated in created a lasting impression, and the positive effect came very soon in the form of new versions and upgrade packages. Thus as early as June 1980 the

Vertical envelopment in action: soldiers jump from a Mi-8MT hovering a few feet above the ground and are ready to engage the enemy immediately.

Mi-8TV got additional armour and armament installed in situ by the manufacturer's technical teams. The upgrade package was built around the Kalashnikov PKT machine-gun – the version designed for armoured vehicles (*poole**myot** Kalashnikova **tahn**kovyy*) – with an electric trigger mechanism (there was a mechanical trigger, too, but electric actuation was far more convenient). While having the same 7.62-mm (.30) calibre as the RPK hand-held version (*rooch**noy** poole**myot** Ka**lash**nikova*), the PKT had the advantage of utilising a different round with a more powerful charge; it was an excellent weapon combining a high rate of fire with a long lethal range and high accuracy (the latter earned it a reputation as a 'sniper's weapon'). It is a noteworthy fact that the Mil' OKB had preferred a tank weapon over purpose-built aircraft weapons, such as the 7.62-mm GShG-7,62 four-barrel Gatling machine-gun (aka TKB-621 or 9A622). The reason was that the latter was too complex and demanding to operational conditions for use on a combat helicopter, considering that the helicopters flew 'lower, slower and over shorter distances than anyone else', as their crews put it (paraphrasing a 1930s slogan, 'fly higher, faster and farther than everyone else'); in these conditions the Gatling guns were prone to overheating and jamming because of the pervasive dust.

In addition to the flexible PKT with a dust protection cover in the nose (fired by the flight engineer), the Afghan upgrade included two more PKTs with ammunition boxes on top of the external stores outriggers and one more flexible PKT installed on a removable mounting frame near the escape hatch in the starboard clamshell cargo door. The latter was the answer to the increasingly frequent attempts to attack the helicopter's unprotected rear hemisphere, especially when the helicopter was completing a firing pass and the pilots could not see what was going on behind them. To remedy the latter situation, car-type rear view mirrors were installed on the flightdeck glazing frame. The tail gun position was manned either by the flight engineer or by an extra crew member acting as the tail gunner.

Interestingly, the nose machine-gun installation affected the aircraft's compass which would go crazy every time the gun was moved, the needle pointing in the same direction as the barrel. The problem was cured by moving the sensitive instrument away from the massive weapon.

Additionally, the upgraded Mi-8TVs could be armed with a 30-mm (1.18 calibre) AGS-17 Plamya automatic grenade launcher. Its undoubted virtues included a high-power round which, despite having the same calibre, packed 50% (!) more explosive than the round of the 2A42 automatic cannon fitted to the BMP-2 IFV. Unsurprisingly, the AGS-17's simplicity and ease of operation also appealed to the armourers, who did not bother to develop a special aircraft version of the weapon and simply installed a stock infantry version complete with the bulky tripod in the helicopter's entry doorway. The only modifications were the addition of wooden clods for the tripod's legs and braces which secured the weapon to the cabin floor, absorbing the AGS-17's powerful recoil. The grenade launcher was fed from a drum-type magazine holding 29 rounds; the latter were either VOG-17A rounds equipped with a 280-gram (9.88-oz) fragmentation grenade or VOG-17M rounds equipped with a 'bouncing' grenade which rebounded on impact and then exploded, raining splinters down on personnel taking cover in trenches and the like.

The grenade launcher found fairly wide use on the Mi-8 in 1980-81. For instance, in the 181st OVP's *Hip* squadron (it should be noted here that OVPs within the 40th Army operated a mix of Mi-8s and Mi-6s, as distinct from the OBVPs operating a mix of Mi-8s and Mi-24s) the daily expenditure of VOG-17 rounds amounted to an impressive 85-300, depending on the intensity of the fighting.

On the minus side, the AGS-17 had a low muzzle velocity – you could actually see the grenade flying after firing it – and a low rate of fire. The rounds, which were equipped with excessively sensitive fuses, were dangerous to handle. Finally, the massive weapon obstructed the doorway, making carriage of troops impossible and complicating crew evacuation in the event of a shootdown. All of this eventually caused the weapon to be 'grounded'. A special helicopter version (AG-17A) designed for installation in the GUV weapons pod did appear eventually, but it did not rate highly for much the same reasons.

The flightdeck armour was augmented by external 5-mm (0.2-in) steel shields attached to the forward fuselage sides by short struts; these were mostly seen on the Mi-8MT/Mi-8MTV. Inside the flightdeck, additional armour panels were attached to the rear bulkhead, the walls (partly obscuring the blister windows from within), the floor and under the instrument panels (ahead of the pilots' feet). The forward shields were originally fixed, rendering the lower row of the flightdeck glazing unusable, which was no good; therefore on later aircraft they were built in several sections, folding away for take-off and landing to maximise visibility – an important point in the dusty conditions of Afghanistan.

In addition to the standard armour weighing 180 kg (400 lb), the pilots often hung bulletproof vests on the flightdeck walls or placed them on the floor under their feet. Bulletproof vests were also used to protect the auxiliary fuel tank in the cabin and provide extra protection for the tail gunner.

For extra survivability some of the helicopters were completed with an inert gas pressurisation system for the fuel tanks reducing the risk of fire and explosion when hit. A carbon dioxide bottle was installed in the cabin, but the CO_2 supply was limited and the flight engineer would open the cock only when there was imminent danger of coming under fire.

Stage B of the 'Afghan upgrade' programme involved installing ASO-2V chaff/flare dispensers, followed by EVU exhaust/air mixers reducing the helicopter's heat signature. These measures were meant to protect the Mi-8 against man-portable air defence systems (MANPADS), such as the General Dynamics FIM-43A Redeye and FIM-92A Stinger, Shorts Blowpipe and, ironically, captured 9K32 Strela-2 (Arrow-2, pronounced *stre**lah***) missiles.

Despite intelligence reports that the Mujahideen had MANPADS, these were not used in the first year of the war, nor were there any amongst the weaponry captured from the enemy. (The numerous reports of 'SAM launches' in 1980-81 were erroneous; actually the rebels had used RPG-7 anti-tank grenade launchers against low-flying helicopters!) This often led the Soviet helicopter units to remove the bulky EVU exhaust/air mixers from Mi-8TVs arriving in Afghanistan. The reason was that the 'first-generation' models were seriously underpowered with respect to the local conditions; thus the 68 kg (150 lb) of the exhaust/air mixers were something the helicopter could do without. It was not until 1983, when the shoulder-launched SAMs became a distinct threat, that the devices became obligatory.

The few 'Afghan improvements' effected by the manufacturers included the design of the sight for the nose-mounted PKT machine-gun. Originally this was a rather crude affair made of thick steel strip; the 'cross-hairs' in fact looked more like 'cross-ropes', obscuring the target and making accurate aim all but impossible. This design later gave way to two concentric rings, which improved accuracy dramatically.

It is a noteworthy fact that the main thrust of the effort to improve the Mi-8's armament was directed at anti-personnel weapons. Machine-guns and grenade launchers had an advantage over FFAR pods: they could be reloaded as long as there was something to reload, permitting prolonged operation with as many firing passes as necessary. In contrast, FFAR pods turned into useless ballast as soon as the rockets were expended. Sometimes, though, when the objective was known to be particularly resistant to damage, the helicopters carried a supply of rockets in the cabin for reloading the pods after landing at a safe spot not far from the target.

The Mi-8's weapons fit made for continuity of fire during an attack, not letting the enemy recollect his wits and fire back. First, a salvo of rockets was unleashed at a safe distance from the target (1,300-1,500 m/4,260-4,920 ft), well out of range of the enemy's air defences, to suppress initial resistance. Then the bombs were dropped on enemy strongholds, the crew spraying the target with machine-gun fire all the while. Considering that sorties were always flown in pairs at the very least (so that if one helicopter went down the other could provide cover for the downed crew), the target was sure to be under fire from at least one helicopter throughout the attack.

Crew workloads were extremely high. The crews made five or six sorties daily, spending 15-18 hours in the air and at the airfield each day; sometimes they relieved each other right in the cockpits to maintain round-the-clock readiness. The flight engineers responsible for the aircraft's condition and the armourers were the worst off. If the overall workload in Afghanistan was doubled as compared to 'Unionside' conditions, the weapons arming workload was 24 (!) times greater. Every available man had to handle bombs, load FFAR pods with rockets, cut open the zinc boxes of machine-gun ammunition and work the 'meat grinder' device which filled ammunition belts with bullets.

This, and the Mi-8's good reliability record, allowed the helicopters to be operated on an 'on condition' basis, with maintenance as required rather than as prescribed by manuals. Time-expired engines were allowed to clock up to 50 hours of 'life after death' before replacement, to say nothing of lesser equipment items which simply worked until they packed up. The same applied to machine-guns; nobody cared any longer how many rounds had been fired as long as the weapon worked. To give credit where credit is due, the PKT turned out to be a highly reliable weapon, working when it was long overdue for overhaul – in spite of the heat and the all-pervading dust. (Incidentally, this dust was a terrible nuisance, clogging filters and eroding engine compressor blades.)

Figures quoted in the Russian popular press give some indication of the intensity of *Hip* operations during the war. On 11th March 1981 a flight of Mi-8s from Faïzabad escorting a supply convoy used up 806 S-5 FFARs, 300 rounds for the AGS-17 grenade launcher and 14,200 rounds of machine-gun ammunition (ie, more than 50 complete ammunition belts!). The flight leader's aircraft came back with just eight bullet holes – an indication that the Mujahideen were taking such a pounding that they were all but unable to return fire.

On 26th May 1981 a group of four Mi-8Ts and Mi-8MTs obliterated a camp used by a Mujahideen gang for rest and recreation. Dropping four 500-kg bombs and firing 255 S-5KO rockets, the helicopters destroyed the house occupied by the bandits and the adjoining buildings, then hosed down the area with 58 VOG-17 grenades and a hail of machine-gun fire. Thus, instead of R & R (rest and relaxation) the guerrillas got some D & D (death and destruction).

However, war is war, and often the helicopter crews found themselves on the receiving end. Recognising the threat posed by enemy aviation, the rebels strengthened their anti-aircraft defences dramatically during the third year of the war. As already mentioned, anti-tank grenade launchers were used – and not unsuccessfully – against low-flying helicopters; if it scored a direct hit, the shaped-charge rocket-propelled grenade could inflict serious damage. Increasingly more often the Mujahideen used 12.7-mm (.50 calibre) DShK HMGs and the even more lethal 14.5-mm (.57 calibre) Vladimirov KPV HMGs (*kroopnokalibernyy poolemyot Vladimirova*). The latter model (which is the main weapon of the Soviet BTR-60PB and BTR-70 armoured personnel carriers) could score a hit against an aerial target at up to 1,300-1,500 m (4,260-4,920 ft) and 1.5-2 km (0.9-1¼ miles) range. (In Afghan contingent slang the HNGs were known as ***svar**ka*, 'welding', because the muzzle flashes looked rather similar to the flashes of arc welding.)

On 31st July 1980 a 250th OVP Mi-8 flown by Capt. M. Groshev was shot up by DShK fire at point-blank range while coming in to disgorge troops south of Ghazni. The fuel tanks and engines were riddled with bullets, and a spark ignited the leaking fuel. The crew barely managed to land the fiercely burning helicopter which exploded as soon as they had jumped clear.

In a duel with enemy air defences the Mi-8TV's externally mounted PKT machine-guns did not perform too well, as the draggy ammunition boxes reduced speed and agility. Aiming them accurately was something of a problem due to their offset position; also, they were cocked by Bowden cables routed to the cabin but could not be revived in flight if they jammed. Hence the externally mounted machine-guns had vanished almost entirely by 1984.

The nose and tail machine-guns, on the other hand, proved their worth, though they had a few drawbacks too. When the nose gun was fired, powder gases filled the flightdeck which had to be aired. The rear gun required the escape hatch to be opened – and on the Mi-8T the cover was simply jettisoned; to prevent unwarranted losses of these covers they were often removed beforehand. On the Mi-8MT the cover opened inwards, but replacing it in flight was impossible all the same; as a result, on landing the helicopter turned into an almighty vacuum cleaner, sucking in dust and debris through the hatch! (To remedy this, various makeshift covers were fabricated, while some Mi-8MTs were field-modified to feature a hinged cover, opened and closed as required.)

The Mi-8's single entry door was another liability. The rear clamshell doors were not normally used for personnel disembarkation because opening them manually took several minutes; this was unacceptable because the incoming helicopters often came under fire and every second was precious. To solve the problem the clamshell doors were sometimes removed and substituted by a safety net. It was not until 1995 that a second entry door was introduced o the Mi-17MD, and it took another two years to incorporate a rapid-action rear loading ramp.

Not all Mi-8 losses in Afghanistan were caused by enemy action. For example, on 20th June 1985 a Mi-8MT crash-landed 62 km (38.5 miles) north-east of Bagram due to pilot error; the crew and troops managed to vacate the aircraft before it was consumed by flames. Another *Hip-H* was damaged beyond repair in similar circumstances on 17th July 1985, landing hard in a tailwind on a helipad 73 km (45.3 miles) north-east of Bagram. On 29th November 1985 one more Mi-8MT was damaged due to brownout (crew disorientation due to dust raised by the rotor downwash) while landing 15 km (9.3 miles) north-west of Kabul.

The advent of MANPADS on the Afghan theatre of operations forced the helicopters up to higher altitudes where the on-board machine-guns were useless. To top it all, the Mujahideen now had early warning posts equipped with mobile radios and mobile anti-aircraft guns installed on jeeps which could pop up unexpectedly almost anywhere. Most often the Mi-8s were damaged by ground fire in the vicinity of landing zones; the flightdeck glazing accounted for 42% of the hits, as the rebels tried to kill the pilots if possible.

The final argument which caused the external machine-guns and the grenade launcher to be removed from the 'first-generation' helicopters was the modifications aimed at improving survivability. These added about 500 kg (1,100 lb) to the Mi-8TV's empty weight, causing the helicopter to become too sluggish; in fact, the helicopter had trouble taking off in hot-and-high conditions. On the other hand, the Mi-8MT with its much more powerful engines and higher performance suffered few changes to the armament, and the reasonable sufficiency principle prevailed.

Starting in the spring of 1980, the Mi-8 was actively used for mining the mountain paths leading into neighbouring Pakistan, used by

First Chechen War casualty. This Mi-8T operated by the Chechen rebels was knocked out at Groznyy-Khankala on 2nd April 1995 by a missile launched by a Russian Air Force Su-25.

the rebels to replenish their supplies. To this end the *Hip* was fitted with the VSM-1 aerial mine-laying system (*vozdooshnaya sistema mineerovaniya*) comprising four pods, each of which featured 29 KSF-1 cassettes with 72 anti-personnel mines apiece. POM-1 fragmentation mines were little used, since they were too conspicuous on the rocks. The PFM-1 high-explosive action mine was much better suited to these conditions; despite a weight of only 80 grams (2.8 oz), its charge of liquid explosive was powerful enough to cripple whoever stepped on it. Within just one minute the Mi-8 could disperse an amazing 8,352 mines, covering an area 2 km (1¼ miles) long and 15-25 m (50-80 ft) wide.

Even though the 40th Army had considerable numbers of heavily armed and armoured Mi-24s, the top brass often preferred to use *Hips*, believing the *Hinds* to be overweight and not agile enough for Afghanistan where the helicopters sometimes had to fly literally down narrow creeks. On the other hand, the Mi-24s often provided cover for the Mi-8s. Even liaison and CSAR aircraft needed helicopter escort, as demonstrated by a tragic incident on 4th March 1987. Two CSAR Mi-8s took off to pick up the crew of a two-seat Sukhoi Su-17UM-3 fighter-bomber which had ejected less than two miles from Bagram. Unfortunately the escorting Mi-24s were delayed; when they belatedly arrived on the scene, both pilots of the jet had been murdered and both *Hips* shot down.

Although Pakistan was not formally involved in the war, it sympathised with the Mujahideen; hence Pakistani Air Force fighters frequently entered Afghan airspace to attack Soviet military aircraft. For self-defence in these situations some Mi-8s were reportedly armed with R-60 short-range air-to-air missiles.

Summing up this section, it would be right to say that Soviet operations in Afghanistan would have been far less successful (remember, we are not touching on the political aspects of the war here) and the death toll would have been much higher if it were not for the trusty Mi-8.

War on home ground

Sadly enough, the Mi-8 has also seen quite a lot of action in its home country – to be precise, mostly in the Commonwealth of Independent States (CIS). Shortly before the breakup of the Soviet Union a spate of bloody ethnic conflicts erupted in the Southern republics. The first of these was over the Nagornyy Karabakh enclave, the subject of a long-standing territorial dispute between Armenia and Azerbaijan.

The seeds of the conflict were planted way back in the early days of the Soviet Union. When the boundaries of the constituent republics were delimited, the Nagornyy Karabakh Autonomous Region populated chiefly by ethnic Armenians became part of the newly-established Azerbaijan Soviet Socialist Republic. While the Armenians and the Azeris had a long history of strife, they had to put up with this, as any dissent would be resolutely squashed. However, when Mikhail S. Gorbachov's *perestroika* loosened the reins, Armenia became increasingly active in its attempts to recapture the lost enclave or turn it into a sovereign state while Azerbaijan, understandably enough, strove to retain its integrity. What started as peaceful demonstrations on both sides quickly escalated into open warfare. As the Soviet Army was put into action to disengage the belligerents, both sides gained access to more weapons, including aircraft.

It is known that Azerbaijan used its Mi-8s in the conflict. On 3rd March 1992 a Russian Army Aviation Mi-26 heavy transport helicopter escorted by Mi-24s delivered 20 tons (44,090 lb) of flour to the Armenian village of Gyulistan, picking up refugees for the return trip. En route the escorting Hinds were forced to drive off an unmarked Azeri Mi-8 which attempted an attack on the transport. Tragically, the Russians' attempts to protect their charge failed – the Mi-26 was shot down by a shoulder-launched SAM near the Azeri village of Seidilyar, 12 of the 50 occupants perishing in the ensuing crash landing.

Another constant source of ethnic strife was in Georgia where two republics, Abkhazia and South Ossetia, tried to gain independence – something which the government in Tbilisi would not tolerate. The Mi-8 was involved in the Georgian-Abkhazi war as well. For instance, in October 1992 an unmarked (probably Abkhazi) Mi-24 unsuccessfully attacked a Mi-8 carrying future Georgian President Eduard A. Shevardnadze to the conflict zone and was driven off by the escorting Russian Mi-24s.

The Chechen Wars

In 1994 the Mi-8 was involved in the first major conflict on the territory of the Russian Federation. The southern constituent republic of Chechnya (Chechenia) – formerly part of the Chechen-Ingush Autonomous SSR – had declared sovereignty after the break-up of the USSR. What with the illegal armed units and separatist tendencies of Gen. Djokhar Dudayev, the self-proclaimed 'Chechen Republic of Ichkeria' was rapidly turning into a rogue state. Deciding it had had enough, Moscow issued an ultimatum demanding compliance with federal laws, which Groznyy ignored. Hence on 11th December 1994 the Russian Federal Armed Forces began an all-arms offensive in Chechnya. It soon turned into a full-scale war which went on for 18 months until a peace accord was signed in Khasavyurt, Ingushetia, on 30th August 1996.

The Mi-8 was actively used throughout the First Chechen war in the transport/replenishment, counter-insurgency (COIN), armed reconnaissance, convoy escort and CASEVAC roles. Two squadrons of assorted *Hips* – Mi-8T and 'MT transport helicopters, Mi-8TV and 'MTV-2 transport/assault helicopters and Mi-9 ABCPs – were in action during the first Chechen campaign, operating from Groznyy-Severnyy airport, Groznyy-Khankala (a former sports airfield) and Mozdok, Ingushetia.

The situation in and around Chechnya was anything but peaceful in 1996-99. Gradually the Russian government grew tired of the constant harassment raids from Chechen territory and the hostage-taking which had turned into a flourishing business in the republic. In August 1999 gangs of Chechen guerrillas captured and briefly held three villages in the Novolaksky, Botlikh and Tsumadi Regions of neighbouring Daghestan. The incursion had been carefully planned and prepared with the objective of instigating mutiny in the republic and turning it into a 'second Chechnya'.

This was the last straw. Determined to put an end to the gangs responsible for this, the government launched what was officially called an anti-terrorist operation – originally on a small scale. However, when Chechen terrorists blew up apartment buildings in Moscow, Volgodonsk and Buinaksk in early September, killing hundreds of civilians, the operation was transferred into Chechen territory and escalated into a full-blown military campaign – the Second Chechen War.

This campaign was different from the First Chechen War. Firstly, the Russian forces were armed with lessons learned during the previous war. Secondly, the First Chechen War was regarded by many as pointless ('we shouldn't have intervened, we should have let those Chechens slug it out between themselves'). The second war was no longer a 'fight for the independence of the Chechen Republic of Ichkeria' but a war of international terrorism against Russia. Besides local warlords like Shamil' Basayev, the guerrillas were led by the Jordanian terrorist Imam Hattab (liquidated by the Russian troops in 2003) and backed by the even more infamous Osama ben Laden, and many were Arab mercenaries. Thus the Russian troops were well aware of what they were fighting for and who they were up against. The general opinion was that 'terrorism cannot be stopped by half-measures and it is necessary to go all the way'.

As of 23rd September 1999 the Russian Army Aviation task force employed in Chechnya as part of the Joint Task Force in the North Caucasus, or OGV (*Obyedi**nyon**naya grooppi**rov**ka voysk na **Sev**ernom Kav**kah**ze*), comprised 68 helicopters – 32 Mi-24s, 26 Mi-8s, eight Mi-26s and two Mi-9 ABCPs. Most of the aircraft and crews came from three North Caucasian Defence District helicopter regiments, with the exception of the Mi-26s (which were normally based elsewhere) and the C3 flight operating the Mi-9s.

As compared to the First Chechen War, Army Aviation utilisation (and its importance) was much higher. In the first three months of the war alone (the autumn of 1999) the Mi-8s, Mi-24s and Mi-26s seconded to the OGV flew more than 9,000 sorties between them, logging nearly 5,000 hours in the skies of Daghestan and Chechnya. In so doing they carried nearly 26,000 tons (57,320 lb) of military materiel and civil cargoes, saving the lives of hundreds of refugees and wounded Russian servicemen.

The Mi-8 had to shoulder the greatest proportion of the Russian Army Aviation task force's in workload during the Second Chechen War. They were in action round the clock, in good or (as was more often the case) bad weather. The *Hips* inserted and extracted commando and recce groups, delivered ammunition and supplies to the battle area. It is also part of their job to pick up what is euphemistically known as 'Cargo 300' (wounded men) and 'Cargo 200' (dead bodies) from the forward area. (The latter name, a coded radio message dating back to the Afghan War or even earlier, is derived from the fact that a body in a government-issue zinc coffin weighs some 200 kg/440 lb.)

As often as not, the Mi-8s had to land on impossible 'hellipads' in the mountains – frequently under concentrated and well-aimed enemy fire. Though it isn't easy to down a helicopter with small-arms fire, many helicopters came back with bullet holes in the fuselage, rotor blades and engine casings. This is where the Mi-8's rugged design really came into its own; the units' tech staff quickly returned such aircraft to fully operational condition, having completed some 150 field repairs by mid-November 1999. This doesn't mean 150 helicopters, of course; some aircraft were veritable 'flak bait', sustaining battle damage eight times a month!

Combat efficiency also improved a lot as compared to the First Chechen War; together with the fixed-wing aircraft and the Russian Army's artillery units the rotary-wing force fulfilled 70-90% of the attack objectives. In so doing the helicopters usually accounted for nearly 50% of the ordnance delivered. Combat tactics and forms of interaction with the ground forces had also changed. As a rule, the helicopters operated as part of a Tactical Air Group (TAG) supporting a ground forces unit – usually a mechanised infantry regiment. Normally the group consisted of two to four Mi-24s and one or two Mi-8s.

During operations a forward air controller was always present at the command post of the regiment to which the TAG was seconded. However, the helicopter pilots kept complaining about the forward air controllers' generally inadequate skills. This was offset to a certain degree by the presence of transport helicopters in the TAG; observing the action from some way off, the Mi-8 crews were able to give more accurate target co-ordinates to the crews of the Mi-24s pounding away at the forward edge of the battle area (FEBA). The transport helicopters also filled the CSAR role, minimising personnel losses in the event of crashes, forced landings, shootdowns etc. Conversely, pairs and flights of Mi-24s supported Mi-8s inserting and extracting tactical airborne assault/reconnaissance groups and provide escort for transport helicopters performing resupply operations to mountainous regions of Chechnya.

Obsolescent avionics were a real problem. Only five OGV Mi-8MTVs which were previously seconded to the UNPF contingent in Angola were equipped with GPS. The crews of the other helicopters had to navigate using the terrain and familiar landmarks, with little to rely on but the basic flight instruments and the Mk 1 eyeball (night-capable helicopters equipped with an optoelectronic system were extremely few and operated in Chechnya on a trials basis only). On the other hand, each of the helicopter pilots accumulated as many hours within those three months as he usually flew in a year.

The accelerated accumulation of flight hours by the helicopters and the unavailability of spares compelled the Russian Army to regroup the rotary-wing force, replacing the old Mi-8Ts of the North Caucasian DD with Mi-8MTs/Mi-8MTVs transferred from other defence districts deep in Russian territory. These were low-time aircraft with an average 400-600 hours' total time since new but with the prescribed service life term in years due to expire in one year. In other cases, service lives had to be extended.

Since main and tail rotor blades were on the most frequently damaged items list, accounting for up to 25% of the battle damage, and the service units lacked the tools and materials to repair them, repair crews were sent to Mozdok (where a repair shop had been set up) from the manufacturing plants. While Mi-26 blades could be quickly delivered from nearby Rostov-on-Don, Mi-8 blades had to be delivered all the way from

A Mi-8MTV-2 operated by the Russian Ministry of Interior troops is started up by means of an APA-5DM ground power unit.

Table 2.

Mi-8 battle damage statistics in the Second Chechen War

Centre fuselage	63 cases
Cockpit section	5 cases
Tailboom	24 cases
Rotors	33 cases
Engines	2 cases
APU	none
Pipelines	3 cases
Fuel tanks	3 cases
Control runs	2 cases
Landing gear	2 cases
Tail rotor drive shaft	1 case

Table 3.

Time required to repair battle damage to Mi-8s in the Second Chechen War (1999-2000)

Sorties flown per case of battle damage	212
Damaged aircraft	22
No of damaged aircraft repairable within:	
24 hours	8
48 hours	2
36 hours	2
more than 36 hours	10

Engels, increasing downtimes for the affected helicopters. Another result was that non-flyable examples (mainly hopelessly damaged ones) were cannibalised for spares to keep the others flying. The shop in Mozdok repaired airframes and main rotor blade pockets, restored electric wiring bundles and so on.

In the course of the anti-terrorist operation the serviceability of the helicopter fleet varied from 75% to 100%. Up to eight helicopters were damaged during each vertical envelopment, reconnaissance or SAR operation, up to four of the damaged aircraft making forced landings every day. The damage was mostly inflicted by small arms fire of 5.45 mm (0.21) calibre from Kalashnikov AK-74 assault rifles and 7.62 mm from Kalashnikov RPK machine-guns, with anywhere between 1 and 56 hits per aircraft.

Battle damage statistics show that the centre fuselage took most of the hits (38%), followed by the rotor blades (25%) and the tailboom/tail rotor pylon (15%). The engines and main gearbox exhibited high resistance to battle damage. Conversely, the main gearbox oil system and the hydraulics proved too vulnerable; three Mi-8s were lost due to hydraulic lines being shot away by 5.45-mm bullets.

Non-combat losses were caused by the crews being unaccustomed to flying nap-of-the-earth (NOE – ie, ultra-low-level terrain-following flight) and in poor visibility conditions, or psychologically unprepared for the mission. Sometimes the pilots would be too optimistic about the weather or the aircraft's capabilities, or misjudge the take-off weight, with overloading as a result. Yet, it should be kept in mind that the pilots were under extreme physical and mental strain, being unaccustomed to flying so much and operating in a real war scenario after all those years of peacetime duty – especially a war on home ground. Just to give you an idea, during tactical commando group insertion some Mi-8 crews made up to 39 landings a day on unprepared landing areas located above 2,000 m (6,560 ft)!

Generally the Mi-8's operational reliability in a combat scenario met the Air Force's requirements, with a 58-hour mean time between failures (or damage). Weapons reliability was very high; a mere nine abnormal FFAR launches involving Mi-8s and Mi-24s were recorded during the Second Chechen War, five of them being caused by rocket motor failures and the others by self-destruction.

Tables 2 and 3 above illustrates Mi-8 battle damage statistics in the active phase of the second Chechen campaign.

Unfortunately, as in any war, losses cannot be altogether avoided. Between August 1999 and June 2000 Russian Army Aviation lost 12 Mi-8s (see Table 4 below).

Table 4. Mi-8 total hull losses in the Second Chechen War 1999-2000

Version	Tactical code	Date	Location
Mi-8MT	41	9-8-1990	Near Botlikh, Daghestan
Mi-8MT	49	11-9-1999	Near Novolakskaya settlement, Daghestan
Mi-8MT	24	1-10-1999	Near Tereklimekteb, Daghestan
Mi-8MT	25	5-10-1999	Near Booynaksk, Daghestan
Mi-8MT	47	24-1-2000	Near Vedeno settlement, Chechnya
Mi-8MTV-1	62	18-2-2000	Near Mt. Rogkort, Chechnya
Mi-8MT	48	18-2-2000	Near Shatoy township, Chechnya
Mi-8MTV-1	61	22-2-2000	Near Mt. Rogkort, Chechnya
Mi-8MTV-2	64	2-3-2000	Near Shatoy township, Chechnya
Mi-8MT	41	14-5-2000	Near Dyshne-Vedeno settlement, Chechnya
Mi-8MTV-2	57	29-5-2000	Near Botlikh, Daghestan
Mi-8MTV-1	83	12-6-2000	Khankala AB, Chechnya

Mi-8 utilisation in the active phase of the Second Chechen War 1999-2000 averaged 160 hours per aircraft, the highest figure being 360 hours. The average number of sorties during this period is 210, the 'record holder' having flown 420 sorties.

Many Russian Air Force Mi-8 pilots earned government awards for their bravery in the Second Chechen War; several of them earned the Hero of the Soviet Union or Hero of Russia titles. Unfortunately some of them received this high title posthumously, including Col. Nikolay Maydanov (HSU), the commander of a North Caucasian DD helicopter regiment. He participated in CSAR operations, saving many downed attack aircraft pilots until he, too, was shot down and killed.

On 15th October 1999 Maj. V. Alimov flew a mission to rescue a group of Russian Ministry of Interior commandos which had been encircled by the Chechen guerrillas near Sernovodsk. Escorted by a pair of Mi-24s, Alimov's Mi-8 arrived on the scene with detail of soldiers to provide cover. The group engaged the bandits immediately. A fierce exchange of fire went on for several minutes as Alimov landed to evacuate the surrounded commandos. He had to take command of both the evacuation proper and direct the actions of the supporting Mi-24s. Even though his aircraft was riddled with bullet holes, Alimov did not leave the scene until he was satisfied that all 'friendlies' were safely on board.

Shortly afterwards, on 7th November, Alimov was tasked with evacuating seriously wounded personnel from Bamut, Chechnya. The weather was poor, and two other crews which had tried to perform the mission earlier that day had failed. Undeterred by this, Alimov took off and headed for Bamut. He was lucky; a gap in the clouds opened just as he approached the town, enabling him to land 1.5 km (0.93 miles) from Bamut where a firefight between the federal troops and the guerrillas was in progress.

No sooner had the chopper landed than it was surrounded by thick fog, and heavy snow started falling. The group of commandos which had arrived with Alimov secured the perimeter of the landing zone, waiting until the wounded men could be brought up. They waited for eight hours; the evacuees – 22 servicemen, 14 of whom were indeed in critical condition – finally arrived and boarded close to midnight. On the way back it turned out that the chopper's home base had shut down due to bad weather and Alimov received instructions to head for Beslan airport at Vladikavkaz, Ingushetia. As if that weren't enough, the helicopter's autopilot failed and heavy icing set in, so that the de-icing system could no longer cope. Still, against all odds the crew managed to reach Vladikavkaz safely and land; the wounded soldiers were rushed off to hospital and their lives were saved. For this heroic deed Maj. V. Alimov received his third Distinguished Service Order in December 1999; on 23rd February 2000 (Homeland Defenders Day) he was awarded the Hero of Russia title.

Other wars

Apart from the wars described above, the Mi-8 and Mi-17 has seen action in numerous other armed conflicts all over the world. For reasons of space we cannot describe them all in detail, but mention has to be made of them.

The **Vietnam War** was probably the first conflict in which the Mi-8 participated. While few details are known, it may be mentioned that, together with Mi-6 helicopters, Antonov An-24 airliners and Il'yushin IL-14 transports, North Vietnamese Air Force *Hips* took part in the major airlift operation between Hanoi and South Vietnam during the North Vietnamese Army's Great Spring Offensive of 1975.

The **Iran-Iraq war** of 1980-1988 became a major chapter in the Mi-8's career. Iraqi Air Force Mi-8TVKs were used for a variety of tasks, including vertical envelopment, destruction of soft-skinned vehicles, personnel, artillery, emplacements and bridges, providing CAS for armoured groups and commandos, aerial mine-laying, reconnaissance and artillery spotting.

In the course of the war there were 118 aircraft/helicopter engagements and 56 helicopter/helicopter engagements, including a few between Iraqi *Hips* and Islamic Iranian Air Force (IIAF) helicopters. The outcome of such engagements depended mainly on the situation and crew skill. By the end of the war Iraqi pilots flying Mi-8TVKs, Mi-24As/Mi-25s and Aérospatiale SA 342L Gazelles had destroyed 53 Iranian helicopters.

The operational career of Iraqi Mi-8s is not limited to this war. IrAF Mi-8TVK and Mi-17-1V troopship helicopters also participated in the **Iraqi invasion of Kuwait** in early August 1990. In so doing 15 Iraqi helicopters, including a few *Hips*, were lost to Kuwaiti air defences during the invasion.

In addition to the Indo-Pakistani war of 1971, Indian *Hips* gained fame during the **Indian Peacekeeping Force operation in Sri Lanka** in 1987-1989, an attempt to put an end to the prolonged civil war in that country. The first operation in that mission was the defence of Jaffna against the rebel Liberation Tigers of Tamil Eelam (LTTE) in October 1987. Escorted by IAF Mi-25s, the Mi-8T and Mi-17 transport/troopship helicopters of the 109th, 119th and 129th Sqns airlifted troops and materiel during Operations *Trishul* (Trident) and *Viraat*.

In late May 1999 **India and Pakistan clashed again** in a renewed conflict around the state of Jammu and Kashmir (called Operation *Vijay*, Victory, by the Indians in an allusion to their victory in the previous war). The Indian Air Force's proven Mi-17 workhorses (the Mi-8Ts were ill-suited for operation in that mountainous area) were used on a large scale, airlifting troops to the border where battles raged between Indian and Pakistani ground troops. This involved operating into airfield located more than 5,000 m (16,400 ft) above sea level adjoining the Siachen Glacier. The *Hips* also attacked Pakistani targets across the border with unguided rockets; the Pakistanis retaliated by shooting down one of the helicopters with a Stinger missile.

Summing up the 49-day Operation *Vijay*, Air Marshal Patnay stated that the IAF helicopters had shouldered the main part of the operation, making 2,185 sorties with a total time of 925 hours.

In **Nicaragua**, Fuerza Aérea Sandinista Mi-17s were in action against the *Contras* guerrillas, operating from Augusto César Sandino Airport (Managua), Punta Huete, Montelimar, Puerto Cabezas, Esteli, La Rosita, Bluefields and El Bluff.

In **Sierra Leone**, where a **civil war** had been going on since 1991, the ill-trained government forces were steadily losing ground to the Revolutionary United Front (RUF) – a bunch of thugs led by Cpl Alfred Foday Sankoh. The tiny Sierra Leone Air Force consisting of a single Mi-17-1V (Mi-8MTV-2) gunship and a single Mi-24V (both flown by Belorussian contract crews) was used against the RUF on armed reconnaissance missions and, while greatly intimidating the rebels, had difficulty finding and attacking them in the dense jungle.

Things got better only when the ruling military junta, the National Provisional Ruling Council (NPRC), hired Executive Outcomes (EO), a proactive security (read: mercenary) organisation based in Pretoria, to conduct operations against the RUF and provide tactical planning and personnel training. This was in 1995 when the rebels were getting dangerously close to the capital, Freetown. In addition to the Sierra Leonean *Hip-H*, EO used its own Mi-17s nominally operated by Ibis Air (9L-LBD/1 Black, ex-G-BVXN, c/n 520M15 and 9L-LBE/2 Black, ex-G-BVXO, c/n 520M16) which inserted and extracted search-and-destroy and mortar teams and carried supplies. The aircraft operated by EO were based at Freetown-Lungi airport, but *ad hoc* helipads were also established near Koidu.

Executive Outcomes also had a hand in the prolonged **civil war in Angola**, in which the Mi-8 had been involved from an early stage. Originally flown by Soviet and Cuban crews, the Angolan *Hips* saw action against the UNITA (*União Nacional por Independencia Total de Angola*) led by Dr. Jonas Savimbi and supported by South African Defence Force (SADF). EO was called upon when the Russian and Cuban instructors left and combat readiness levels in the Angolan AIr Force became rock-bottom.

Coming back to **Sri Lanka**, starting on 15th Mach 1993 the Sri Lankan Air Force took delivery of 12 Mi-17s. Serving with the newly formed 6th Helicopter Sqn, they were immediately put into action against the LTTE rebels in the north of the island, airlifting troops into the war zone – specifically, to the bases at Elephant Pass, Mannar, Mullaittivu and Poonerin. Previously the government troops some- times had to make the perilous journey by road, as the SLAF's Bell 212s could not provide an adequate tactical airlift capability.

The Mi-17s were normally based at Katunayake AB near Colombo, although two helicopters were stationed at Vavuniya AB in the north. Interestingly, no more than three of the helicopters were operational at any one time, the rest sitting in storage.

The *Hips* were used with considerable success in a major air/land/sea assault called Operation *Riverisa* (Sunshine) and later in *Riverisa* II and *Riverisa* III. Manufacturer's specifications notwithstanding, the helicopters usually operated with a crew of four and carried up to 30 'passengers'. The helicopters featured some local modifications, including installation of GPS and metal sheeting in the cargo cabin. The latter was meant to preclude corrosion caused by the blood of wounded soldiers – a problem which had affected the SLAF's Harbin Y-12 II Panda light transports which, like the *Hips*, were used for CASEVAC duties.

One of the SLAF's Kazan'-built Mi-17s, CH-587, was lost with all hands when it ditched and sank in the Indian Ocean – presumably after being shot down. After this the surviving examples were retrofitted with a flotation system installed by FPT Industries in Portsmouth, UK. Also, from then on the *Hips* operated with the clamshell cargo doors removed to speed up evacuation. Another Mi-17 was damaged by a SAM over the Kokilai Lagoon on 10th November 1997 but managed a forced landing. One of the escorting Mi-24Vs was less lucky, being destroyed by the same missile.

The **Colombian Army** used its Mi-17s against the infamous Medellín drug cartel in the north. These operations were risky, as the drug mafia put up armed resistance. On one occasion an Ejército de Colombia Mi-17-1V received 22 direct hits by HMG fire but managed to return to base and was repaired, flying several more missions on the same day!

Similarly, **Peruvian Army** Mi-8Ts/Mi-17s saw action against the local drug cartels, the infamous Sendero Luminoso (Shining Path) Maoist terror organisation and the equally radical Tupac Amaru Liberation Movement.

Above: A gaggle of Russian Air Force/16th VA special mission *Hips*, including a Mi-8PPA and a Mi-8SMV, at Kubinka AB. Some of these aircraft had been stationed in East Germany.

Above: Ukrainian Air Force Mi-8MTs, including '123 Black', were used by the United Nations Peace Forces in support of the United Nations Transitional Authority in Eastern Slavonia (UNTAES).

Croatian Mi-8TVKs inherited from the Yugoslav Air Force were used in the civil war in ex-Yugoslavia, operating against the army of 'the current Yugoslavia' (Serbia and Montenegro). However, the *Hip-Cs* could not provide adequate battlefield support for the Croatian Army and several were shot down on CAS missions. Thus they were soon supplanted by Croatia's newly -acquired Mi-24V in this capacity.

In March 2000 **Chad** received a couple of Mi-8MTV from the Ukraine. Flown by Ukrainian mercenary pilots, the helicopters were put into action against rebels in the north. On 3rd October 2002, however, both *Hips* (TT-OAJ and TT-OAK) were destroyed by the rebels who overran Faya Largeau AB.

In March 2001 the Macedonian Air Force put its Mi-8MTVs into action when, at President Boris Traikovsky's orders, the Macedonian Army began Operation *Metla* (Broom), an all-arms offensive against Albanian insurgents (remnants of the officially-disbanded Kosovo Liberation Army, or UÇK – *Ushtara Çilimatare Kosovës*) attacking the borderside town of Tetovo. The operation was successful; on 27th March, Macedonian forces had gained the hills around the town and captured the terrorists' main base, a fortress on Kali Hill, forcing the Albanians back into Kosovo. Soon afterwards, however, the fighting resumed.

Earlier in this book, we compared the Mi-8/Mi-17 with the Kalashnikov assault rifle. Now we hope you can see why.

Another view of '123 Black' sitting under threatening skies at Klisa airport in company with a sister ship coded '124 Black'. Read more about UNPF operations in Chapter 6.

Chapter 6

Peaceful Duties

Aeroflot started taking delivery of the Mi-8 in late 1966. Service tests in the Tyumen' Civil Aviation Directorate (CAD), the Moscow Territorial CAD and the Kremenchug Civil Aviation Flying School began in February 1967, flight training commencing the following month. On 20th August 1967 the Ministry of Civil Aviation (MGA – *Mini**ster**stvo grazh**dahn**skoy avi**ah**tsii*) cleared the Mi-8 for internal and external cargo carriage in normal operation.

It should be noted that Aeroflot's organisation closely resembled an air arm's order of battle – which is hardly surprising, considering that the Soviet civil air fleet constituted an immediately available military reserve (and considering the militarisation of the Soviet economy at large). There was a number of Civil Aviation Directorates (UGA – *Ooprav**len**iye grazh**dahn**skoy avi**ah**tsii*), several of which were in the Russian Federation and one in each of the other Soviet republics. These were broadly equivalent to the air forces of the USAF or the air armies of the Soviet Air Force. Each CAD consisted of several United Air Detachments (OAO – *obyedi**nyon**nyy aviaot**ryad***) based in major cities; these were equivalent to an air group (USAF) or an air division (SovAF). Each UAD had several Flights (LO – ***lyot**nyy ot**ryad***) similar to an air wing (USAF) or an air regiment (SovAF). Finally, a Flight comprised up to four, or maybe more, squadrons (yes, squadrons – *aviaeskad**ril'**ya*!); not infrequently different squadrons of the same Flight operated different aircraft types.

The Azerbaijan CAD – more specifically, the 109th Flight of the Zabrat United Air Detachment based at Baku-Zabrat heliport – was among the first Aeroflot subdivisions to operate the type. Its missions included maintaining communication between the mainland and the famous and unique Neftyanyye Kamni ('Oil Stones') industrial settlement not far from Baku. This was a large group of offshore oil rigs in the Caspian Sea connected with each other and with similar 'islands' accommodating the oil workers' living quarters etc. by elevated driveways. Like the Mi-4Ps used earlier for this purpose, the Mi-8Ps landed on special 'islands' serving as helipads to perform workforce rotation, bring mail and urgent cargoes and, if necessary, take sick persons to hospitals on the shore.

The Mi-8 was actively involved in the development of oil deposits in the oil-rich Tyumen' Region. Here, Mi-8T CCCP-24197 (c/n 98943809) belonging to the Tyumen' CAD/Nefteyugansk UAD passes over a KAvZ-3275 Stalker experimental four-wheel drive bus at Nefteyugansk airport in July 1990.

The very first Mi-8Ps delivered to Aeroflot were 24-seaters featuring six rows of seats. Almost concurrently with the launch of commercial Mi-8 operations in the USSR, however, the Aviaexport All-Union Agency started offering the Mi-8P to foreign customers. Export aircraft had the seating capacity increased to 28 by adding a seventh row of seats, and this layout was standardised. At any rate, on 24th December 1967 the *Izvestiya* daily reported that *'Adler airport has taken delivery of the new 28-seat Mi-8 passenger helicopter. This is a good gift to tourists, skiers and nature lovers. The new machines will be employed on new leisure routes in the Caucasian Mountains.'* One of the aircraft in question must be Mi-8P CCCP-25250 (c/n 0213) manufactured on 30th October 1967 and delivered to the North Caucasian CAD/Sochi Airport/59th Independent Air Squadron. (Sochi and Adler are served by the same airport, just like Köln and Bonn, and the 59th IAS was assigned to the airport, not to a United Air Detachment as was customary.) Incidentally, this particular aircraft served for 20 years, staying in service at least until June 1987!

Speaking of registrations, civil Mi-8s were normally registered in the CCCP-22xxx, -24xxx, -25xxx and -27xxx blocks. A few early-production examples received registrations in the CCCP-11xxx block normally reserved for Antonov An-12 transport aircraft (as were the first civil Mi-6 heavy-lift transport helicopters); they were presumably all reregistered later. Some industry-operated Mi-8s received registrations in the CCCP-061xx, -693xx, -708xx, -709xx, -791xx and -939xx blocks. To confuse things considerably, many registrations were reused in time due to the large production scale as older aircraft were struck off charge. Additionally, some registrations were in fact only radio callsigns allocated to Mi-8s in full military markings when these were operated by the Ministry of the Interior.

Pilots noted that the new helicopter was easy to fly, albeit somewhat more demanding than the Mi-4, especially at the hover. Shortcomings pointed out at the service introduc-

Mi-8P RA-25244 (c/n 3228) was one of several Mi-8s operated by the Central Regions CAD/Myachkovo UAD/305th Flight, a specialised air services unit based at Moscow-Myachkovo.

tion stage were the lack of cargo handling equipment on the Mi-8T and the lack of an auxiliary power unit (the latter did not appear until the advent of the Mi-8MT).

When aircraft factory No.99 in Ulan-Ude also launched Mi-8 production in 1970, delivery rates to both Aeroflot and the Soviet Air Force were stepped up dramatically, speeding up the re-equipment of units flying the Mi-4. (Curiously, most export Mi-8s were Kazan'-built aircraft, the aircraft built in Ulan-Ude being intended chiefly for the home market.) By the mid-1970s the Mi-8 had been taken on strength by virtually all Civil Aviation Directorates, as well as the Training Establishments Directorate (UUZ – *Oopravleniye oochebnykh zavedeniy*) controlling the civil aviation flying and technical schools.

The following table lists known civil aviation units operating the Mi-8 in Soviet times.

Civil Aviation Directorate	United Air Detachment & Constituent Flight	Home base	New name
Arkhangel'sk CAD	2nd Arkhangel'sk UAD	Arkhangel'sk-Vas'kovo	2nd Arkhangel'sk UAD
	Nar'yan-Mar UAD/73rd Flight	Nar'yan-Mar	Nar'yan-Mar Air Enterprise
Armenian CAD	Yerevan UAD/113th Flight	Yerevan-Erebuni	Armenian Airlines
Azerbaijan CAD	Zabrat UAD/109th Flight	Baku-Zabrat	AZAL-Avia Helicopters
Central Regions CAD	Myachkovo UAD/305th Flight	Moscow-Myachkovo	MAUS – Myachkovo Air Services
	Yaroslavl' UAD/319th Flight	Yaroslavl'	Aviatsiya Yaroslavlya
East Siberian CAD	Bodaibo UAD/133rd Flight/2nd Sqn	Bodaibo	Bodaibo Air Enterprise
	Bratsk UAD/245th Flight/4th Sqn	Bratsk	Bratsk Air Enterprise
	2nd Irkutsk UAD/3rd Flight*	Irkutsk-1	Baikal Airlines
	Kirensk UAD/135th Flight	Kirensk	Kirensk Air Enterprise
	Ulan-Ude UAD/183rd Flight	Ulan-Ude/Mookhino	Buryatia Airlines
	Ust'-Kut UAD/364th Flight	Ust'-Kut	Ust'-Kut Avia
Far Eastern CAD	Kamchatka CAPA/Khalaktyrka UAD/2nd Flight*	Petropavlovsk-Kamchatskiy/Khalaktyrka	Khalaktyrka Air Enterprise
	Kamchatka CAPA/Koryak UAD/285th Flight	Manily?	Koryak Avia
	Kamchatka CAPA/2nd Petropavlovsk-Kamchatskiy UAD/149th Flight	Petropavlovsk-Kamchatskiy/Yelizovo?	2nd Petropavlovsk-Kamchatskiy AE
	Sakhalin CAPA/Okha UAD/359th Flight/2nd Sqn	Okha	SAT – Sakhalinskiye Aviatrassy
	Blagoveschchensk UAD/414th Flight/4th Sqn	Blagoveschchensk	Blagoveschchensk Air Enterprise
	2nd Khabarovsk UAD/249th Flight/2nd Sqn	Khabarovsk-MVL	Vostok Airlines
	Nikolayevsk-na-Amure UAD/378th Flight	Nikolayevsk-na-Amure	Nikolayevsk-na-Amure Air Enterprise
Georgian CAD	Kutaisi UAD/230th Flight/1st Sqn	Kutaisi-Osnovnoy (?)	
	Tbilisi UAD	Tbilisi-Lochini	AISI
Kazakh CAD	Alma-Ata UAD	Alma-Ata	
	Burundai UAD/137th Flight	Alma-Ata/Burundai	Burundai-Avia
	Burundai UAD/191st Flight	Alma-Ata/Burundai	Burundai-Avia
	Goor'yev UAD/424th Flight/1st Sqn	Goor'yev	
	Mangyshlak UAD/361st Flight/3rd Sqn	Mangyshlak	
Kirghiz CAD?§	Frunze UAD?§	Frunze	Kyrghyzstan Airlines
Komi CAD	Pechora UAD/338th Flight	Pechora	Komiavia (Pechora AE)/Komiaviatrans
	Ukhta UAD/233rd Flight	Ukhta	Komiavia (Ukhta AE)/Komiaviatrans
	Vorkuta UAD/445th Flight	Vorkuta	Komiavia (Vorkuta AE)/Komiaviatrans
Krasnoyarsk CAD	Igarka UAD/251st Flight	Igarka	Igarka Air Enterprise
	Kezhma UAD/131st Flight	Kezhma	Kezhma Air Enterprise
	Khatanga UAD/221st Flight/1st Sqn	Khatanga	Khatanga Air Enterprise
	Khatanga UAD/221st Flight/Dudinka Independent Air Squadron	Dudinka	Dudinka Air Enterprise
	Noril'sk UAD	Noril'sk-Alykel'	Noril'sk Airlines
	Tura UAD/362nd Flight	Tura-MVL	Tura Air Enterprise
	Tura UAD/Vanavara Independent Air Squadron	Vanavara	Vanavara Air Enterprise
	Turukhansk UAD/399th Flight	Turukhansk	Turukhansk Air Enterprise
	Tuva UAD/132nd Flight	Kyzyl	Tuva Airlines
	Yeniseysk UAD/127th Flight	Yeniseysk	Yeniseyskiy Meridian

Civil Aviation Directorate	United Air Detachment & Constituent Flight	Home base	New name
Leningrad CAD	2nd Leningrad UAD	Leningrad-Rzhevka	Baltic Airlines; Air Len
	Murmansk UAD?§	Murmansk-Murmashi	Murmansk Airlines
	Petrozavodsk UAD/69th Flight	Petrozavodsk-Peski	Petrozavodsk Air Enterprise
Magadan CAD	Anadyr' UAD/150th Flight/1st and 3rd Sqns†	Anadyr'-Oogol'nyy	
	Bilibino UAD/316th Flight	Bilibino	Bilibino Air Enterprise
	Chaunskoye UAD	Chaunskoye	Chaunskoye Air Enterprise
	2nd Magadan UAD/258th Flight‡	Magadan-13th km/56th km	2nd Magadan Air Enterprise
	Seymchan UAD/194th Flight	Seymchan	Seymchan Air Enterprise
North Caucasian CAD	Makhachkala UAD	Makhachkala-Uitash	Daghestan Airlines
	Sochi Airport/59th Independent Air Squadron	Sochi/Adler	Sochispetsavia
	Stavropol' UAD?§	Stavropol'	SAAK
Tajik CAD	Dushanbe UAD	Dushanbe	Tajikistan Airlines (Tajik Air)
Turkmen CAD	Ashkhabad UAD/166th Flight/3rd Sqn	Ashkhabad	Turkmenistan Airlines/Khazar
	Chardzhou UAD/443rd Flight	Chardzhou	Turkmenistan Airlines
Tyumen' CAD	Khanty-Mansiysk UAD/284th Flight	Khanty-Mansiysk	Khantyavia
	Mys Kamennyy UAD	Mys Kamennyy	Tyumen'AviaTrans (UTair)
	Nadym UAD	Nadym	Tyumen'AviaTrans (UTair)
	Nefteyugansk UAD	Nefteyugansk	Nefteyugansk Air Enterprise
	Nizhnevartovsk UAD/331st Flight (and 441st Flight?§)	Nizhnevartovsk	Nizhnevartovsk Air Enterprise
	Novyy Urengoy UAD/413th Flight	Novyy Urengoy-Yaghel'noye	Tyumen'AviaTrans (UTair)
	Salekhard UAD/315th and 388th Flights	Salekhard	Tyumen'AviaTrans (UTair)
	Surgut UAD/121st Flight	Surgut-Pobedit	Tyumen'AviaTrans (UTair)
	Surgut UAD/Noyabr'sk Independent Air Squadron	Noyabr'sk	Noyabr'sk Air Enterprise
	Tarko-Salé UAD	Tarko-Salé	Tarko-Salé Air Enterprise
	Tazovskiy UAD/389th Flight	Tazovskiy	Tazovskiy Air Enterprise
	1st Tyumen' UAD/255th Flight	Tyumen'-Plekhanovo	Tyumen'AviaTrans (UTair)
	Urai UAD/345th Flight	Urai	Urai-Avia
Ukrainian CAD	Zavodskoye UAD/252nd Flight	Simferopol'-Zavodskoye	
Urals CAD	Berezniki Air Enterprise?§	Berezniki	Berezniki Municipal AE
	2nd Perm' UAD/10th Flight*/2nd Sqn	Perm'-Bakharevka	2nd Perm' Air Enterprise
	2nd Sverdlovsk UAD/3rd Flight*/1st and 2nd Sqns	Sverdlovsk-Uktus	2nd Sverdlovsk Air Enterprise
Volga CAD	2nd Kazan' UAD?§	Kazan'	2nd Kazan' Air Enterprise
	2nd Kuibyshev UAD/333rd and 449th Flights	Kuibyshev-Smyshlyayevka	
	Ufa UAD	Ufa	BAL Bashkirian Airlines
West Siberian CAD	Kolpashevo Air Enterprise/257th Flight	Kolpashevo	Kolpashevo Air Enterprise
	Novosibirsk UAD/116th Flight	Novosibirsk-Severnyy	Novosibirsk Airlines
	Strezhevoy UAD/244th Flight	Strezhevoy	Strezhevoy Airlines
Yakutian CAD	Aldan UAD	Aldan	Novosibirsk Airlines
	Batagai UAD	Batagai	Batagai AE (Polar Airlines)
	Kolyma-Indigirka UAD/248th Flight	Cherskiy?	Cherskiy Air Enterprise?
	Kolyma-Indigirka UAD/Chokurdakh Independent Air Squadron	Chokurdakh	Chokurdakh AE (Polar Airlines)
	Magan UAD/288th Flight	Yakutsk-Magan	Sakha Avia
	Magan UAD/Olyokminsk Independent Helicopter Squadron	Olyokminsk	Sakha Avia
	Magan UAD/Sanghar Independent Air Squadron	Sanghar	Sakha Avia
	Mirnyy UAD/402nd Flight	Mirnyy	Almazy Rossii – Sakha (Alrosa)
	Mirnyy UAD/Lensk Independent Air Squadron	Lensk	Almazy Rossii – Sakha (Alrosa)
	Neryungri UAD	Neryungri-Chool'man	Delta-K
	Nyurba UAD/270th Flight	Nyurba	Nyurba Air Enterprise
	Tiksi UAD	Tiksi	Tiksi Air Enterprise
	Ust'-Nera UAD/404th Flight	Ust'-Nera	Ust'-Nera Air Enterprise
	Zhigansk UAD/276th Flight	Zhigansk	Zhigansk Air Enterprise
	Zyryanka UAD	Zyryanka	Zyryanka Air Enterprise
235th Independent Air Detachment		Moscow-Vnukovo	Rossiya State Transport Company
Training Establishments Directorate (UUZ)	Kremenchug Civil Aviation Flying School/3rd and 4th Flights	Kremenchug-Bol'shaya Kokhnovka	
State Civil Aviation Research Institute (GosNII GA)		Moscow/Sheremet'yevo-1	

* The numbers are as per official documents but these are clearly *not* the true numbers; there is duplication and triplication and quadruplication of the Flight numbers from 1 to 10!

† The 2nd Sqn of the 150th Flight operated Antonov An-26 transports.

‡ Number as per official documents; however, in reality this may be the 258th Flight.

§ Unconfirmed (the reference to the Tyumen' CAD/Nizhnevartovsk UAD/**441st** Flight is most probably in error, as this Flight operated Mi-6s!)

Above: Mi-8P CCCP-11094 (presumably operated by the Azerbaijan CAD/Zabrat UAD/109th Flight) installs a dust filter at the Kirovabad Aluminium Foundry, Azerbaijan, in March 1969.

EMERCOM of Russia Mi-8T '018 Orange' in a non-standard colour scheme demonstrates firefighting techniques with a VSU-15 'Bambi Bucket' fitted with an annular spraybar for checking the spread of a fire.

As can be seen from the table, the majority of Aeroflot units operating the type was based east of the Urals Mountains and in the northern regions of the Russian Federation – notably in the Tyumen' Region rich in oil and natural gas deposits and in the Yakutian Autonomous SSR abundant in diamonds and gold. This is no coincidence: the Mi-8 was actively used in support of geological prospecting teams and the oil, natural gas and mining industry, proving indispensible in the development of the remote regions of the Soviet Union. The helicopters hauled bulky and heavy equipment and carried shifts of workers to the gas and oil fields from nearby major airports, carrying them back again when the shift changed. (Due to the harsh Siberian climate people could only work at the gas and oil fields for a few months at a time, whereupon they needed lengthy rest and recreation.) The Mi-8s also kept up communication with the floating oil rigs in the Arctic Ocean, such as M/V *Sevastopol'*.

The rugged and dependable helicopter was the main means of communication between small settlements scattered in the taiga which, to quote a line from a popular Soviet song, 'only an aeroplane can reach' (meaning that there are no roads in those parts!). Actually sometimes only a helicopter could reach the spot, as the terrain around an oil rig lost in the woods or near a river where a gold mining dredge was anchored would daunt even the Antonov An-2 biplane renowned for its ability to operate from minimal airstrips. The Mi-8 also found much use in a similar capacity in the Central Asian republics – for instance, for supporting the Gaz-Achak gas field in Turkmenia. (Incidentally, Mi-8Ts operated in the desert regions of the USSR – for example, CCCP-22290 of the Turkmen CAD/Ashkhabad UFD – were sometimes retrofitted with Mi-8MT-style dust/debris filters to reduce wear and tear on the engines.)

Until the mid-1970s Aeroflot's colour schemes were as disparate as the aircraft it operated; each type had its own livery, and sometimes more than one. Aeroflot's first Mi-8Ps left the Kazan' factory in the same livery as worn by late-production Mi-4Ps; the fuselage was mostly white with a red cheatline, grey undersurfaces and grey trim on the engine/main gearbox 'superstructure'. The early version of the Mil' OKB logo was painted under the flightdeck blister windows. Some Mi-8Ts, however, wore a dark green 'camouflage' scheme, and the registration (which was usually applied in black) was almost illegible against the green background – especially because the tailboom was often black with soot from the engine efflux.

By the early 1970s the airline's management rightly decided to do something about this 'identity crisis'. Hence a common fleet-wide standard livery was developed and endorsed by MAP and MGA in March 1973, featuring a blue cheatline and a grey belly; in the case of the Mi-8 there was also a grey stripe along the tailboom with a gap for the registration. Under the new standard, aircraft operated in the High North and the Far East received a modified colour scheme with a red cheatline, a red/white vertical tail and red outer wings/horizontal tail for high definition against white backgrounds in the event of a forced landing. In the case of helicopters, however, a different approach was chosen; the cheatline was still blue but the white and grey colours on the fuselage were replaced by a brilliant orange and the tailboom trim was blue. (It has to be said, however, that sometimes Aeroflot's northern and eastern CADs took delivery of aircraft in ordinary blue/white colours which really should have the 'Polar livery', while some 'oranges' ended up in the southern CADs where their high-visibility colour scheme was of no use at all.)

Aeroflot's 235th Independent Air Detachment (otdel'nyy aviaotryad) – the Soviet federal government flight – operated Mi-8PS VIP helicopters as 'flying limos' when the head of state had to be whisked away from the airport after arriving from somewhere, or when high-ranking politicians were visiting the province and had a tight schedule. Occasionally these helicopters would land in the middle of Moscow (in Red Square), which many people were unhappy about. A little-known fact is that the 235th IAD also had a few Mi-8Ts, presumably used for carting special communications equipment around – or GAZ-24 Volga sedans, as the cargo cabin was a bit too small for the government garage's GAZ-13/GAZ-14 Chaika and ZiL-117 limousines (to say nothing of the ZiL-114).

It was common practice in the Soviet Union that a single aircraft overhaul plant (ARZ – ***a****viare***mont***nyy* ***z****avod*) would repair all aircraft of a given type, regardless of where they were based. Given the huge numbers of Mi-8s produced, one plant was not enough. Thus, civil Mi-8s were handled by ARZ No.21 at Leningrad-Pulkovo (now called SPARC – St. Petersburg Aircraft Repair Co.), ARZ No.26 at Tyumen'-Plekhanovo, ARZ No.41 in Omsk and ARZ No.73 in Magadan, while TV2-117 engines and VR-8 main gearboxes were overhauled by ARZ No.404 in Sverdlovsk (now the PRAD Company in Yekaterinburg). Military examples were refurbished by the Russian Air Force's ARZ No.419 at Gorelovo AB near St. Petersburg (since 1992), ARZ No.810 in Chita, the plant in Konotop, the Ukraine (now known as Aviakon) and the maintenance facility at Rangsdorf AB, East Germany. Additionally, foreign Mi-8s were refurbished by the Polish Air Force's overhaul

Above: 2nd Kazan' Air Enterprise Mi-8T RA-06175 (c/n 8621) in a grey/green colour scheme demonstrates how rescuees can be hoisted aboard with the LPG-150 hoist.

In post-Soviet times many aircraft belonging to the various new airlines retained Aeroflot colours for a while, such as these orange/blue Myachkovo Air Services Mi-8Ts RA-22641 (c/n 8026) and RA-25954 (c/n 5593). The latter aircraft was once based aboard the research vessel M/V *Mikhail Somov*.

plant No.1 (WZL-1) at Lódz-Lublinek, the overhaul plant at Tököl, Hungary and, more recently, Helisota in Kaunas, Lithuania. The Hungarian plant served not only domestic needs but also refurbished aircraft from the neighbouring Eastern Bloc nations, as well as from the Middle East and Africa.

Mission variety: anyplace, anytime

Flying crane operations were one of the Mi-8T's principal missions both in the USSR and abroad. Initially even Mi-8Ps sometimes performed flying crane operations – presumably because deliveries to Aeroflot were slow at first, as the transport version was acutely needed by the military. For instance, in March 1969 a Mi-8P with the non-standard registration CCCP-11094 flown by F. Belooshkin, I. Grigoryan and D. Bokarev installed 28 vortex-type air filters with an aggregate weight of about 400 tons (881,830 lb) at the aluminium foundry in Kirovabad, Azerbaijan. The job was completed within four days – 2.5 times less than would have been required, using conventional means. Gradually, as production gained tempo and more Mi-8T helicopters became available to Aeroflot, such cases became increasingly rare.

The East German airline Interflug and the Czechoslovak airline Slov-Air tasked with various utility missions modified their Mi-8Ts by fitting a makeshift observation blister to the entry door. Moreover, the Germans devised a special technique to assist accurate positioning of the slung load. A tetrahedral object called HOP (*Hilfsorientierungspunkt* – auxiliary reference point) was installed on a short arm right next to the place where the load was to be set down, and the pilot was to position the helicopter so that he would see an equilateral triangle.

From 1969 onwards the Mi-8 was actively used in setting up high-voltage power lines (and was the first Soviet helicopter to find use in this role). The first such line was the one between Tyumen' and Surgut; the helicopters erected power line pylons in places ground vehicles could not reach and paid out the wires by means of externally slung BRU-1 inertia-less drums (*bezinertsionnoye raskahtochnoye oostroystvo*). The technology was devised by the Krasnodar-based All-Union Research Institute for the Application of Aviation in the National Economy (VNII PANKh – *Vsesoyooznyy naoochno-issledovatel'skiy institoot primeneniya aviahtsii v narodnom khoziaystve*).

Also, starting in 1969, the Mi-8 was used for heli-logging operations. Trials in this capacity were held in December 1969 in the Adler logging company (Krasnodar Region). Once again, 1969 was the year when the type first found use for fighting forest fires. Apart from landing teams of firefighters, the helicopter could carry two tons (4,410 lb) of water in an underslung cylindrical metal container and dump them on the fire. On one occasion it delivered a small bulldozer to assist the firemen!

In the Pamir Mountains of Tajkistan, the Mi-8 was used for monitoring the large Medvezhiy Glacier. Every ten to 15 years, parts of the glacier break away, causing mudslides which can do great damage, so advance warning needed to be given when the situation became dangerous.

Mi-8Ts were used on the Northern Sea Route along the Soviet Union's northern coastline, performing resupply operations for ships at sea and occasionally flying ice reconnaissance missions for the nuclear-powered icebreakers leading ship convoys. For the latter mission, however, the smaller and less fuel-thirsty Mi-2 light utility helicopter was usually used.

The Mi-8 also made its mark in the research of the Polar regions. These helicopters were used for communications and supply flights in support of Soviet drifting research stations in the Arctic Ocean (called ***Sev**ernyy **Pol**yus*, North Pole) and were based at the Soviet research stations in Antarctica – Molodyozhnaya, Mirnyy etc. The helicopters usually belonged to the Central Regions CAD/Myachkovo UAD/305th Flight based at Myachkovo airfield a short way south of Moscow. (In case you are surprised, the Myachkovo UAD was habitually tasked with Polar support missions in addition to its other duties.)

The type's Antarctic debut was in 1971 when two helicopters left Leningrad aboard M/V *Ob'* in late October as part of the 17th Soviet Antarctic Expedition which reached the goal in December. The Mi-8Ts operating in support of Soviet Polar research stations sometimes featured observation blisters in the rearmost window on each side.

Some of the Mi-8s involved, however, were based aboard Soviet Polar research vessels which were normally used to carry the personnel of the Soviet Antarctic Expeditions to and from the glacial continent. For instance, M/V *Akademik Fyodorov* had two Mi-8Ts, CCCP-24403 and CCCP-24468, while the helicopter flight of M/V *Mikhail Somov* comprised four such aircraft – CCCP-22246, CCCP-22568, CCCP-25954 and CCCP-27788). The ship would get as close to the shore as the floating ice would permit, whereupon the helicopters would make shuttle flights. When M/V *Mikhail Somov* was trapped by ice 20 km (10.8 nm) from the Antarctic coast in 1991 as she was due to pick up the personnel of the 35th SAE from Ice Station Molodyozhnaya, the Far East Shipping Company sent the icebreaker *Vladivostok* to the rescue. She was carrying a specially equipped Mi-8 featuring additional navigation systems for overwater flights down south. Due to time constraints the helicopter had to be airlifted all the way from Moscow to Vladivostok by a Soviet Air Force Antonov An-22 Antey heavy transport.

305th Flight Mi-8s were also stationed full-time on Spitsbergen where a Composite Air Detachment of the Central Regions CAD was formed to support the operations of the Soviet coal mining concession on Svalbard, the main island of the archipelago. These aircraft flew 'shuttle bus' and cargo services, linking the Piramida (Pyramid) mining settlement with Longyear airport and other parts of the island. The Myachkovo UAD had the distinction of being the first commercial operator of the Mi-8MT, and several early-production Mi-8MTs wearing non-standard registrations in the CCCP-0615x block were seconded to the Composite Air Detachment around 1988. Interestingly, these aircraft were also the first Mi-8s to feature a weather radar – an absolute necessity on Spitsbergen with its mountainous terrain and frequent bad weather. Tragically, one of these helicopters, CCCP-06155 (c/n 93397), crashed near Piramida in below-minima conditions on 27th March 1991 due to white-out, killing both pilots.

In late 1987 a Mi-8 was temporarily based aboard the new freighter M/V *Vitus Bering* which brought supplies to the Chukotka Region of the Soviet Far East. The ship's aviation component was to consist of two Kamov Ka-32S helicopters, but these had not yet been delivered to the Far East CAD/Vladivostok UAD by the time the Vitus Bering was to start on her maiden voyage. Thus the Mi-8 had to act as a stand-in for the contra-rotating Kamovs, carrying containers from the ship to the shore.

As a less serious occupation, Mi-8Ts often carried hunting parties – both professional hunters working full-time for the state and people hunting for their own enjoyment. Incidentally, it was a time-honoured tradition of some local Communist party bosses – and some illegitimate poachers as well – to use helicopters for hunting in the literal sense, shooting through the open door as the poor animals scared out of their wits by the roaring helicopter were running for their lives! Occasionally such hunting outings led to flight incidents when the passengers carried loaded shotguns aboard (which was against the rules) and somebody accidentally loosed off a shot in the cabin; fortunately no lives and no helicopters were lost that way.

The Mi-8's large payload and rugged dependability turned it into an indispensible aircraft for various law enforcement agencies. A large fleet of Mi-8s was operated by the Ministry of the Interior; sometimes, as noted earlier, they were ex-military machines still retaining full military colours but allocated civil

Above: EMERCOM of Russia Mi-8MTV-1 RA-27181 (c/n 96183) illustrates the livery worn by the Mi-8s of the ministry's Moscow-based Tsentrospas flying division. This aircraft is named 'Andrey Rozhkov'. The clamshell cargo doors have been removed for paradropping.

Another EMERCOM of Russia Mi-8MTV-1 in the same red/white colour scheme, RA-27180 (c/n 96182), has had the Tsentrospas titles removed.

registrations. In the Far East the activities of these helicopters included drug busting operations in the areas adjacent to the Chinese border where poppy was commonly cultivated by the locals as a source of opium.

In post-Soviet days the type was actively used by the State Customs Committee of Russia, serving with the regional Customs offices in St. Petersburg, Novosibirsk etc. To increase their range and endurance some of the Customs service's Mi-8MTVs were upgraded with six external tanks on outriggers similar to those of the armed assault versions; this enabled the helicopters to patrol the economic exclusion zone and land inspection parties on suspicious ships in case of need.

Mi-8s equipped with laser scanners or multi-mode observation systems were used to patrol oil and gas pipelines, checking for cracks and leaks which could cause a fire and explosion. Several Mi-8Ts, presumably including RA-22948 and RA-22974, were fitted with thermal imaging equipment and used for locating leaks in hot water mains in Moscow.

Unfortunately no aircraft type is guaranteed against attrition, and the Mi-8 had its share of fatal and non-fatal accidents. Given the huge number of aircraft built, the accident statistics appear quite horrifying – but percentage wise they are probably no worse than with any other mass-produced helicopter type.

The causes of the accidents vary widely. Admittedly sometimes hardware failure was the case. For instance, on 11th February 1976 Mi-8 CCCP-22538 (exact version unknown, c/n 1638) of the Yakutian CAD/Kolyma-Indigirka UAD/248th Flight crashed 87 km from Bulun airport, Yakutia, when the port engine's free turbine disintegrated due to a manufacturing defect, causing a massive fire. The crew managed a forced landing but all six passengers died in the blaze.

On 20th June 1991 Mi-8T CCCP-22235 (c/n 6377) of the Central Regions CAD/ Myachkovo UFD/305th Flight was flying at 150 m (490 ft) in the southern outskirts of Moscow when one of the artificial horizons failed, causing longitudinal instability. The helicopter started 'seesawing' (rocking fore and aft), and the main rotor blades struck the tailboom, severing it; the Mi-8 crashed out of control in a wooded area 260 m (850 ft) from the Moscow Ring Motorway, killing all three crewmembers. Artificial horizon failures were among the most common technical causes of Mi-8 accidents.

On 9th April 1991 the abovementioned Mi-8T CCCP-22290 (c/n 6978) of the Turkmen CAD/Ashkhabad UFD crash-landed near Bakhardok, Turkmen SSR, after a control system actuator failed, causing longitudinal and lateral imbalance. Luckily the crew escaped unhurt.

More often than not, however, the accidents were caused by the tell-tale human factor (crew or ATC error and breaches of discipline), adverse weather, a combination of these, or other reasons. For example, on 26th April 1993 Mi-17 RA-70948 (c/n 95465) operated by the Russian-Belgian joint venture Skylink ran out of fuel near Battambang, Cambodia, suffering damage in the ensuing forced landing in a rice paddy. It was later evacuated to Russia and repaired.

On 22nd July 1991 Mi-8T CCCP-22368 (c/n 7256) of the Far Eastern CAD/Kamchatka CAPA/Khalaktyrka UAD/2nd Flight was damaged in a landing accident at Izluchina helipad near Petropavlovsk-Kamchatskiy. As the helicopter hovered before landing, the main rotor downwash kicked up foreign objects. Trying to avoid being hit by these objects, the pilot moved the helicopter backwards; in so doing the tail rotor struck a wooden building and the tail rotor pylon snapped off, causing the helicopter to come down and roll over on the starboard side. Nobody was hurt and the helicopter was repaired. The crew of a Mi-8MTV-1 leased by the South African airline Heyns Helicopters from Tyumen'AviaTrans was not so lucky in similar circumstances. As the helicopter was installing an air handling unit on the roof of a building in Cape Town, the tail rotor struck an advertising billboard erected on the same roof; the uncontrollable machine fell on the roof and exploded, killing all four occupants. Incidentally, the aircraft (c/n 95954) was registered ZS-RIP. Talk about spooky reggies!

As an example of poor discipline, on 26th October 1980 Mi-8T CCCP-25961 (c/n 5807) of the Far Eastern CAD/Sakhalin CAPA crashed into Mt. Shakhtyor 17 km (10.5 miles) from Komrvo settlement, Sakhalin Island when the pilots intentionally departed from the predesignated route in bad weather; the crew of three was killed. On 11th July 1991 Mi-8T CCCP-22569 (c/n 7814) of the Yakutian CAD/Batagai UAD was damaged beyond repair near Deputatskiy airport during an SAR mission while trying to locate a vehicle with a power line repair crew which had gone missing. The helicopter, which was overloaded with too many passengers, lost speed while making a U-turn after locating the vehicle and 'fell through', hitting the ground hard and snapping off the tailboom. Luckily there were no fatalities this time but the number of rescuees rose dramatically! However, these cases are as nothing compared to what happened at Tarko-Salé, Tyumen' Region, on 14th May 1987 while Central Regions CAD/Myachkovo UFD/305th Flight Mi-8T CCCP-25731 (c/n 4235) was on temporary duty there. After the crew had had a small 'party', the drunken flight engineer tried to steal the helicopter and flipped it over during an unsuccessful attempt to take off! Fortunately the 'pilot' was unhurt and the aircraft was repairable.

Sometimes air traffic controllers were to blame. This was the case on 1st November 1974 when Mi-8T CCCP-25686 (c/n 3771) belonging to the federal government flight (235th Independent Flight Detachment) collided in mid-air with An-2 CCCP-70766 (c/n 1G132-21) of the Tyumen' CAD/Surgut UFD/121st Flight near the An-2's home base.

Rotors of hope

Search and rescue missions take an important place among the Mi-8's multifarious activities. For instance, devotees of winter fishing are a perennial headache for the airmen of the Leningrad Region. Ignoring repeated warnings, they pursue their hobby to the last – and frequently find themselves trapped on ice floes in the Gulf of Finland, on Lake Ladoga and Lake Onega as the ice starts breaking up in the spring. The only way of rescuing these castaways is by helicopter – and such rescue missions aren't cheap.

Helicopters belonging to the Georgian and North Caucasian CADs often had to undertake a different kind of rescue mission, taking sick or injured mountain climbers to hospitals. On one occasion the Mi-17 set a world record of an unusual kind, landing at 6,200 m (20,340 ft) above sea level on Mt. Everest to pick up an injured mountain climber – a difficult and dangerous operation because of the rarefied air at that altitude.

A new page in this chapter of the Mi-8's biography was opened in 1992 when a new government agency was formed. Its function was to promptly provide relief in the event of natural disasters or major accidents. The agency's units would fight major fires, disassemble collapsed buildings to extract survivors and/or bodies, provide medical aid, deliver goods to areas cut off from regular supply routes, evacuate people from dangerous areas etc. Originally called GKChS (*Gosoo**dar**stvennyy komi**tet** po chrezvy**chay**nym sitoo**ah**tsiyam* – State Committee for Emergencies, ie, emergency control), the agency became a full-fledged ministry in 1993 and the abbreviation was changed to MChS (M for *mini**ster**stvo*). Apart from a boost of status, this was probably done to avoid associations with the infamous GKChP (*Gosoo**dar**stvennyy komi**tet** po chrezvy**chay**nomu polo**zhen**iyu*) – the National Emergency Committee that briefly held power during the failed hard-line communist coup of 19th-21st August 1991 which brought an end to the Soviet Union's existence. To the English-speaking world the agency is known as EMERCOM of Russia.

EMERCOM's aviation detachment started life in March 1992 when the Central Airmobile Rescue Unit, or Tsentrospas, was formed at Zhukovskiy (the Russian acronym is derived from the official name – *Tsen**trahl'**nyy **aero**mo**bil'**nyy spa**sah**tel'nyy ot**ryad***). Initially it operated a handful of Mi-8MT helicopters leased from civil operators. One of the first major operations they were involved in was in 1992 when civil war broke out in Georgia as Abkhazia, an autonomous republic within Georgia, wished to secede. Five orange-painted GKChS Mi-8MTV-1s wearing Aeroflot titles and large Red Cross markings (to stop them from being fired upon by the Abkhazi separatists) shuttled back and forth between Sochi, Russia, and the Abkhazi town of Tkvarcheli, delivering humanitarian aid and airlifting refugees out of the war zone on the way back. The flights had to be suspended at the end of the year but resumed when Georgia, Abkhazia and Russia reached an agreement to this effect on 7th February 1993.

Later, EMERCOM built up its own fleet of Mi-8MTV-1s, plus at least one Mi-8T and one Mi-8PS VIP helicopter; these serve with five regional centres (flight detachments) based in Moscow (Tsentrospas), Krasnodar (Southern Regional Centre), Krasnoyarsk (Siberian Regional Centre), Chita (Transbaikalian Regional Centre) and Khabarovsk (Far Eastern Regional Centre). While some of the helicopters are civil-registered, many of EMERCOM's helicopters have three-digit serials testifying to the agency's paramilitary nature. They wear a distinctive livery with an orange/blue/orange cheatline and orange/blue roundels (the same as, for example, on French Securité Civile aircraft) incorporated into a windrose.

The ministry's Mi-8s have to perform a wide range of tasks when tackling emergencies – which seem to be thrust upon Russia with relentless regularity. Thus in May 1998 EMERCOM's air wing was put to the test during a major emergency in the Republic of Sakha (Yakutia). A huge ice jam had formed on the Lena River 40 km (24.8 miles) downstream from the city of Lensk. As a result, Lensk and the republican capital Yakutsk, as well as more than 100 smaller settlements, were flooded or cut off from supply routes; millions of people were in danger. While EMERCOM's Il'yushin IL-76TD transports delivered food, medicines etc. to Yakutia, measures were taken to eliminate the cause of the flood.

First, four Sukhoi Su-24M tactical bombers of the Russian Air Force's 76th Air Army deployed to Mirnyy from where they were to fly sorties, attacking the ice jam with general-purpose bombs. However, the idea was dropped because the area was heavily populated and bomb splinters could kill someone.

Above: A most unusual-looking *Hip* – this Mi-8MTV-3 (c/n 95156) seen at Moscow-Tushino on 9th May 1995 (complete with pylons) wears the civil registration CCCP-83964 (even as late as this) and the scrubbed-out titles of the Russian airline Transaero! In reality it is a Russian Air Force machine, of course.

Hence the Mi-8MTVs of EMERCOM's Transbaikalian Regional Centre were called upon to do the job. With the helicopter hovering just a dozen feet above the ice, the crew dropped 25-kg (55-lb) charges of high explosive; powerful explosions at short intervals demolished the ice, breaching the jam, and the following day the water had receded sharply. The operation was supervised by Aleksandr Moskalets, Deputy Minister of Emergencies. Meanwhile, other Mi-8MTVs and the ministry's Mi-26T heavy-lift helicopters airlifted people out of the flooded areas, evacuating nearly 40,000 people.

Another standing task for the helicopters stationed in the eastern regions of Russia is fighting forest fires which occur annually in the Khabarovsk Region and Eastern Siberia during the summer season. Together with the mighty Mi-26T the Mi-8MTVs equipped with VSU-5 'Bambi buckets' holding 5 tons (11,000 lb) of water are used for firefighting duties. You may say 5 tons of water isn't much, but the helicopter can refill the bucket in seconds and come back – and there's plenty of rivers and lakes in those parts.

All white

Again, due to its considerable capabilities and the ability to operate in the harshest environments with a minimum of support facilities the Mi-8 has become a favourite with the United Nations which actively use the type during peacekeeping operations in various parts of the world. For instance, in 1992 the UN chartered several Mi-8MTVs from the Russian Air Force (masquerading in Aeroflot markings for appearance's sake) for assistance in the holding of Angola's first free elections.

In early 1993 the abovementioned Mi-17 RA-70948 was operated for the United Nations Transitional Authority in Cambodia (UNTAC). United Nations aircraft operated into Cambodia from Thailand (U-Tapao Royal Thai Air Force Base) until Prince Norodom Sihanouk, head of Cambodia's Higher National Council, imposed a moratorium on timber exports to stop the country's national resources from being plundered by the Pol Pot junta – which ran contrary to the interests of Thai companies working hand-in-glove with the notorious Khmer Rouge. As a result, Thailand denied further use of its bases, demanding that further operations be conducted from Cambodian territory.

Also in 1993, Mi-8MTV-1 RA-27171 of the Russian airline UTair was operated for United Nations Mission in Sierra Leone (UNAMSIL). Incidentally, UTair (known as Tyumen'AviaTrans until 1st October 2002) is the world's

'028 Yellow', a Russian Ministry of the Interior Mi-8MTV (note the vertical white stripe on the tailboom) based at St. Petersburg-Pulkovo. The aircraft is equipped with six external fuel tanks.

Brand-new Mi-8T RA-22151 (c/n 99357581) in full Aviaenergo colours at Mineral'nyye Vody airport in February 1993.

largest commercial helicopter operator (and the largest commercial operator of the Mi-8) and has won international recognition for its expertise in rotary-wing operations. Hence the airline has developed a long-standing partnership with the United Nations and the contracts for UNPF support operations are being periodically prolonged. As of now UTair supports UN missions in Ethiopia and Eritrea, Western Sahara, Sierra Leone and Eastern Timor (UNPROFET – United Nations Protection Force in Eastern Timor). The turnover from the UN contracts in 2001 was an estimated US$ 35 million.

In the spring of 1996 the specially-formed 8th Combat Helicopter Squadron of the Ukrainian Army Aviation equipped with Mi-8MTVs was seconded to the United Nations Transitional Administration in Eastern Slavonia (UNTAES). This body had been established in June 1996 to oversee the transition of this fertile and oil-rich enclave occupied by separatist Serbs since 1991 back to Croatian rule (the local Serb minority had raised a rebellion when Croatia declared independence from federal Yugoslavia).

Operating from Klisa airport located between Osijek and Vukovar, the helicopters were duly painted in the United Nations Peace Force (UNPF) all-white colour scheme. Since there was considerable danger of being fired upon by Serbs and Croats alike, the Mi-8s were escorted by Ukrainian Army Aviation Mi-24P gunships (also seconded to UNTAES). It quickly turned out that the language barrier hampered operations, so translators were drafted in from the Ukrainian armed forces and tactical interpreters were carried for communication with NATO forces. By May 1997 UNTAES *Hip-Hs* and *Hinds* had flown a total of 2,500 hours, carrying some 7,000 passengers and earning praise from the UNPF commander, the Belgian Maj. Gen. Jozef Schoups. The deployment not only provided the crews with some very welcome flying practice (which was rather scarce at home) but earned equally welcome hard currency (the UN contract amount for the first six months in Eastern Slavonia was US$ 8 million).

At least two Mi-8MTV-1s leased from the Russian airline Vladivostok Avia (RA-25463 and RA-25464) were seconded to the UN Police Mission in Haiti (MIPONUH – *Misión de Policia de Naciónes Unidas en Haiti*) in 1996-1999, operating from Port-au-Prince. Tajik (EY-25169) and Russian (RA-27067) Mi-8MTV-1s were seconded to the United Nations Mission in Ethiopia and Eritrea (UNMEE) in 2003, operating from the Eritrean capital Asmara.

In 1998 at least one Czech Air Force/ 62 Helicopter Squadron (62. VrLt) Mi-17 was operated for the UN Stabilisation Force in Bosnia-Herzegovina (SFOR). Unfortunately this aircraft crashed on 25th October 1998; it turned out that the power train had failed after being serviced with the wrong grade of oil and that the prescribed maintenance had not been performed for the last 460 hours, although it should be done every 100 hours.

Other operations under the auspices of the United Nations included Ukrainian civil Mi-8Ts (such as UR-24275) operated for the United Nations Preventive Deployment Force in Macedonia (UNPREDEP) which was to prevent the civil war from spreading to this part of former Yugoslavia. Ukrainian Mi-8MTV-1s were operated by the UNPF during the effort to stop the civil war in Tajikistan in 1999 when Islamic fundamentalists attempted to topple the government in Dushanbe.

Unfortunately the white UN colours do not give any form of protection against hardened criminals with a total disregard for human life. In a wanton act of terrorism, on 8th October 2001 Chaika Aircompany Mi-8T UR-24229 was shot down by an Igla shoulder-launched surface-to-air missile fired by Chechen rebels who had taken refuge on Georgian territory. The helicopter, which was seconded to United Nations Observation Mission in Georgia (UNOMIG) monitoring the Georgian-Abkhazi confrontation, crashed on Mt. Golova 14.5 km from Sukhumi-Babushara airport, killing all on board.

World records

Even as the trials progressed the Mi-8 demonstrated its capabilities for the world to see by setting a series of internationally recognised records in its class. The first two achievements were made on 19th April 1964, using the second prototype (the unregistered V-8A c/n 0201). To this end the seats in the cabin were replaced by two long-range tanks; the take-off weight was exactly 14 tons (30,864 lb). A crew consisting of captain Vasiliy P. Koloshenko, co-pilot Nikolay V. Lyoshin, navigator Semyon I. Klepikov and flight engineer Vsevolod A. Koposov covered a distance of 2,465.736 km (1,531.5 miles) on a closed circuit – a big triangle formed by Moscow-Tushino airfield and the towns of Tikhonova Poostyn' and Vyaz'ma – within 12 hours 3 minutes 34 seconds. The previous record established by USAF pilots G. Bush and W. Singer in 1956 was 1,929 km (1,198 miles). Concurrently the helicopter set a world speed record, averaging 201.839 km/h (125.365 mph) on a 2,000-km (1,242-mile) stage.

More records followed soon after the Mi-8's service entry. An early-production Mi-8T with the non-standard registration CCCP-11067 (possibly the second *production* aircraft, c/n 0201?) painted in the dark green Aeroflot colour scheme was used to set a world speed record for women. On 23rd August 1967 a crew comprising pilots Inna Kopets and Lyudmila Isayeva, navigator Yuliya Stoopina and flight engineer Tat'yana Russiyan attained an average speed of 273.507 km/h (169.88 mph) over a 500-km (310-mile) closed circuit (Moscow-Tushino – Vyaz'ma – Kalooga). The helicopter was modified for the record flight by fitting wheel spats and removing the external tanks and KO-50 heater to cut drag (all fuel was carried in auxiliary tanks in the cabin).

Five days later the same machine with almost the same crew – Isayeva was captain this time, with Kopets as co-pilot and flight engineer Russiyan – set another speed record for women, clocking 258.666 km/h (160.66 mph) over a 1,000-km (621-mile) closed circuit, bettering the previous record by 121 km/h (75 mph). On 14th September 1967 another all-woman crew – captain Inna Kopets, co-pilot Lyudmila Isayeva, navigator Gamilya Galimova and flight engineer Valentina Volkova – set two records at once, attaining a range of 2,082.224 km (1,293.3 miles) and averaging 235.119 km/h (146.036 mph) on a 2,000-km closed circuit. The Kokchetav Region of Kazakhstan was the scene this time, with the town of Kzyl-Tu as the start/finish point. Finally, on 15th August 1969 a crew captained by Inna Kopets set a female range record, covering a distance of 2,232.218 km (1,386.47 miles) in a straight line.

Chapter 7

The E-Mi-grants

Foreign customers were quick to see the potential of the Soviets' new twin-turbine helicopter unveiled at the 1965 Paris Air Show, and orders for the Mi-8 started coming in immediately after the show. The first export order came from the least likely quarter – a Dutch company ordered a single Mi-8T from Aviaexport. Later the helicopter was resold to the United States where it was operated by Petroleum Helicopters, Inc. The first order was quickly followed by others from the United Arab Republic, Iraq, Yugoslavia and other Socialist and third world countries. The dependable, highly survivable and fuel-efficient helicopter soon attracted interest not only in the world's poorer regions where lacking infrastructure made rugged reliability and autonomous operation a prime requirement but also in industrially developed countries, including some with an aircraft industry of their own.

Fifteen years later the Mi-8 was in service with more than 50 nations. As of now the list has further grown; Aviaexport alone has delivered more than 4,000 new Mi-8s and Mi-17s which at one time accounted for nearly 50% of the agency's hard currency earnings.

(Now that we mention Aviaexport, this agency also had a hand in complicating things for the Western intelligence community – and for aviation enthusiasts at large. From 1970 onwards all Mi-8s delivered abroad via Aviaexport were issued special construction numbers under what may be called the 'Aviaexport system'. This is more intelligible than the 'damn fool system' with the famous five digit computer numbers but still does not reveal the batch number, number of aircraft in the batch, year of manufacture or plant – for exactly the same reason. The first three digits are a country code, the first one supposedly indicating the region where the helicopter is to be delivered. For instance, 104 = Hungary (1 equals Europe), 202 = China, 226 = Iraq (2 equals Asia and the Middle East), 368 = Ethiopia (3 equals Africa), 407 = Cuba (4 equals Central America and the Caribbean), 515 = Guyana (5 equals South America) and so on. The other two (or three) digits are the number of the aircraft built for the country in question. Thus, Kazan'-built MIAT Mongolian Airlines Mi-8T BNMAU-410 (c/n 20410) is the tenth example delivered to Mongolia; judging by the manufacture date (25th March 1986), it is a Batch 86 aircraft.

In the case of the 'second-generation' Mi-8MT/Mi-17 series the country designator is followed by an M for Kazan'-built aircraft (or sometimes a P in the case of ECM versions) or a C for Ulan-Ude built examples. For instance, Mi-8MTV-1 RA-70869 built for China but not delivered is c/n 202M29. Quite often, however, this logic does not work, as the first digit does not match the continent – probably because aircraft were diverted from a different order. For instance, India is 223 (which is OK) but some Indian Mi-172s have c/ns prefixed 356C; Turkey is 792, Peruvian Mi-8s have c/ns prefixed both 419M and 520 etc.)

More often than not the foreign operators of the Mi-8/Mi-17 were military ones and the type has seen action in countless armed conflicts all over the world (see Chapter 4). Thus the Mil' workhorse, like the equally famous Kalashnikov assault rifle, has come to epitomise both the Soviet/Russian design school and the Soviet Union's (Russia's) foreign trade efforts. In terms of sales success and longevity it is on a par with the famous Volkswagen Beetle and the Douglas DC-3/C-47.

Moreover, the collapse of the Warsaw Pact military bloc and subsequent political changes in Eastern Europe as the former Socialist countries strove to join the NATO and re-equip their air arms with Western hardware led to large-scale sales of second-hand Mi-8s to countries which had not operated the type before. Many aircraft popping up in out-of-the-way parts of the world, especially in the zones of regional conflicts, have obscure origins and the legality of their purchase is often questionable (the use of companies established as a front for weapons smuggling operations is all too common).

Of course, this is not to lessen the merits of the battle-proven, adaptable and extremely durable helicopter – and of those who design and build it. The incessant and concerted efforts of the Mil' Moscow Helicopter Plant, Kazan' Helicopters and the Ulan-Ude Aircraft Production Association to improve their product by developing and certificating new versions make sure that the good old *Hip* will remain the world's most widely used helicopter for a decade or two yet. In 1975 the Mi-8's designated service life was 21,500 flight hours and 25 years, with a 1,500-hour limit within a seven-year period up to the first major overhaul and a 1,500-hour/four-year time between overhauls (TBO). Yet some aircraft have remained operational for nearly 30 years – a fact which testifies to the helicopter's sturdy design.

The following is a brief rundown of Mi-8/Mi-17 operators abroad (ie, outside the former Soviet Union). Full fleet lists cannot be given for reasons of space, and only brief operational details are given for the same reason.

Afghanistan

Starting in 1968, the Afghan Republican Air Force (*Afghan Hanai Qurah*) took delivery of at least 14 armed Mi-8Ts and 12 Mi-8MTs – mostly transferred from the Soviet Air Force. The former version was allocated serials in the 2xx range, while the Mi-8MTs were serialled in the 5xx, 6xx and 7xx blocks. A single Mi-8PS serialled T-003 was also supplied to the government flight.

Later, when Soviet troops pulled out of Afghanistan in 1989, hostilities continued as the various warlords scrambling for power tore the Afghan AF apart and started using its remnants against each other. A number of Mi-8Ts and Mi-8MTVs, all in poor condition, were operated by the Northern Alliance (the anti-Taliban coalition led by Gen. Abdul Rashid Dostum). These include Mi-8T '00 37' and Mi-8MTV-2 '563'.

Algeria

The Algerian Air Force (Al Quwwat al Jawwiya al Jaza'eriya/Force Aérienne Algerienne) took delivery of 12 Mi-8s (versions unknown) in the late 1980s. One aircraft wore both a civil registration, 7T-WUX, and the Air Force serial 693. Others wore two-digit serials prefixed SV, suggesting they were operated by the Police Air Wing.

Angola

The Angolan Air Force (FAA – Força Aérea Angolana) was a major operator of the *Hip*, operating both the Mi-8T/TB and the Mi-8MTV. A few were civil-registered (known examples are D2-EUF, -EUH, -FMH, -FMI and -TAD). Most, however, had overt military markings; the *Hip-B/Cs* were serialled H-01

'792 Red', an Afghan Air Force Mi-8MT. The helicopter displays late-style Communist-era roundels.

through H-99, while the *Hip-Hs* were serialled H-500 through H-594. Some of the Mi-8TBs (for instance, H61) were equipped with Mi-8MT-type intake filters.

Attrition among the Angolan Mi-8s was consistently high. Much of it was due to the ongoing civil war and combat losses inflicted by the UNITA; other losses, however, were caused by poor airmanship and the frequent dust storms in desert areas.

Bangladesh

The Bangladesh Air Wing (*Biman Bahini*) took delivery of at least 18 Mi-8Ts (including 405 and 410) and one Mi-8P (805) and four Mi-17s. The aircraft were based at Zahurul Haque AB in Chittagong and Tezgaon (also referred to as Tejgaon) AB near Dacca (Dhaka). However, the Mi-8s proved to be underpowered in the hot climate of Bangladesh and the surviving examples were progressively traded in for 15 new Mi-17s built in Kazan'. The Mi-17s are mostly used in the utility role, although some have four weapons pylons plus gun fittings.

Belgium

Skytech Helicopter Services operated Mi-8MTV-1 RA-25402, Mi-171 RA-25750 and Mi-8MTV-1 RA-27041 leased from Russian airlines in 1996-97.

Bosnia and Herzegovina

The Bosnia and Herzegovina Federation Army (VF – *Vojska Federacije*) operated at least eight Mi-8s. Originally all of them were quasi-civil, being registered T9-HAA, -HAB, -HAD, -HAF, -HAG to -HAI and -HAL. Later, Mi-17 T9-HAG gained overt military markings and the serial VF-1804. Additionally, the Vojska Federacije operated Mi-8Ts '60306', '60401', '60402' and Mi-8MTV-1s '60404' and '60405' which were later reserialled VF-3813, VF-1801, VF-3812, VF-1802 and VF-1803 respectively.

Mi-8P '862' (c/n 20255?), one of many delivered to the Civil Aviation Administration of China.

Bulgaria

Starting in late 1969, the **Bulgarian Air Force** (BVVS – *Bolgarski Voyenno Vozdooshni Seeli*) purchased at least ten armed Mi-8Ts and two Mi-8Ps. In 1985 they were augmented by at least 24 Mi-17-1Vs and four Mi-17TPB communications jamming helicopters. Part of the fleet was operated by the 24th VPBV (*vertoleten polk boyni vertoleti* – combat helicopter regiment) based at Plovdiv; others operated from Dobrich AB and Krumovo AB where they were used for SAR duties, replacing the BVVS's last Mi-4As in 1985. The helicopters wore at least two different camouflage schemes – a simple dark green/dark earth scheme with pale blue undersides or a three-tone camouflage with green greyish-blue undersurfaces).

Additionally, the **government VIP flight** of the 16th Airlift Regiment operating from Sofia-Vrazhdebna airport included at least eight Mi-8P/Mi-8S helicopters; these wore the livery of the national flag carrier Balkan Bulgarian Airlines and the civil registrations LZ-CAB, -CAC, -CAE, -CAG, -CAK, -CAM, -CAP and -CAT. The latter example was retrofitted with a weather radar to enhance flight safety, as it was presumably used by the head of state, Todor Zhivkov.

The 'real' **Balkan Bulgarian Airlines** also had a small fleet of *Hips*, including Mi-8Ts LZ-CAA, -CAF and -CAL; the first of these was configured as a flying ambulance and wore appropriate Red Cross markings. Later they were apparently joined by Mi-8Ss LZ-CAC and -CAE transferred from the government flight; this is based on the fact that both helicopters were used for flying crane operations at one time!

Sofia-based charter carrier **Hemus Air** operated Mi-8T LZ-CAF in 1988. Other Bulgarian operators of the type were **ICONA** which operated a mix of Mi-8Ts/Mi-8MTVs (LZ-MSF/-MSG/-MSS and LZ-MSQ/-MSR/-MSY) in 1995 and **Scorpion Air** (also called Air Scorpio) with a similar mix (LZ-MOL/-MON/-MOO/-MOQ/-MOS/-MOT/-MOW/-MOX and LZ-MOE to -MOG/-MRL/-MRO to -MRU/-MSF/-MSG/-MSI) bought/leased from 1998 onwards.

Burkina Faso

Starting in 1990, the Burkina Faso Air Force acquired at least one Mi-8S VIP helicopter (XT-MAU) for government use and four Mi-17s. One of these was also civil-registered (XT-MCV) while the others had military serials.

Chad

In 2000 the Chad Air Force (*Force Aérienne Tchadienne*) bought two used Mi-8MTVs from the Ukraine. Registered TT-OAJ and TT-OAK/4321 (in spite of their ownership and camouflage scheme), the helicopters were based at

Faya Largeau. On 3rd October 2002 both machines were destroyed there on the ground by enemy action.

China (People's Republic of China)

China was one of the largest foreign customers for the Mi-8. Early deliveries, which began in 1971, were to the **Civil Aviation Administration of China** (CAAC), the 'Chinese Aeroflot', which received at least 55 examples (mostly Mi-8Ps). There are speculations, however, that many of these aircraft were actually military. At first the helicopters wore simple three-digit registration numbers ranging from 752 to 864 (even numbers only) without the B- nationality prefix adopted in 1972, since they never left the country. In 1988 part of the fleet was reregistered under the new four-digit system as B-7801 through B-7814; subsequent civil Mi-8s received registrations in the new format.

Starting in 1984, when deregulation set in, further deliveries were made to some of the new airlines (often based on CAAC's regional divisions – the equivalent of Civil Aviation Directorates in the USSR) which tore up the old CAAC fleet and appropriated the aircraft based in their hometowns. These include **China Northern Airlines** which bought four Mi-8s (B-7815 to B-7818) and five Mi-171s (B-7851 to B-7855), and **China General Aviation** which operated four Mi-8s (B-7816 to B-7822). Other operators are **Qingdao Helicopter Airlines** with three Mi-8Ts (B-7825 to B-7827) and **Eastern General Aviation Co.** with five Mi-171s (B-7856 to B-7860).

The **People's Liberation Army** (PLA) also operated the type in large numbers. From early 1990 onwards some PLA Mi-8s sported four- or five-digit serials prefixed LH instead of the customary four-digit format. Moreover, in 1996 the PLA started taking delivery of the Mi-17MD. These aircraft wear two-tone camouflage and two-digit serials prefixed CUA, which purportedly stands for **China United Airlines** (the commercial division of the People's Liberation Army Air Force)!

Colombia

Mi-8 operations in this South American country started in 1992 when **Helitaxi Colombia** leased 12 Mi-8MTV-1s (HK-3730X to HK-3732X, HK-3758X to HK-3782X and HK-3862 to HK-3865) from Tyumen'AviaTrans. **Helicol** (Helicopteros Nacionales de Colombia) joined in a year later with 12 more Mi-8MTV-1s (HK-3879X to HK-3882X, HK-3888X to HK-3890X, HK-3897X, HK-3898X, HK-3908X, HK-3910X and HK-3911X). A third commercial operator appeared in 1998 when **Heliandes** acquired two Mi-8MTV-1s (HK-4160X and HK-4164X).

The *Hip-H* was also operated by the **Colombian Army Aviation** (*Ejército de Colombia*) which took delivery of ten Mi-17-1Vs on 25th April 1997; these include EJC-175, EJC-176 and EJC-477. Around 2000 the Colombian Army ordered the more capable Mi-17-V5; one example serialled EJC-389 has been identified so far.

Congo-Brazzaville

The Congo Air Force (*Force Aérienne Congolaise*) operated at least three Mi-8s; all three had been withdrawn from use by 1991.

Costa Rica

The Costa Rican Ministry of Public Security (MSP – *Ministerio de Seguridad Publica*) operated at least one Mi-8MT serialled MSP016 in late 1994.

Croatia

After the disintegration of Yugoslavia the newly-established Croatian Air Force (HRZ i PZO – *Hrvatsko Ratno Zrakoplovstvo i Protizracna Obrana* – Croatian Air Force/Air Defence Force; later renamed HZS – *Hrvatske Zracne Snage*) inherited an unspecified number of armed Mi-8Ts (and a few Mi-8PSs) from the Yugoslav Air Force. Known serials are H-101, H-102, H-104 to H-106 and H-151 (H-102 and H-106 are Mi-8PSs).

Starting in 1993, the HZS bought a number of Mi-8MTV-1s from Russian airlines. Known examples were serialled H-201 to H-207, H-210 to H-213, H-215, H-217, H-251 and H-252. Some of the helicopters had names; for instance, H-101, the oldest aircraft in the fleet, was named 'Stara Frajla' ('Old Maid' in Croatian). H-205 was christened 'Sveti Ivan' (St. John the Baptist), while H-211 was 'Sveti Donst' (St. Dunstan). The *Hips* operated from Pleso AB near Zagreb, Zadar, Lucko, Divulje and Velika Gorica.

Additionally, the HZS operated a small number of quasi-civil examples. These included Mi-8Ts 9A-HAA, -HAB, -HAE and -HIH, Mi-8S 9A-HHH which was the presidential aircraft, and Mi-8MTV-1s 9A-HAC, -HAD and -HRH. The latter machine was converted into a VIP aircraft representing a strange cross-breed between a Mi-8MT and a Mi-172, with rectangular windows but large rear clamshell doors and a normal sliding entry door.

Cuba

The fleet of the Cuban flag carrier Empresa Consolidada **Cubana de Aviación**, commonly known simply as Cubana, included at least 18 Mi-8s registered CU-H400 to CU-H412, CU-H414, CU-H415 and CU-H417 to CU-H420. After 1990, when Cuba also went in for deregulation, many of these helicopters were transferred to a new airline called **Aerogaviota** ('gaviota' is Spanish for seagull).

The **Cuban Air Force** (FAR – *Fuerza Aérea Revolucionaria*) operated more than 20 Mi-8Ts in armed configuration. At least two Mi-17s were added later. The total number delivered to the FAR is probably much higher, as the *Hips* appear to be serialled consecutively from at least 65 to 133; the Mi-8s were based at Varadero, Santiago de Cuba, Holguín and Girón.

Czechoslovakia/Czechia (Czech Republic)

The country then known as Czechoslovakia was the first foreign operator of the Mi-8, receiving its first examples of the type in 1967 when the 'rational' c/n system was still applied to export aircraft such aircraft are marked with an asterisk). By 1989 Czechoslovakia had taken delivery of 39 'first-generation' Mi-8s, followed by 50 Mi-8MTs (in both pure transport and armed assault configurations) in 1989-91.

The **Czechoslovak Air Force** (CzAF or CVL – *Ceskoslovenské Vojenské Létectvo*) operated a total of eight Mi-8Ps/PSs (0210*, 0815, 0829, 0830 and 0834 to 0837) and 18

Czechoslovak Police Mi-8P B-8427 (c/n 10827) displays the characteristic Czech MoI roundels. This aircraft passed to the Slovak Police in 1993.

Above: Tiger-striped Mi-8MT 0837 (c/n 108M37) saw service with the Czech component of the United Nations' Stabilisation Force in Bosnia and Herzegovina (SFOR).

Mi-8Ts (0610*, 0910*, 0313*, 2832*, 3932*, 1032* to 1232*, 1532*, 1632*, 1932*, 2032*, 0133* and 0816 to 0820), while the Mi-8MT serials ran in sequence from 0801 to 0850. The Mi-8Ps saw service with the 3. DLP (*dopravni létecky pluk* – transport air regiment) based at Prague-Kbely AB, whereas the transport and assault versions were operated by the 4. VrP (*vrtulnikovy pluk* – helicopter regiment) at Sliac, Squadron 2 of the 11. VrP at Plzen-Líne, Squadron 2 of the 51. VrP 'Dr. Eduard Benes' at Prostéjov and an unidentified unit at Ostrava-Mosnov. Apart from regular transport duties, the Mi-8s were tasked with aerial photography and SAR duties – although these were more commonly performed by the lighter Mi-2 utility helicopter. Additionally, the CzAF received three Mi-8PPA ECM helicopters serialled 7520, 7522 and 7523, as well as a single Mi-9 ABCP serialled 0001.

The second operator of the type was the **Federal Government Flight** (LOMV – *Letecky oddíl ministerstva vnitra*; also called LS FMV – *Letecká spolecnost federalního ministerstva vnitra*, Airline of the Federal Ministry of the Interior) which received two Mi-8PSs registered OK-BYK and OK-BYL in 1970. The aircraft were operated only briefly, going to the Police Air Wing in 1970 as B-8021 and B-8022 respectively; the police also operated 11 other Mi-8Ps and 'PSs serialled B-8123, B-8426 to B-8428, B-8829, B-8130, B-8231, B-8532, B-8733, B-8938 and B-8939.

(Note: In keeping with the then-current – and still current – Czech practice the CzAF Mi-8s received serials matching the last four digits of the c/n; for instance, Mi-8T '1632 White' is c/n 1632, Mi-8T '0816 White' is c/n 10816 and Mi-8MT '0850 White' is c/n 108M50. ('2832 White' and '3932 White' are an exception to the rule, being c/ns 020832 and 030932.) The Police Air Wing used a different system looking like Chinese civil registrations if it were not accompanied by characteristic quasi-triangular insignia. The B prefix stood for [*Verejná*] *bezpecnost* – 'public security' (ie, police); the first digit matched the type, the second indicated the year of production and the last two were the last two digits of the c/n. Thus the former OK-BYL (c/n 10822) manufactured in 1970 originally had the serial applied in error as B-8122 (because it was transferred in 1971!) but this was later amended to the correct serial, B-8022.)

Finally, **Slov-Air**, the Slovak subsidiary of CSA Czechoslovak Airlines which was tasked with feeder traffic and various aerial work, took delivery of two Mi-8Ts (OK-DXN and -DXO) in 1973. Later they were supplemented by two former Czech Police Mi-8Ps (OK-ZXP and -EXR). Nearly all of these, along with the two Mi-8Ts operated by **Air Transport Europe** (OK-MYN and -OYO), passed to Slovakia after 1st January 1993. Other civil operators in Czechia were **Air Transa** (Mi-8Ts OK-EXC/-YXB/-YXC) and **Aerocentrum** (Mi-8Ts OK-EXC/-FXA/-FXE).

Djibouti

The Djibouti Air Force operated five second-hand Mi-8Ts bought in the CIS in unarmed utility configuration in the early 1990s and

Radar-equipped Mi-8PS HS-6 (c/n 13306) of the Finnish Air Force.

refitted to assault configuration. They were assigned the quasi-civil registrations J2-MAJ, -MAL, -MAM, -MAR and -MAS; only the last two letters were carried visibly.

Ecuador

In Ecuador the type saw service with two airlines – **Heliservicios**, which operated two Mi-8Ts (HC-BUK and -BUL), and **Helipet** (Helicopteros Petroleros), which operated two Mi-8MTV-1s (HC-BSG and -BSH) in support of oil industry operations in 1994. The **Ecuador Army** (*Ejército Ecuatoriana*) had at least four Mi-171s (E-480, E-483, E-484 and E-486) on strength, delivered in 1997;

East German Air Force Mi-8PS '739 Black' (c/n 10599) was delivered to TFG 44 (the government VIP flight) in May 1981, later passing to KHG 3. It became 93+60 after German reunification.

Egypt

Starting in the late 1960s, the **Egyptian Air Force** (*al Quwwat al-Jawwiya il-Misriya*) took delivery of 68 Mi-8Ts in transport/assault configuration and at least one Mi-9. Known serials are 880 to 887, 1010,1025, 1036, 1046, 1051, 1217, 1256, 1311, 1320, 1330, 1406, 1419, 1468, 1476, 1483 and 1486. The helicopters operated from Cairo-West AB. Some were retrofitted with air intake filters supplied by the British company APME (Aircraft Porous Media Equipment). Later, deliveries were curtailed when Egypt's new allegiance to the West; not until post-Soviet times did the *Hip* make a comeback in these parts when Kazan' Helicopters began deliveries of 20 Mi-17-1Vs.

Additionally, an **unknown Egyptian airline** operated Mi-8PS SU-BML leased in Russia in the late 1990s.

El Salvador

The Salvadorean airline Helica operated two second-hand Mi-8s – an ordinary Mi-8T (YS-1005P) and a rare Mi-8TS VIP helicopter registered YS-1006P. Both were leased to New Zealand in 1993, the former aircraft being lost in a crash during the lease.

Estonia

The aviation detachment of the Estonian Ministry of the Interior (*Piirivälve Lennusalk*) operates Mi-8S ES-PMA and three Mi-8Ts (ES-PMB to -PMD) acquired from Germany in 1995.

Ethiopia

More than 30 Mi-8Ts and more than ten Mi-8MTs were delivered to the Ethiopian Air Force (*ye Etiopia Ayer Hail*), starting in 1977 when the pro-Soviet regime of Mengistu Haile Mariam seized power. Some of the helicopters came from Hungarian surplus stocks. The *Hip-Bs* were apparently serialled consecutively from 850 to at least 869, while the *Hip-Hs* had serials in the 16xx and 20xx ranges.

Several of the helicopters fell into enemy hands during the border conflict with Eritrea.

Equatorial Guinea

Six ex-Czech Air Force Mi-8MTs were registered to an unidentified operator in Equatorial Guinea in 2002 as 3C-QSD to -QSI. All six were probably never delivered and were eventually sold to the USA.

Finland

Maintaining a non-aligned status and being positioned geographically between the NATO nations and the USSR, Finland purchased military equipment from the East and the West alike. Between May 1973 and August 1983 the **Finnish Air Force** (*Suomen Ilmavoimat*) took delivery of eight Mi-8Ts (serialled HS-1 to HS-4 and HS-11 to HS-14) and a pair of Mi-8Ps (HS-5/HS-6).

The aircraft were operated by the transport squadron (*Kuljetuslentolaivue*) at Utti AB. In due course most were retrofitted with Western weather radars in undernose pods. HS-11, HS-13 and HS-14 were operated by the **Finnish Border Police**, wearing appropriate titles in Finnish (Rejavartiolaitos) to port and in Swedish (Gränsbevakningen) to starboard; for a while they were placed on the civil register as OH-HVA to -HVC before reverting to their original serials. One helicopter was lost in a crash on 13th April 1982 – and it was not the unlucky number, as you might think, but HS-12.

France

Heliglobe Finet France Cargo leased several Mi-8s from the Mil' OKB, including Mi-8MTV RA-70934.

Germany (East/West)

East Germany was probably the largest foreign operator of the Mi-8, receiving no fewer than 116 'first-generation' aircraft. Between mid-1967 and March 1984 the East German airline **Interflug** took delivery of six Mi-8Ts (DM-SPA to -SPC, -SPE, -SPF, DDR-SPP and DDR-SJA). Used mostly for flying crane work, originally they belonged to the utility division, **Interflug Spezialflug** (IF/SF) but were transferred to the photo survey department (**Interflug Bildflug** or IF/BF) in 1978. Among other things, they were instrumental in converting the East German railroad network from diesel to electric power, performing a huge amount of work setting up the overhead power cables.

By far the most Mi-8s, however, saw service with the **East German Air Force** (LSK/LV – *Luftstreitkräfte und Luftverteidigung der Deutschen Demokratischen Republik*), and the East German Navy (*Volksmarine*). The armed forces took delivery of 37 Mi-8Ts (serialled 389 to 391, 394 to 400, 626, 627, 630 to 634, 636, 902, 903, 906, 907, 909 to 913, 921 to 928, 930 to 932), 38 Mi-8TBs (124 to 126, 128 to 135, 750 to 752, 755, 763, 764, 768, 807, 808, 810, 812, 814, 818, 820, 824, 827, 830, 831, 834, 933 to 940) and 26 Mi-8Ss (396, 397, 732, 735, 739, 773, 911 No.2, 914, 915, 945, 950, 960 to 962, 966, 970 to 977, 990, 993 and 998).

HG 31 at Brandenburg-Briest, later redesignated HG 34, was the first to introduce the type in July 1968; like their civil colleagues, the LSK/LV flight and ground crews took their training at the Kremenchug Civil Aviation Flying School. The more heavily armed Mi-8TB saw service from 1977 onwards to HG 5 (*Hubschraubergeschwader* – helicopter wing) at Basepohl AB, which became KHG 57 and then KHG 5 (*Kampfhubschraubergeschwader* – combat helicopter wing) 'Adolf von Lützow', and with KHG 67 at Cottbus AB, later redesignated KHG 3 'Ferdinand von Schill'. These two units also operated Mi-24D and Mi-24P assault helicopters; together the *Hip* and the *Hind* would have made a deadly duo over the battlefield.

The Mi-8Ss served with STS-29 (*Selbständige Transportfliegerstaffel* – independent airlift squadron) at Marxwalde AB tasked with government VIP flights which received

Above: In 1990 several East German Air Force Mi-8Ts, including '930 Black' (c/n 10545), were assigned to SAR duties and received appropriate markings. This aircraft was serialled 93+16 after German reunification and ultimately scrapped in September 1994.

the first two of the type in 1968. On 1st January 1973 STS-29 was reorganised, becoming TFG-44 'Arthur Pieck' (*Transportfliegergeschwader* – airlift wing), and the Mi-8s were taken over by a special helicopter squadron within the wing. Originally they wore an attractive red/white colour scheme; however, after a fatal crash in 1975 the helicopters were no longer used by the East German leader Erich Honecker and his closest aides, carrying government officials of lower rank and the army top brass; also, they reverted to camouflage colours. After logging a certain number of flight hours the Mi-8Ss were transferred to other units and converted to Mi-8PSs, so that no more than seven were in service with the government flight at any one time.

Also in 1977, HS 16 of the **East German Border Guards** (*Grenztruppen*) received two Mi-8PSs augmented by a Mi-8T in 1982. Additionally, eight Mi-9 airborne command posts (serialled 402, 405, 407, 409, 411, 416, 426 and 482) were delivered to KHG 57/KHG 5 in 1983-84; later, four of them were transferred to KHG 67/KHG 3. Still later the ABCPs were operated by two Command and Reconnaissance Helicopter Squadrons formed within these units, known as HSFA-5 and HSFA-3 respectively (*Hubschrauberstaffel der Führung und Aufklärung*) at Basepohl and Cottbus.

The **East German Navy** had several Mi-8Ts and 'TVKs serving with MHG 18 (*Marinehubschraubergeschwader* – naval helicopter wing) at Parow since 1976. Two of these helicopters were lost in a mid-air collision in January 1981. In the latter days of East Germany a number of *Hips* was set aside for SAR/MEDEVAC duties.

When Germany reunited on 3rd October 1990, the united **German Armed Forces** (*Bundeswehr*) took over most of former East Germany's military aircraft, including 101 *Hips*. These received four-digit serials ranging from 93+01 to 93+20, 93+30 to 93+46, 93+50 to 93+55, 93+60 to 93+76, 93+80 to 93+98 and 94+01 to 94+24. Some Mi-8s and Mi-9s were briefly operated by HFS 400 (*Heeresfliegerstaffel* – Army aviation squadron) at Cottbus and LTG 62 at Wunstorf. Others saw service with Squadron 3 of the Luftwaffe's government VIP flight known as FBS (*Flugbereitschaftstaffel*, lit. 'duty squadron') and based at Köln-Wahn.

Seven Mi-8Ts and two Mi-8Ss were transferred to the **German Police**, receiving the registrations D-HOZB through D-HOZJ, but never actually used.

In 1994 the Bundeswehr retired the type; most aircraft were placed in storage and eventually sold or scrapped. The civil Mi-8Ts, too, found further use with the newly formed airline **Berliner Spezial Flug**, becoming D-HOXA to -HOXC, -HOXF, -HOXP and -HOXQ respectively.

Armed Mi-8T ('Mi-8TVK Mk I') '10442 Red' (c/n 10442) of the Hungarian Air Force was operated by the UN Stabilisation Force in Bosnia and Herzegovina (SFOR) as a MEDEVAC helicopter.

Guinea

The **Guinean government flight** operated three Mi-8Ss registered 3X-GDF, -GDT and -GVB. The latter aircraft was delivered not later than 1975. Additionally, Mi-8S 3X-GDI was operated by **Air Guinée**.

Guinea Bissau

An airline called Bipal operated at least two Mi-8s, including Mi-8MTV1 J5-GAA delivered in August 2002.

Guyana

The Guyana Defence Force took delivery of at least three quasi-civil Mi-8Ps registered 8R-GDH, -GGC and -GGD. Another example serialled GDF-1 is also known but this may be one of the above three.

Hungary

Starting in 1968, 60 'first-generation' *Hips* – 53 Mi-8Ts and seven Mi-8P/Mi-8Ss – were delivered to the Hungarian Air Force (MHRC – *Magyar Honvedseg Repülö Csapatai*) by the Soviet Union. However, only 47 of them (Mi-8Ts serialled 827, 927, 228 to 428, 628, 130 to 330, 730, 736 to 936, 036, 136 and 10417 to 10444, plus Mi-8Ss '416', '10446' and '10447') were actually taken on strength by the MHRC. The others sat in storage at the maintenance facility in Tököl until sold off, some of them going back to the CIS. Oddly enough, however, Hungary later seized a Mi-8S and nine Mi-8Ts intended for Iraq due to sanctions imposed against Saddam Hussein's regime, and these were later pressed into Hungarian Air Force service as 2639, 2656, 6200, 6204, 6206, 6207, 6212, 6215, 6220 and 6223. The 'first-generation' assault/ transport and VIP versions were operated by the 'Borz' Helicopter Squadron based at Szentkirälyszabadja and the 'Sarkany' Training Squadron at Szolnok.

Additionally, in 1991 the Hungarian Air Force took delivery of one Mi-9 (001), five Mi-17s (701 to 705) and two Mi-17TPB ECM helicopters. These belonged to the 'Fönix' Helicopter Squadron, also based at Szentkirälyszabadja.

India

The **Indian Air Force** (IAF, or *Bharatiya Vayu Sena*) is one of the largest Mi-8 operators. Known serials (which run in the Z 1xxx, Z 2xxx and Z 3xxx series) suggest that about 120 Mi-8Ts/Mi-8PSs were delivered, supplemented later by about 40 Mi-17s. The Mi-8 served with the Nos 109, 118, 119 and 121 Squadrons stationed at New Delhi, Bangalore-Yelahanka, Jodhpur and Jessore, as well as other units in India's vast territory.

Some Indian Mi-8Ts/Mi-8PSs have been upgraded locally by installing a weather radar in a thimble radome. For many years the *Hips* wore olive drab or two-tone camouflage patterns; the Mi-8PSs were an exception, sporting a smart grey/dark blue/white livery. From late 2000 onwards the IAF started introducing a common overall light grey low-visibility colour scheme which is applied to the helicopters as well. in 2000 the IAF started taking delivery of an additional batch of Kazan'-built Mi-8MTV-5-1s featuring a one-piece cargo ramp/door, and these wear the new livery from the start.

Additionally, **Mesco Airlines** took delivery of three Mi-172s registered VT-MAE to -MAG, while **Pawan Hans** Helicopters operated three sister ships (VT-ASM, -PHF, and -PHG). The latter airline also leased Mi-8s in Russia, including Mi-8Ts RA-24243, -24467, -25944 and -25974.

Iran

While Russian types are generally popular with Iranian airlines, it is mostly fixed-wing aircraft that are operated (usually on a lease basis). Navid Air was one of the few exceptions to the rule, operating two Mi-8Ts, a Mi-8MTV-1 and a Mi-8AMT from Karaj-Payam airport in 1997-98.

Iraq

The **Iraqi Air Force** (*al Quwwat al-Jawwiya al-Iraqiya*) was easily the largest foreign customer for the *Hip*, ordering more than 220 'first-generation' Mi-8s (including a few Mi-8PPAs) and more than 200 Mi-8MTs. There is no reliable information as to how many were actually delivered, as many were embargoed or diverted to other customers when UN sanctions were imposed on Iraq after the First Gulf War of 1989; some sources, however, say only 36 were in service in 1982. Known examples are Mi-8PPA '25', Mi-8Ts '200', '204', '206', '207', '212', '215', '220',' 223', '641', '650', '651', '656', '687' and Mi-8MTV '1435'.

A few Mi-8s wore the livery of **Iraqi Airways**; one example registered YI-ACS is known.

Israel

Israel Aircraft Industries operate a single Mi-17 coded IAI 817 converted as an avionics/weapons upgrade demonstrator.

Gloss olive green/medium grey Mi-8T ('Mi-8TVK Mk I') Z 2451 (c/n 223112?) displays one of the camouflage schemes worn by Indian Air Force *Hips*.

Above: Aero Asahi Mi-8PA JA9549 (c/n 26001) corresponded to the Mi-8S as far as the airframe was concerned. Note the mounting rails for the removed air conditioner aft of the entry door.

Japan

The Asahi Koyo (Aero Asahi) air services agency purchased a single Mi-8PA registered JA9549. Among other things, the aircraft was used for flying crane work.

Jordan

Royal Wings (note that this is not the government flight) operated a single Mi-8T registered JY-RWM.

Kenya

In 1999 the Kenya Police Air Wing operated two Mi-8s registered 5Y-EDM and -UKW, presumably bought second-hand in Russia. Later they were augmented by two new Mi-17s (5Y-STA and -SFA) based at Nairobi-Wilson.

Kampuchea (Cambodia)

The **Kampuchean Air Force** operated at least 15 *Hips*, some of which wore **Kampuchean Airlines** titles, despite being painted in camouflage colours. Known examples are Mi-8Ts XU 811 and XU 814, Mi-8PSs XU.801 and XU.802, Mi-17s XU-023, XU-171, XU 174, XU-178, XU-179 and XU-184, Mi-17-1Vs XU-170, XU.175, XU-176 and XU-177 (note the variations in registration style). A further example, XU 812 (version unknown), was destroyed by the Khmer Rouge at Anlung Veng on 9th February 1997.

North Korea (Korean People's Democratic Republic)

An unspecified number of Mi-8Ts (the armed assault version) was supplied to the North Korean Air Force not later than 1979. Little is known about the fleet because of North Korea's obsession with security.

South Korea (Republic of Korea)

A number of Mi-17MDs with rectangular windows was delivered to the South Korean Police by 2001.

Laos

The Laos Government (ie, the obviously the **Lao People's Liberation Army Air Force**) operated at least 14 Mi-8Ts/Mi-8Ps and at least nine Mi-8MTs from the early 1990s onwards. All of them were civil-registered (known identities range from RDPL-3.4040 to RDPL-3.4076, though the intervening registrations were probably Mi-8s as well) and some were nominally operated by the state airline **Lao Aviation**, but the camouflage finish worn by most of the helicopters spoke for itself.

According to Russian sources, the LPLAAF had ordered 12 Mi-17-1Vs from Kazan' Helicopters for delivery in 1997-99 as replacements for the existing Mi-8Ts. However, deliveries were halted after the fourth aircraft due to non-payment.

Latvia

The Latvian Air Force (*Aviacijas Pretgaisa Aizsardzibas Speki*) operates two Mi-8MTVs, '101 White' and '102 White', which were purchased from Russian airlines and refurbished in Lithuania. The helicopters are based at Riga-Spilve.

Lithuanian Air Force Mi-8MTV '01 Blue' (ex-CCCP-27075?, c/n 95911) shortly before landing.

Libya

The Libyan Arab Republic Air Force (LARAF, or *al Quwwat al-Jawwiya al-Libiya*) reportedly had had 12 armed Mi-8Ts on strength in 1982. By 1998 most of them were presumably unserviceable because spares supplies were cut off in 1992 due to UN sanctions. These were imposed when Libyan terrorists blew up Pan American Airlines Boeing 747-121A N739PA over Lockerbie, Scotland, on 21st December 1988. However, more Mi-8s/Mi-17s may have been delivered after the sanctions were lifted on 5th April 1999. Only one example serialled 8230 has been identified to date.

Lithuania

The **Lithuanian Air Force** (*Karines Oro Pajegos*) has at least nine *Hips* in service with the helicopter squadron at Pajouste. Known examples are Mi-8MT '01 Blue', Mi-8PS '11 Blue' and Mi-8Ts '02 Blue', '03 Blue', '09 Blue', '10 Blue', '12 Blue' and '14 Blue'. All the Mi-8Ts are former civil examples converted to transport/assault configuration by Helisota; the helicopters have been fitted with state-of-the-art Western communications equipment, Nitesun SX-16 searchlights and other add-ons enhancing their capabilities. Some have been configured for SAR operations are are deployed at Klaipeda.

On the civil side, Vilnius-based **AviaBaltika** operated Mi-8Ts LY-HAJ and LY-HAO to -HAQ; the abovementioned Helisota company had a Mi-8PS registered LY-HBB. Other civil examples were registered LY-HAD, -HAX, -HAY, -HBC, -HBD and -HBF.

Macedonia

The Macedonian Army Aviation (VAM – *Vazduhoplovstvo Armeisko Makedonija*) operated at least three Mi-8MTVs serialled VAM-301 (formerly on the civil register as Z3-HHC), VAM-302 and VAM-304.

Madagascar (Malagasy Republic)

The Malagasy Air Force (Armée de l'Air Malgache) operated at least four quasi-civil Mi-8s registered 5R-MOD to -MOG; the former aircraft is a Mi-8T.

Malaysia

In 1998 the Fire and Rescue Department of Malaysia purchased a single new Mi-17-1V and a single used Mi-8MTV-1 (serialled M49-01 and M49-02 respectively) from Russia. Based at Langkawi, the helicopters can be equipped with water cannons for fighting fires in high-rise buildings – a modification made by the local company Airod.

Malta

Malta Aircharter, a subsidiary of Air Malta, leased two Mi-8s from the Bulgarian government flight (Mi-8P LZ-CAP in 1992 and Mi-8T LZ-CAE in 1997-2000), plus three Mi-8Ts (LZ-CAH, -CAX and -CAZ) in 1997 and Mi-8P LZ-CAR in 2000-03. Mi-8P RA-24637 was also leased from Sochispetsavia.

Maldives Islands

Heli Air and **Hummingbird Helicopters** operated Mi-8P/Mi-8S helicopters leased from the Bulgarian government flight (LZ-CAB, -CAC, -CAK, -CAM, -CAO and -CAP) in the 1990s for carrying tourists between the islands of the archipelago. For overwater operation the helicopters were retrofitted with an emergency flotation bag system.

Unfortunately three of the 'hummingbirds' were lost in crashes (LZ-CAP in 1994, LZ-CAC in 1996 and LZ-CAK in 1999).

Mexico

Mexico became a Mi-8 operator in 1986 when the Ulan-Ude aircraft factory delivered the first 12 Mi-8Ts. Currently the **Mexican Navy** (*Aviaciõn Naval Mexicana*) operates at least 16 Mi-8Ts and Mi-8MTV-1s (MR-350 through MR-366; however, MR-362 is a VIP aircraft).

The helicopters came from both Kazan' and Ulan-Ude production lines. The Mi-8 is in service with 1° *Grupo Aéronaval*/1° *Escuadrõn de Appoyo Tãctico y Logistico* (1st Naval Air Group/1st Tactical & Logistical Support Squadron) at Veracruz, the capital of the identically named state; 2° *Grupo Aéronaval*/3° EATL at Chetumal, Quintana Roo; and 2° EATL at Teacapan, Sinaloa.

Later, additional deliveries were made to the **Mexican Air Force** (*Fuerza Aérea de Mexico*), which has at least two Mi-8Ts (FAM-1802/FAM-1803) and presumably up to 21 Mi-8MTV-1s (FAM-1701 to FAM-1721); some of them are stationed at Acapulco. The **Mexican Police**, too, operates up to six Mi-8MTV-1s with military-style serials (presumably PF-301 to PF-306) and four civil-registered examples (XC-PFD to -PFG).

Mi-8P LZ-CAX (c/n 7666) in full Malta Aircharter colours at Malta-Luqa. This is reportedly ex-Aeroflot (Yakutian CAD) CCCP-22847.

'1024 Yellow' (c/n 1024), the sixth Mi-8T delivered to the Pakistan Army. Interestingly, it has a nose-mounted machine-gun but no pylons.

The Russian helicopters earned high praise both from the men flying them and from the local press. The so-called 'Russian squadron' of the Air Force even received a special award from the authoritative Latin American aviation magazine *Revistaero* for services rendered in dealing with the aftermath of a hurricane which swept through several Mexican states in the autumn of 1997. For nearly 20 days the Mi-8s were in operation round the clock, transporting 1,400 tons (3,086,400 lb) of cargo and airlifting hundreds of civilians out of the affected areas.

Mongolia

The **Mongolian People's Army Air Force** operated an unknown number of Mi-8s. Some were former Soviet Army aircraft; the helicopters wore serials based on the c/ns and had the national *zoyombo* markings painted over the existing red stars. Known serials are 711, 910, 0719 (Mi-8S), 3118, 3194 and 4747. At least 12 others were quasi-civil; some of these were camouflaged while others wore the colours of **MIAT Mongolian Airlines** – which, true enough, also operated several Mi-8Ps/Mi-8Ts on feeder routes. It is known that at least 11 examples were delivered new to Mongolia.

Mozambique

More than 25 Mi-8s of an unspecified version (probably armed Mi-8Ts) were delivered to the Mozambique Air Force (FPA – *Força Popular Aérea de Moçambique*). The helicopters appear to be serialled consecutively from 050 to 075.

Myanmar

The Myanmar Air Force (*Tamdaw Lay*) took delivery of 12 *Hips* in October 1997, including Mi-8MTs serialled 66-07 and 66-08.

Nepal

This country with extreme hot-and-high conditions and lots of 'hellipads' (ie, helipads with extremely difficult approach conditions!) is one place where the Mi-17 really comes into its own. In the mid-1990s 12 examples of the type were operated by a selection of Nepalese airlines, including **Nepal Air Helicopters**, **Asian Airlines**, **Everest Air**, **Air Ananya** and **Gorkha Airlines**.

Additionally, a number of Mi-17-1Vs was delivered to the **Royal Army of Nepal**; these include RAN-36 and RAN-37.

New Zealand

Heli Harvest operated three Moldovan-registered Mi-8MTV-1s (ER-MHA, -MHH and -MHZ) leased in 2000, plus a sister ship registered RA-25488 leased from Ikar Aircompany and Mi-8MTV RA-70870 leased from the Mil' OKB.

Nicaragua

The Nicaraguan Air Force (FAS – *Fuerza Aérea Sandinista*) took delivery of an estimated 26 Mi-8TVKs by 1988 (apparently serialled from 261 to 286). From that year onwards they were followed by 48 *Hip-Hs* (mostly armed Mi-17-1Vs) serialled 287 to 334. The helicopters operated from Augusto César Sandino Airport, Managua.

After the end of the war and the ousting of Daniel Ortega the Nicaraguan Air Force was renamed *Fuerza Aérea Ejército de Nicaragua* and some of the Mi-8s were sold as surplus. An example serialled EPS 334, however, served as the presidential helicopter of the new head of state, Violeta Barrios de Chamorro.

Pakistan

The Pakistan Army Aviation Corps was one of the more unlikely customers for the Mi-8. Starting in 1968, the No.4 Army Aviation Squadron at Rawalpindi-Qasim AB took delivery of at least 23 Mi-8Ts, two Mi-8MTVs and seven Mi-17-1Vs.

Papua New Guinea

Hevi Lift (*sic*) operated Mi-171 RA-27101 leased from Vladivostokavia.

The Palestine

In 1994, as the Middle Eastern peace process progressed to the point of Israel allowing the Palestinian state striving for sovereignty to have its own aviation, the Palestinian Administration received two ex-Yemeni Mi-8PSs (which had been operated for the Palestine Liberation Organisation up to then, as it was). Under the arrangement agreed upon by ICAO the helicopters were placed on the Egyptian civil register as SU-YAA and SU-YAB; there have been speculations that the letters 'YA' reserved for Palestinian aircraft stood for Yasser Arafat! Two more VIP *Hips*, Mi-8MTs SU-YAF and SU-YAG, joined the fleet in 1996, and a fifth (Mi-8MT SU-YAL) was added shortly afterwards. Regrettably all three Mi-8MTs were destroyed at Gaza Strip airport on 3rd and 13th December 2001 in an Israeli punitive attack launched in the wake of terrorist attacks against civilian targets in Haifa and Jerusalem.

Peru

Peru was the first South American nation to operate the Mi-8. The country was traditionally on good terms with the Soviet Union, and the first two Mi-8Ts delivered in September 1970 were ex-Aeroflot machines supplied free of charge 'to strengthen the ties of friendship', which was not uncommon in Soviet times.

The vast majority of Peruvian Mi-8s were military operated. The **Peruvian Air Force** (FAP – *Fuerza Aérea del Peru*, also called *Fuerza Aérea Peruana* in some sources) received at least ten Mi-8Ts with serials ranging from FAP-626 to FAP-678; four quasi-civil examples are also known, though they probably had military serials before. Similarly, they were followed by at least ten Mi-8MTs in full military markings (known serials range from 603 to 626 and 636), plus at least ten quasi-civil examples. The *Hips* are operated by Grupo Aéreo 3 at Lima-Callao AB.

Most military examples were delivered to the **Peruvian Army** (*Ejército Peruano*) which operated nearly 100 Mi-8Ts serialled in the EP-5xx series and at least 60 Mi-8MTs serialled in the EP-6xx series. At least three ex-Hungarian examples, including 471, are known to be in service with the **Peruvian Navy** (*Marina Peruana*). The **Peruvian Police** (*Policia Nacional del Peru*) also received two Mi-8MTs and six Mi-8MTV-1s (PNP-501 to PNP-508).

Civil operators included **Helisur** with at least two Mi-8MTV-1s (OB-1585/OB-1586), **Helicusco** with Mi-8MTV-1s OB-1581/OB-1691 and Mi-171 OB-1639, **Aviasur** with Mi-8AMT OB-1582 (later reregistered OB-1668), Mi-8MTVs OB-1662 and OB-1663, and **Amazon Helicopters** with Mi-8AMT OB-1646. Also, the **government flight** operated a Mi-8S with the old-style registration OB-E-966.

Poland

The Mi-8's Polish history began in December 1967 when the **Polish Air Force** (PWL – *Polskie Wojsko Lotnicze*) took delivery of its first

Above: Orange-painted Peruvian Air Force Mi-8T OB-E-996 at Lima-Callao. The flightdeck section is painted a lighter Dayglo orange.

Mi-8T SP-SWU (c/n 10638) was one of six operated by the Polish Aeropol air services agency. It was previously operated by the Instalbud construction agency as SP-ITK.

Seen here in the smart red/white livery with Rzeczpospolita Polska (Republic of Poland) titles it currently wears, Mi-8PS '620 Red' (c/n 10620) is one of several operated by the so-called 'Papal squadron' of the Polish Air Force's Government flight (36. SPLT) at Warsaw-Okecie.

two Mi-8Ts. Of the 62 'first-generation' *Hips* delivered by mid-1983, most were Mi-8Ts in armed assault configuration operated by the 37. PST (*Pulk Smiglowców Transportowych*) at Leznica Wielka and the transport helicopter regiment at Warsaw-Bemowo. These were serialled 314, 414, 0614, 720, 523, 606 to 612, 614 to 616, 621 to 626, 628, 636 to 645, 647 to 649 and 651 to 661. Mi-8Ts serialled 902, 908 and 8151 have also been reported.

13 other examples (613, 617 to 620, 627 and 629 to 635) were Mi-8Ps and Mi-8Ss, and all but two of them served with the 36. SPLT (*Specjalny Pulk Lotnictwa Transportowego* – special transport air regiment) at Warsaw-Okecie tasked with government VIP transport duties. These helicopters wore a colour scheme patterned on that of LOT Polish Airlines, later replaced by a smart livery in the national colours of red and white with 'Rzeczpospolita Polska'/'Republic of Poland' titles. The helicopter squadron of the 36. SPLT was known colloquially as the *papieska eskadra* ('papal squadron') because on several occasions it supported the travels of Pope John Paul II during his pilgrimages to Poland (including 2nd-10th June 1979 and 4-17th June 1999).

Between December 1987 and December 1989 the PWL purchased eight new Mi-8MTs from Aviaexport (serialled 602 to 608 and 701). The coinciding serials gave rise to considerable confusion, causing some Mi-8Ts to be reported as Mi-8MTs '609' to '618' which never existed.

Currently most military examples have been transferred to the Polish Army and are operated by the 37. DL (*Dywizjon Lotniczy* – aviation division) at Tomaszów-Mazowiecki and the 1. PZSL (*Pulk Zmieszany Smiglowcowy Łącznikowy* – Composite Liaison Helicopter Regiment). A single example ('656') converted to Mi-8RL CSAR configuration serves with the LGPR (*Lotnicza Grupa Poszukiwawczo-Ratownicza* – SAR Air Group) at Bydgoszcz.

Several Mi-8Ts and Mi-8MTs were transferred to the Polish Navy, serving with Squadron C of 1. DLMW (*Dywizjon Lotniczy Marynarki Wojennej* – naval aviation division) at Gdynia-Babie Doly and performing SAR duties. These include Mi-8MT '0608' dubbed 'Big Brother' (and sometimes referred to as 'Mi-17T') and Mi-8MTV-1 '5528' bought second-hand in the CIS.

Additionally, several *Hips* went to the Polish Ministry of the Interior (MSW – *Ministerstwo Spraw Wewnątrznych*). They served with the 103. PL NJW MSW (*Pulk Lotniczy Nadwislanskich Jednostek Wojskowych* – Air Regiment of the Wisla Armed Forces Formations); outwardly the MoI helicopters could be identified by the blue/white band around the tailboom. In 2003 Mi-8S '635' and Mi-8T '659' were registered PL-40XP and PL-41XP respectively, using the special PL- prefix allocated to police aircraft (instead of the official SP- nationality prefix).

In addition to their primary duties (transportation of military personnel and materiel), the PWL Mi-8Ts quickly found use as flying cranes in the interests of civilian organisations. The first such operation took place on 15th April 1969 when a crew captained by Col. Boleslaw Andrychowski installed floodlights on the roof of a railway depot in Grochów. Perhaps the most interesting cases when PWL *Hips* were used in this capacity were in 1972 when military pilots performed Operations *Palisada* I and *Palisada* II, installing 150 lightning protection masts at the Czechowicy oil refinery; each mast was 27 m (88 ft) tall and weighed 3 tons (6,610 lb). On another occasion a Mi-8 lifted power lines crossing the harbour channel at Gdansk to let a floating dock pass; the entire operation took 15 minutes.

In 1973 the **Instalbud** (ie, *instalacja i budowa* – installation and construction) organisation was established in Nasielsk near Warsaw for performing complex construction work. Among other things, it operated Mi-8s leased from the PWL as required, including a Mi-8T registered SP-ITK. The largest civilian operator of the type in Poland was the **Aeropol Air Services Agency** (*Przedsiebiorstwo Uslug Lotniczych Aeropol*) which operated Mi-8Ts SP-SWR, -SWU and -SZT, plus Mi-8Ps SP-SWS, -SWT (later reregistered SP-SWW) and -SZR. Another air services provider flying the type was the **Dakomat Air Services Enterprise** (*Zespol Uslug Lotniczych Aeropol*) operating Mi-8Ts SP-FEF to -FEI, -FEK, -FEL, -FER and -FES (all but the latter one were leased from the Air Force). These enterprises undertook various duties, such as urgent delivery of spares when combine harvesters went unserviceable in the field and time was crucial.

Mi-8T SP-SWR was later sold to the **Polish Medical Aviation** (*Lotnicze Pogotowie*

Ratunkowe) and accordingly reregistered SP-SXR; the second individual letter of the registration on Polish ambulance aircraft is always an X, symbolising the Red Cross. In 1997-98 the airline **White Eagle Aviation** operated Mi-8T SP-FSZ leased in the Ukraine.

Romania

Starting in mid-1968, the **Romanian Air Force** (*Fortele Aeriene ale Republicii Socialiste Române*) received 22 Mi-8Ts (04, 05, 10, 705 to 707 and 712 to 727) and 13 Mi-8PSs (03, 08, 708 to 711, 728 to 732, 735 and 736). The utility version saw service with *Grupul* 94 *Elicoptere* at Alexeni, while the VIP helicopters belonged to the Air Force's Presidential Flight based at Bucharest-Baneasa.

In 1984-85 the fleet was expanded by the purchase of five Mi-8MTs serialled 102, 103 and 107 to 109. To these was added a rather unusual *Hip-H* serialled 110; bought second-hand via Hungary, the aircraft was originally a Mi-17-1VA flying hospital but was converted to VIP configuration with external tanks from a MiG-21 fighter (!) to extend range!

In 1991 two Mi-8PSs and two Mi-8MTs were transferred to the recently established airline **Romavia** (the Romanian government flight) as YR-MLA to -MLD, returning to the Air Force and regaining their former serials in 1992. Eight *Hips*, including the abovementioned Mi-17-1VA, were transferred to the **Romanian Police** in 1991.

Apart from that, the Mi-8s were occasionally operated by civil organisations. Thus, an agency named **CSS** leased Mi-8P YR-EVP No.1 and Mi-8T YR-EVR No.1 in 1971-76. With the Romanian flag carrier **TAROM** (*Transporturile Aeriene Române*), it was vice versa: YR-EVP No.2 was a 'T and YR-EVR No.2 was a 'P (the time frame in this case was 1983-85). **Aviaţia Utilitara** leased Mi-8T YR-EVB and Mi-8P YR-EVI in 1971-76.

Rwanda

On 24-27th October 1999 the Rwandan Air Force (*Force Aérienne Rwandaise*) took delivery of two Mi-17MDs serialled RAF-1707 and RAF-0210. Two more Kazan'-built Mi-17s, including a radar-nosed Mi-172 in presidential VVIP configuration (RAF-1907), were delivered later. Together with two Mi-24s purchased earlier these were the first aircraft operating in Rwanda after the civil war of 1994 in which every previously existing aircraft had been destroyed.

Sierra Leone

In 1995 **Ibis Air Transport** owned two Mi-17s registered 9L-LBD/'1 Black' and 9L-LBE/'2 Black'. Delivered via the UK, these were operated by the mercenary organisation Executive Outcomes during the civil war in Sierra Leone, taking part in combat operations against the Revolutionary United Front rebels.

Starting in 1997, **Paramount Airlines** operated at least three Mi-8s – 9L-LBO No.1 (the registration was reused twice on other aircraft types), 9L-LBT No.2 (registration previously used on a different types) and 9L-LBX.

Slovakia

With the division of the Czech/Slovak Federal Republic into two separate states on 1st January 1993 and the division of the 'old' CzAF, the 'new' **Slovak Air Force** (*Slovenské Vojenské Létectvo*) received a substantial portion of the *Hip* fleet – six Mi-8Ts (0817/1132/1932/2032/2832/3932), two Mi-8Ps (0210 and 0837), one Mi-8PPA (7520) and 17 Mi-8MTs. Most of the *Hip-Hs* continued in service with the 4. VrP at Sliac, which later moved to Presov when the latter base reopened after repairs in December 1992. The others and the *Hip-Bs* were operated by the 2. ZmDLP (*zmiesany dopravni létecky pluk* – composite transport air regiment) at Presov. Two of the Mi-8MTs were converted locally to the indigenous Mi-17Z-2 ECM version.

The **Slovak Police** likewise inherited three Mi-8Ps – B-8231, B-8427 and B-8532.

On the civil scene, the Mi-8 was operated by **Air Transport Europe** (OM-DXO, -EVA, -MYN, -OYO, -YZO and -ZXP) and **Tech-Mont Helicopter Co.** (Mi-8T OM-AXZ).

South African Republic

A large number of Mi-8MTVs leased from Russian airlines was operated by **Court Helicopters**, **Eagle Airways** and **Heyns Helicopters** in 1995-99, operating from Cape Town and Nelspruit. Eight of them received South African registrations (ZS-RIP and -RIR to -RIX) while operated by the latter lessee – and, as already mentioned, ZS-RIP crashed (Rest In Peace!).

'0843 White' (c/n 108M43), a Slovak Air Force Mi-8MT.

Spain

In addition to its own helicopter fleet, **Helicopteros de Sureste** operated several Bulgarian-registered Mi-8MTVs wet-leased from Air Scorpio in 1995. Also, the **Spanish Civil Protection Agency** (*Protección Civil*) leased Mi-8MTV-1 RA-25471 from Sochispetsavia in mid-1996; the helicopter was stationed on the Canary Islands for the duration.

Sri Lanka

In 1993-98 the **Sri Lanka Air Force** (SLAF) obtained 12 Mi-17s serialled CH-587 to CH-599; the first three machines arrived on 15th March 1993 from Kazan' aboard an An-124-100 Ruslan heavy-lift aircraft belonging to Volga-Dnepr Cargo Airlines. The last six were built by U-UAPO and wore a different camouflage scheme initially (the Kazan'-built aircraft were brown, while the Ulan-Ude built examples had a bluish hue), although all surviving SLAF Mi-17s were later repainted to a common standard. The *Hips* were operated by the 6th Helicopter Wing based at Vavuniya.

Additionally, a Mi-8P registered 4R-ATK was operated by **Ace Air Tours** in 1995. This airline also leased Mi-8P RA-24296 from the Mil' OKB.

Sudan

At least 11 Mi-8s were in service with the Sudanese Air Force (*al Quwwat al-Jawwiya as-Sudaniya*; also reported as *Silakh al-Jawwiya as-Sudaniya*). Their origin is unclear, since Sudan did not have 'friendly nation' status with the Soviet Union and it is highly improbable that so many could have been captured from Libya during the war of 1983-87 and retained.

Swaziland

Air Pass operated two Mi-8PSs registered 3D-MIA and -MIO in 1998. 'Pass' was an acronym for Pietersburg Aviation Services & Systems; this was because, though nominally a Swazi company, the airline was based at Pietersburg-Gateway International airport, South Africa.

Syria

About 50 Mi-8s, at least some of which were ex-Soviet Army Aviation aircraft, were delivered to the Syrian Air Force (*al Quwwat al-Jawwiya al Arabiya as-Suriya*). The helicopters are based at Aleppo. Known serials are 354, 365, 376, 381 to 383, 390 to 392, 641, 650, 1281, 1289, 1295, 1358, 1370, 1390, 1395 and 1396.

Turkey

The Turkish civil air scene changes almost too rapidly to keep track of it. Starting in the late 1980s, several airlines (many of which are no longer extant) leased Mi-8s in the Soviet Union and CIS as required. These were **Han Air** (TC-HAK, -HAL), **Doruk Air** (TC-HDA to -HDH, -HDK), Emair (TC-HEM, -HER), **Karadeniz Hava Yollari** (TC-HNA), **Mas Air** (TC-HSA, -HSB), **PAN Havacilik**, **Saglam Air** (TC-HAG, -HIS) and **Trans Air** (TC-HTC, -HUA and -HUS).

On 27th March 1991 Mas Air Mi-8PS-11s TC-HSA and TC-HSB were involved in a bizarre incident at Istanbul-Ataköy heliport when members of the Dev-Sol leftist organisation tied up the local guards and placed explosives under the helicopters, destroying 'HSB and causing minor damage to 'HSA. This terrorist attack was an act of revenge against the airline's owner Ali Sen, the boss of Sen Holding, for firing workers in Izmit.

However, Turkey also has its own *Hips*. On 25th November 1995 the **Turkish Rural Police** (*Jandarma*) took delivery of 19 Mi-17-1Vs serialled J792M01 to J792M19. Two examples (J792M03 and J792M18) were delivered in MEDEVAC configuration, three others (J792M06, J792M11 and J792M19) were in armed assault configuration; the others were ordinary utility helicopters.

Uganda

At least two Mi-8Ts were supplied to the Uganda Army Air Force before 1982. By 1996 they were replaced by seven Mi-17s serialled AF 601 through AF 607.

United Kingdom

Four Mi-8s were placed on the UK register in 1995. A company called **Corporate Management** had two Mi-17s registered G-BVXN and G-BVXO; both were sold to Sierra Leone in 1995. Another company, **Orbit Resources**, registered Mi-8Ts G-BWHX and G-BWHZ; both were sold to Swaziland in 1997 and their subsequent fate is unknown (they did *not* become 3D-MIA and -MIO mentioned above).

USA

The **US Army's Operational Test and Evaluation Command** (OPTEC) established in November 1990 – or, more precisely, the OPTEC Threat Support Activity (OTSA) at Biggs Army Air Field, Fort Bliss, Texas – obtained a pair of Mi-8Ts and three Mi-8MTVs/Mi-17s in armed assault configuration. Their origins and previous identities are mostly classified, although one of the Mi-17s is a captured Iraqi aircraft. Besides their home base, they operate from Fort Polk, Louisiana, and are widely used to represent the adversary during various exercises such as *Red Flag*, *Green Flag* and *Roving Sands*.

On the civil scene, back in 1967 **Petroleum Helicopters, Inc.** purchased a Mi-8 registered N16555, using it to support oil prospecting operations in Peru. Much later, in 2002, a company called **R. J. Harroff Businesses** reserved the registrations N353MA and N393MA for two Mi-8MTV-1s, while the registrations N26197, N26277, N26281, N26299, N26308, N26330 were similarly reserved for six sister ships by **Delaware Corp.**; it is not known if these registrations were actually taken up.

Venezuela

An airline called **Helicopteros del Caribe** had three Mi-8MTV-1s registered YV-866C, YV-867C and YV-868CP. Another Mi-8 in service with an **unidentified Venezuelan operator** was registered YV-960C.

Vietnam

The **Vietnam People's Air Force** (VPAF, or *Không Quan Nham Dan Viêt Nam*) took delivery of more than 60 Mi-8Ts and 'PSs. The helicopters wear four-digit serials which may appear to match the c/ns but actually have nothing in common with them; for instance, '7812 Red' is not Kazan'-built c/n 7812 but Ulan-Ude built c/n 9732601!

The other Mi-8 operator in the country was **Hãng Không Viêt Nam** (Vietnam Airlines); in the 1990s its helicopter component became a separate entity called **Service Flight Corporation of Vietnam** (T.C.Ty Bay Dich Vu Viêt Nam). Its fleet included Mi-8Ts VN-8402/VN-8404, Mi-8MTV-1 VN-7846, Mi-17s VN-8408, VN-8410 to VN-8412 and VN8417 (no dash), and Mi-172 VN8420.

North Yemen (Yemen Arab Republic)

The Yemen Arab Republic Air Force (YARAF) received more than 30 Mi-8Ts and 'PSs – all of them after 1982. The serials appear to run sequentially from 801 to at least 832, plus 710 and 722 (the latter two are ex-Romanian aircraft).

South Yemen (People's Democratic Republic of Yemen)

The South Yemen Air Force (PDRYAF) got the type ahead of its northern counterpart, with 15 Mi-8s in service by 1982; only one aircraft serialled 110 is known.

Yugoslavia

The Yugoslav Air Force (JRV – *Jugoslovensko Ratno Vazduhoplovstvo*) operated the Mi-8T and Mi-8PS in huge numbers. Judging by the known serials running sequentially from 12202 to 12411, about 220 were delivered. Known bases are Zagreb, Bjelasnica and Vrsac. After the breakup of the Socialist-era Yugoslavia most of the *Hips* were apparently retained by the **'new' Yugoslavia (Serbia and Montenegro)**.

Zambia

Seven Mi-8s serialled AF751 to AF757 were delivered to the Zambian Air Force in 1975.

Chapter 8

...and the Rest of the Gang

Mi-8 Versus the Competitors

In today's world, all-out military confrontation between superpowers and World War Three are no longer a likely scenario but regional conflicts, international drug trafficking and, in recent years, international terrorism have become the principal threats. In these conditions most nations view the formation of rapid reaction forces as a top priority; hence measures have to be taken to enhance the armed forces' ability to rapidly deploy to a given spot for safeguarding national interests. This includes such tasks as drug control operations and operations against illegal migration or infiltration by guerrilla forces. These tasks are best solved by modern multi-role medium-lift helicopters which can carry personnel and materiel alike, as well as perform riot control and counter-insurgency (COIN) operations.

For several years the Mi-8MTV (Mi-17-1V) and its more modern derivatives have been competing in this market segment with the Sikorsky S-70 (UH-60A Black Hawk) and its versions and the Eurocopter (née Aérospatiale) AS 332L Super Puma/AS 532UL Cougar. These are twin-turbine helicopters of somewhat smaller size and weight possessing comparable engine power to that of the 'first-generation' Mi-8 (but slightly smaller than that the Mi-8MT/Mi-17). Developed under the UTTAS (Utility Tactical Transport Assault System) as a Bell UH-1 replacement, the UH-60A first flew in 17th October 1974 and entered production in 1978, finding wide use with the US armed forces and being supplied to a few selected nations. The AS 332 was brought out as a 'bigger and better SA 330 Puma', making its first flight on 13th September 1978 and achieving production status in 1980.

In terms of numbers the Soviet helicopter got ahead of the competitors; as already noted, more than 4,000 copies of the Mi-8/Mi-17 family have been exported, seeing service in various regions of the world with widely varying terrain and climatic conditions. Apart from the earlier development/service entry dates, this is partly due to political reasons and... er... aggressive pricing.

As mentioned previously, the Mi-8MT/Mi-8MTV (Mi-17) is available in basic transport, armed assault/transport (Mi-8MTV-2/Mi-17-1V), anti-tank capable (Mi-8AMTSh/Mi-17Sh), flying surgery hospital (Mi-17-1VA), passenger (Mi-172) and specialised ECM and command/control versions. The foreign competitors offer comparable mission variety: the H-60 comes in basic transport and assault/transport configurations, the latter featuring an external stores support system (ESSS); other versions include the HH-60 Night Hawk combat search and rescue (CSAR) version, the MH-60 special forces version, the EH-60A ECM version, the VH-60A VIP helicopter for Presidential use, the very different SH-60 Seahawk ASW version etc. The Super Puma is offered as the AS 332B1 and AS 332M1 military transport version seating 23 or 25 troops respectively, the AS 332F1 naval anti-shipping strike version, the AS 332C commercial passenger/cargo helicopter and the stretched AS 332L1 heliliner seating up to 24 passengers, and so on. The more advanced

Five brand-new Mi-17MDs await delivery to the Chinese People's Liberation Army at Kazan'-Osnovnoy (note that the 'Danger, VHF' inscription on the radomes is in Chinese characters).

The Aérospatiale AS 332M1 Super Puma is the Mi-8MT's French counterpart. This is Swiss Air Force/4th Air Regiment T-317 (c/n 2337) performing at the RIAT-2000 airshow at RAF Cottesmore on 23rd July 2000.

AS 532 Cougar can carry up to 27 persons or haul up to 4.5 tons (9,920 lb) of cargo.

If we compare some design features of the three helicopters, the bigger Mi-8 has a rather larger cabin and was conceived for straight-in loading from the start, with rear clamshell doors allowing it to carry bulky loads such as vehicles and field guns internally. In contrast, the French and American machines have side loading doors only and can only carry bulky loads such as vehicles externally slung. On the other hand, the AS 332/AS 532 and the UH-60 have two sliding cabin doors for quicker embarkation/disembarkation while transporting troops, compared to which the single port side entry door and rear clamshell doors of the Mi-8 may be less convenient. The Russian engineers have learned this lesson: the latest versions (the Kazan'-built Mi-8MTV-5/Mi-17MD and the Ulan-Ude-built Mi-171) feature a second entry door to starboard.

The Mi-8MT *et seq*. and the S-70 (H-60) both feature an auxiliary power unit, while the AS 332 has none. The Mi-8MTV's APU is a valuable asset, allowing reliable engine starting at up to 4,000 m (13,120 ft) ASL. Also, the Mi-8MT *et seq*. and the Super Puma have dust/debris filters fitted as standard, whereas on the Black Hawk they are an optional feature and are not fitted to the commercial S-70 and the VH-60A.

Fuel system design is another aspect. The Mi-8 family has strap-on fuel tanks as standard; these reduce the risk of an internal fire if hit by ground fire but are vulnerable in the event of a crash landing when the helicopter rolls over. In contrast, the AS 332/AS 532 and the S-70 (H-60) have underfloor fuel tankage as standard; in the case of the UH-60 the tanks are made crashworthy and protected by armour (crash-resistant/self-sealing fuel tanks are optional on the AS 332). All three types have provisions for internal long-range tanks. Additionally, the AS 332/AS 532 and the UH-60 have provisions for external tanks (in the case of the Black Hawk, if the ESSS is installed); the Mi-17's external stores pylons are 'dry', but special-mission or VIP Mi-8/Mi-17s can be fitted with external tanks to order. Additionally, unlike the Russian and French machines, the HH-60A CSAR version features in-flight refuelling capability.

As regards weapons, the UH-60 comes closer to the Mi-8/Mi-17 than the French counterpart, featuring provisions for pintle-mounted 7.62-mm machine-guns firing through the cabin doors while the ESSS allows 16 TOW or Hellfire ATGMs to be carried. The AS 332B1 and AS 332M1 can carry gun and rocket pods, while the AS 332F1 is armed with the powerful AM39 Exocet anti-shipping missile. The military versions of all three helicopters have provisions for active and passive IRCM equipment for protection against heat-seeking missiles (IR jammers and exhaust/air mixers to reduce the heat signature).

As a transport helicopter the Mi-17-1V is about equal to the AS 332M1 and has about 15-20% better performance than the UH-60. This is because the American helicopter's payload is nearly 35% less and the higher cruising speed cannot make up for this. The situation changes if the mission to be fulfilled is assault or troop insertion/extraction. Here the Mi-17-1V comes out on top, which is evident during hot-and-high operations. The latest versions of the Mi-8 can land reconnaissance and search groups at altitudes up to 4,000 m – performance that still has to be matched by foreign counterparts.

Yet, however super the Super Puma may be, both it and the Black Hawk were developed more than 20 years ago, and of course Western helicopter design does not sit idle. During the last decade three new medium-lift helicopters have been developed and flight-tested both sides of the Atlantic Ocean – the NH90 ('new helicopter for the '90s') developed by the NH Industries four-nation consortium, the Sikorsky S-92 Helibus and the three-engined EH Industries (now Westland-Agusta) EH101. The latter type is in production and has entered service in the UK (as the Merlin) and Canada (as the CH-149 Cormorant), while the other two are due to complete trials imminently. In addition to the latest state of the art in avionics and engine design

The Westland-Agusta (née EH Industries) EH101 is one of the more modern competitors. Here, Canadian Forces/103rd Sqn CH-149 Cormorant 149906 is seen at Farnborough International 2000.

these aircraft incorporate some of the thinking that went into the Mi-8, featuring a rear loading ramp/door. As if this were not enough, a competitor looms on the home market – the Mi-38 (which, true enough, has been making slow progress because of the post-Soviet chaos and economic problems).

Of course, the foreign helicopters have their strong points, including more fuel-efficient engines, more capable avionics and better overall manufacturing standards. (It is true that Soviet aircraft generally lack finesse; however, it is equally true that surface finish matters little in a war where the reputed Soviet design philosophy of 'make it simple, make it strong, but make it work' comes into its own.) Also, the Mi-8/Mi-17 may well qualify for the title of the World's Most Heavily Armed Chopper, and the weapons arsenal is periodically updated to meet the requirements of modern warfare.

Thus, casting aside the political motives which inevitably influence military equipment sales, we can say with assurance that the Mi-17-1V and its follow-on versions stand a fair chance against their Western counterparts because they surpass them in a number of important parameters. These include the ability to withstand harsh environments and tolerate rough handling. The Mi-8's durability and ease of maintenance and repair have become legendary. Any failed component, even the main gearbox, can be replaced in the field, using a minimum of support facilities and tools. No Western helicopter can boast the same.

The price factor is not to be dismissed, too. Currently the Mi-8 is underpriced on the world helicopter market, with a flyaway price around US$ 3.7 million; some industry experts claim the price could be easily increased by at least 50%. In comparison, the closest present-day competitor – the AS 332 – costs around US$ 11 million while being inferior to the Mi-8 in certain respects.

Specifications comparison of modern medium-lift helicopters

	Mil' Mi-17MD (Mi-8MTV-5)	Eurocopter AS 332L2	Sikorsky UH-60L Super Puma Mk II	NH Industries NH90	Westland-Agusta EH101	Sikorsky S-92	Mil' Mi-38 (provisional)
Country of origin	Russia	France	USA	Germany / France / Netherlands / Italy	UK/Italy	USA	Russia
Maiden flight	n.a.	6-2-1987	10-1974	18-12-1995	9-10-1987	23-12-1998	–
Production entry	1998	1992	n.a.	n.a.	2000	n.a.	–
Crew	2-3	2	2	2	2	2	2
No.of troops	36	29	14	20	30*	22	30*
Powerplant	2 x Klimov TV3-117VM	2 x Makila 1A2 Turboméca	2 x General Electric T700-GE-700	2 x Rolls-Royce/ Turboméca RTM.322-01/9 or General Electric T700-GE-T6A	3 x Rolls-Royce/ Turboméca RTM.322-01/8 or General Electric T700-GE-T6A	2 x General Electric CT7-8	2 x Pratt & Whitney Canada PW127T/S†
Take-off power, shp	2 x 2,200	2 x 1,845	2 x 1,560	2 x 2,200(2 x 2,040)	3 x 2,240 (3 x 2,040)	2 x 2,520	n.a.
Normal TOW, kg (lb)	n.a.	8,350 (18,410)	9,185 (20,250)	9,100 (20,065)	13,000 (28,660)	n.a.	13,460 (29,670)
MTOW, kg (lb)	13,500 (29,760)	9,300 (20,500)	11,100 (24,470)	10,000 (22,040)	14,600 (32,190)	12,840 (28,300)	15,600 (34,390)
Length, rotors turning	25.24 m (82 ft 9¾ in)	18.73 m (61 ft 4½ in)	n.a.	19.56 m (64 ft 2 in)	22.81 m (74 ft 10 in)	20.88 (68 ft 6 in)	n.a.
Fuselage length	18.99 m (62 ft 3⅝ in)	n.a.	12.6 m (41 ft 4 in)	16.14 m (52 ft 11½ in)	19.53 m (64 ft 1 in)	17.12 m (56 ft 2 in)	19.7 m (64 ft 7½ in)
Height on ground	4.755 m (15 ft 7½ in)	4.92 m (16 ft 1¾ in)	n.a.	5.31 m (17 ft 5 in)	6.62 m (21 ft 8⅝ in)	5.46 m (17 ft 11 in)	5.13 m (68 ft 10¾ in)
Main rotor diameter	21.294 m (69 ft 10⅜ in)	15.6 m (51 ft 2⅛ in)	16.36 m (53 ft 8 in)	16.3 m (53 ft 4 in)	18.59 m (60 ft 0 in)	17.71 m (58 ft 1½ in)	21.0 m (68 ft 10¾ in)
Tail rotor diameter	3.908 m (12 ft 9½ in)	3.05 m (10 ft 0 in)	n.a.	3.2 m (10 ft 6 in)	4.01 m (13 ft 2 in)	3.35 m (10 ft 11⅝ in)	3.84 m (12 ft 7¼ in)
Internal payload, kg (lb)	4,000 (8,820)	4,000 (8,820)	2,560 (5,640)	2,000 (4,410)	5,440 (12,000)	n.a.	6,000 (13,230)
Payload, kg (lb)	5,000 (11,020)	2,730/4,500 §	(6,010/9,920)	3,630(8,000)	2,500 (5,510)	3,120(6,880)	n.a.
Cabin volume, m^3 (cu. ft)	23 (812)	19 (670)	11.6 (409)	11.8 (416)	27.5 (971)	16.9 (596)	28.94 (1,022)
Hovering ceiling, m (ft)	4,000 (13,120)	3,100 (10,170)	3,200 (10,500)	3,500 (11,480)	3,900 (12,795)	3,300 (10,830)	2,990‡ (9,000)
Service ceiling, m (ft)	6,000 (19,685)	5,200 (17,060)	5,800 (19,030)	4,250 (13,940)	3,100 (10,170)	4,600 (15,090)	6,500 (21,325)
Top speed, km/h (mph)	262 (162)	280 (174)	296 (184)	290 (180)	309 (192)	290 (180)	275 (170)
Cruising speed, km/h (mph)	240 (149)	250 (155)	260 (161)	260 (161)	260 (161)	260 (161)	n.a.
Range, km (miles)	n.a.	870 (540)	600 (373)	796 (494)	1,019 (633)	n.a.	1,300 (805)

* Number of passengers in airline configuration

† Klimov TVa-3000 turboshafts with a take-off rating of 2,500 shp and a contingency rating of 3,750 shp envisaged originally

‡ Out of ground effect

§ Internal/slung load

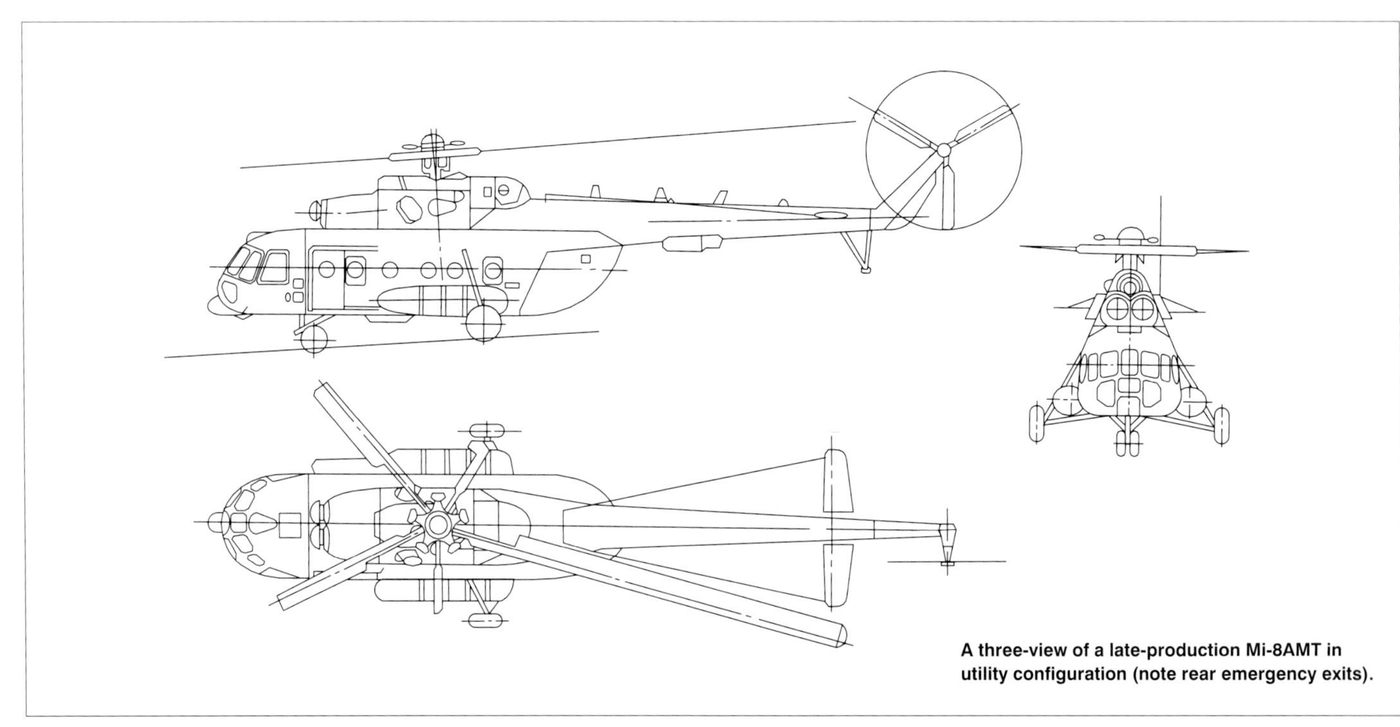
A three-view of a late-production Mi-8AMT in utility configuration (note rear emergency exits).

A three-view of the Mi-8AMTSh.

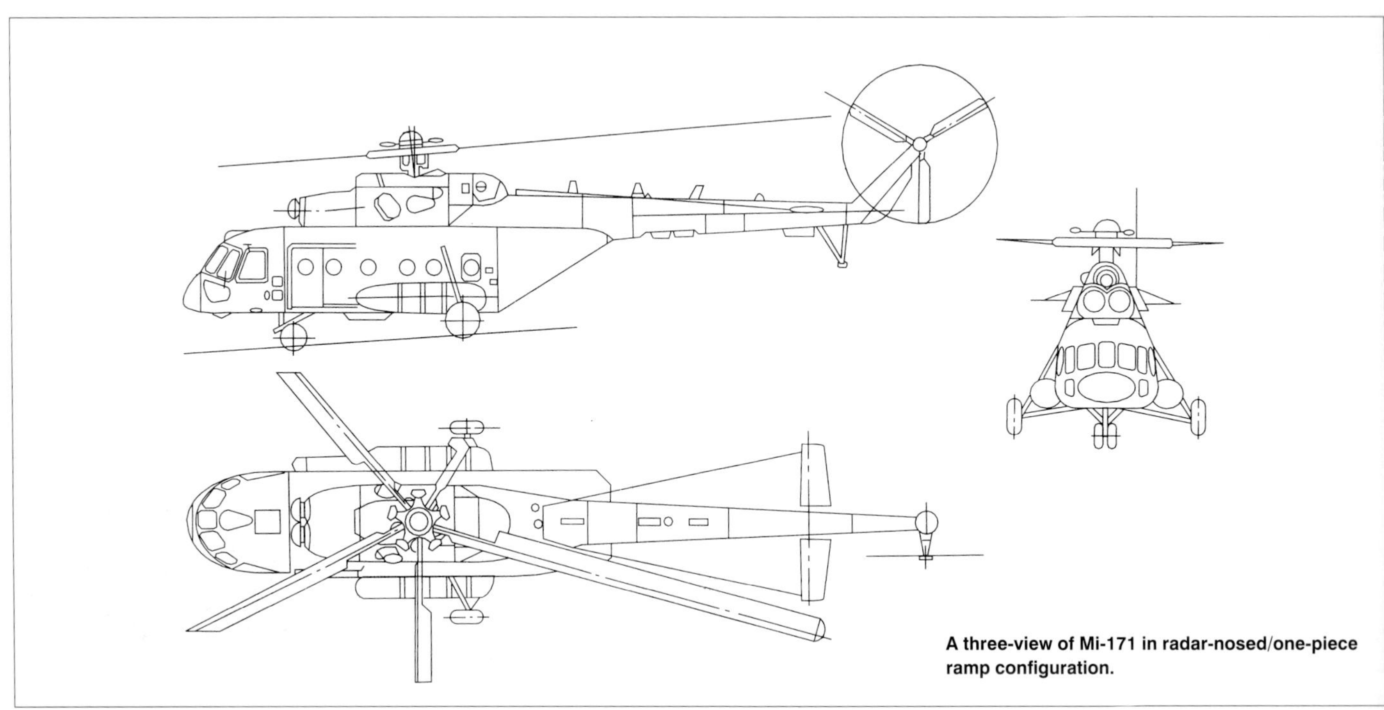
A three-view of Mi-171 in radar-nosed/one-piece ramp configuration.

Above: The V-8 single-engined prototype (c/n 0101) during an early stage of trials. The basic colour scheme is patterned on that of late-production Mi-4Ps.

The second prototype (V-8A, 0201) in an early test flight with a four-bladed main rotor and a Mi-4 wooden-bladed tail rotor. Note the unfaired main gear struts.

Above: The V-8AP (CCCP-06181) during trials. This colour scheme was used as standard for production Mi-8Ps until 1973.

An early-production armed Mi-8T (/1968-standard Mi-8TV') in olive drab camouflage with blue undersides; note the flightdeck boarding step to starboard.

Above: A Russian Naval Air Arm Mi-8T coded '51 Yellow' taxies at Ghelendjik, Russia, during one of the biennial Hydro Aviation Shows.

'07 Red', a recently overhauled Russian Air Force Mi-8T in pure utility configuration, takes off past the control tower at Savostleyka AB, an Air Defence Force airfield near Nizhniy Novgorod. The chocolate brown/foliage green camouflage is decidedly non-standard.

Above: Russian Air Force Mi-8S '01 Yellow' (c/n 8433) on display during one of the open days at Kubinka AB where it is based. The unusual olive drab/blue camouflage is noteworthy.

The as-yet uncoded second prototype Mi-18 (later coded '84 Red'; c/n 93114) in armed configuration during initial flight tests.

Above: Mi-8MT '74 Yellow' displays a rather unusual configuration with weapons outriggers but no pylons. The housings for the ASO-2V-02 chaff/flare dispensers on the fuselage sides are empty.

An extremely weathered Russian Air Force Mi-8MTV armed with six UB-32A FFAR pods 'unbuttoned' for maintenance at Ghelendjik. Like the other *Hip* and the Kamov Ka-29TB in the background, it is operated by the Federal Border Guards (note the white identification stripes on the clamshell rear doors or fuselage).

Above: B-8733 (c/n 10833), a Czech Police Mi-8PS, caught by the camera a few seconds before landing. The Czech/Slovak Police Mi-8s wear this red/white colour scheme.

Mi-8S RA27189 (c/n 99357636) in the early days of its 'second life' after rebuild from a crashed Mi-8T. It is seen here at the MAKS-99 airshow in the colours of Krylo Airlines shortly after return from lease to an Egyptian airline which operated it as SU-BML. The helicopter already has a radar but no air conditioner yet.

Above: Polish Air Force Mi-8T '414 White' (c/n 0414) in typical PWL three-tone tactical camouflage at a tactical airfield. This aircraft became an instructional airframe at the technical school in Olesnica, Poland, after retirement.

The first production Mi-8TG, RA-25364 (c/n 98206842), in the static park at the MAKS-93 airshow. Note the absence of the rescue hoist, the yellow-painted LNG pipelines partly protected by covers, and the filament-wound fragmentation prevention layer which prevents the LNG tanks from exploding, should they crack.

Above: Ukrainian Air Force Mi-8T armed with four UB-16-57UMP FFAR pods in the static park of the Aviasvit-XXI airshow at Kiev-Svyatoshino in September 2000. The freshly painted helicopter has been overhauled and upgraded by the Aviakon company in Konotop.

East German Air Force Mi-8PS '739 Black' (c/n 10599) on a paved parking spot in a dispersal area which is just big enough for the aircraft.

Above: This view of Civil Aviation Administration of China Mi-8P 862 (c/n 20255?) clearly shows that the CAAC livery incorporates some elements of the Mi-8Ps' pre-1973 Aeroflot livery (see page 114).

Lithuanian Air Force Mi-8T '03 Blue' (c/n 99253775) makes a demonstration flight at an air fest in Poland; the weapons outriggers are not yet fitted – or already removed. This is another 'undead' aircraft which was rebuilt after a crash at Zoknai on 24th July 1997.

Above: The Mi-8MTV-K flying crane (c/n 95583) at the MosAeroShow-92. The water tanks in the background are meant to be carried by the Mi-26, not the Mi-8.

Hungarian Air Force Mi-8T '10443 Red' (c/n 10443) in post-Communist era markings. The bronze/green camouflage was typical of Mi-8s overhauled at Tököl.

Above: German Navy (Bundesmarine) Mi-8T 93+03 (ex-East German Navy '907 White', c/n 10536) in a special farewell colour scheme.

Mi-8T RA-24282 (c/n 98734415) was converted into a radar-equipped Mi-8S for Moscow-Domodedovo based East Line. It is seen here at its home base during the Civil Aviation 2002 airshow in August 2002; note the external tanks.

Above: EMERCOM of Russia/Tsentrospas Mi-8MTV-1 RA-27181 'Andrey Rozhkov' (c/n 96183) seen flying at Zhukovskiy in 1999 with the clamshell doors removed.

Ukrainian Air Force Mi-8MTV '20 Black' seconded to the United Nations Transitional Authority in Eastern Slavonia (UNTAES) shortly before departing to Klisa.

Above: Gaudily painted Mi-8S RA-24181 of Spetsneftegaz (c/n 98943287) fitted with external tanks is another converted Mi-8T. Note the unusual bulge in the port clamshell door and the twin boxes under the tailboom housing the flight data recorder and cockpit voice recorder.

The Mi-17LL (RA-70880) at the MAKS-95 illustrates the orange/blue version of Aeroflot's 1973-standard livery. Note 'Flight Research Institute' titles and logo.

Above: Malaysian Fire Department Mi-17 M49-02 (c/n 459M01) at Langkawi with flotation bags fitted. The 'BOMBA' titles mean Fire Service. Note the drawing of the local bird known as Pekaka in Malay after which the helicopter is named.

The Mi-17M prototype, RA-70937 (c/n 95448), at the 1993 Paris Air Show with the starboard side flotation bags inflated for demonstration purposes.

Above: Mi-8MTKO '29 Yellow' (c/n 94309) on the display line at Zhukovskiy on 13th August 1999, the day before the official opening of the MAKS-99 airshow.

Mi-8AMTSh RA-25755 No.3 (c/n 59489611121) at Le Bourget in 1999; the helicopter is already repainted but not yet modified. Note that the type has been misspelled as 'Mi-8AMTS'.

We hope you enjoyed this book . . .

Midland Publishing titles are edited and designed by an experienced and enthusiastic team of specialists.

We always welcome ideas from authors or readers for books they would like to see published.

In addition, our associate, Midland Counties Publications, offers an exceptionally wide range of aviation, military, naval and transport books and videos for sale by mail-order worldwide.

For a copy of the appropriate catalogue, or to order further copies of this book, and any other Midland Publishing titles, please write, telephone, fax or e-mail to:

Midland Counties Publications
4 Watling Drive, Hinckley,
Leics, LE10 3EY, England
Tel: (+44) 01455 254 450
Fax: (+44) 01455 233 737
E-mail: midlandbooks@compuserve.com
www.midlandcountiessuperstore.com

US distribution by Specialty Press – see page 2.

Vol.1: Sukhoi S-37 & Mikoyan MFI
1 85780 120 2 £18.95/US $27.95
Vol.2: Flankers: The New Generation
1 85780 121 0 £18.95/US $27.95
Vol.3: Polikarpov's I-16 Fighter
1 85780 131 8 £18.95/US $27.95
Vol.4: Early Soviet Jet Fighters
1 85780 139 3 £19.99/US $29.95
Vol.5: Yakovlev's Piston-Engined Fighters
1 85780 140 7 £19.99/US $29.95
Vol.6: Polikarpov's Biplane Fighters
1 85780 141 5 £18.99/US $27.95

Red Star Volume 7
TUPOLEV Tu-4 SOVIET SUPERFORTRESS

Yefim Gordon and Vladimir Rigmant

At the end of WW2, three Boeing B-29s fell into Soviet hands; from these came a Soviet copy of this famous bomber in the form of the Tu-4. This examines the evolution of the 'Superfortresski' and its further development into the Tu-70 transport. It also covers the civil airliner version, the Tu-75, and Tu-85, the last of Tupolev's piston-engined bombers. Also described are various experimental versions, including the Burlaki towed fighter programme.

Softback, 280 x 215 mm, 128 pages, 225 black/white and 9 colour photographs, plus line drawings
1 85780 142 3 **£18.99/US $27.95**

Red Star Volume 8
RUSSIA'S EKRANOPLANS
Caspian Sea Monster and other WIG Craft

Sergey Komissarov

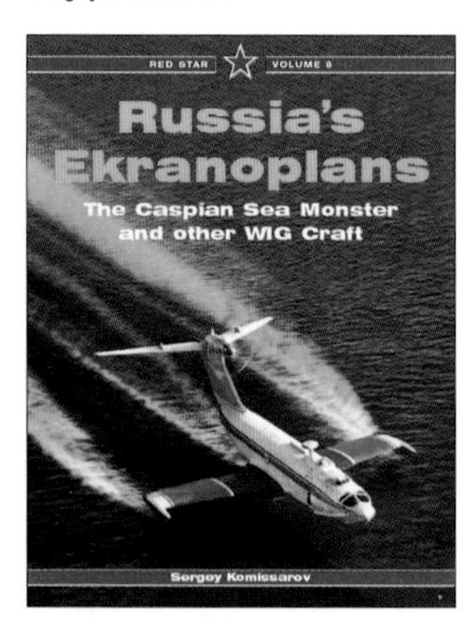

Known as wing-in-ground effect (WIGE) craft or by their Russian name of ekranoplan, these vehicles operate on the borderline between the sky and sea, offering the speed of an aircraft coupled with better operating economics and the ability to operate pretty much anywhere on the world's waterways.

WIGE vehicles by various design bureaus are covered, including the Orlyonok, the only ekranoplan to see squadron service, the Loon and the KM, or Caspian Sea Monster.

Softback, 280 x 215 mm, 128 pages 150 b/w and colour photos, plus dwgs
1 85780 146 6 **£18.99/US $27.95**

Red Star Volume 9
TUPOLEV Tu-160 BLACKJACK
Russia's Answer to the B-1

Yefim Gordon

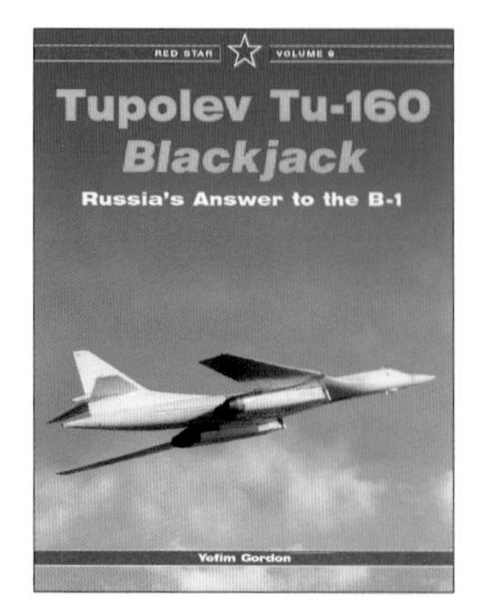

How the Soviet Union's most potent strategic bomber was designed, built and put into service. Comparison is made between the Tu-160 and the Sukhoi T-4 ('aircraft 100', a bomber which was ahead of its time), the variable-geometry 'aircraft 200' – and the Myasishchev M-18 and M-20.

Included are copies of original factory drawings of the Tu-160, M-18, M-20 and several other intriguing projects. Richly illustrated in colour, many shots taken at Engels.

Sbk, 280 x 215 mm, 128pp, 193 col & b/w photos, dwgs, colour side views
1 85780 147 4 **£18.99/US $27.95**

Red Star Volume 10
LAVOCHKIN'S PISTON-ENGINED FIGHTERS

Yefim Gordon

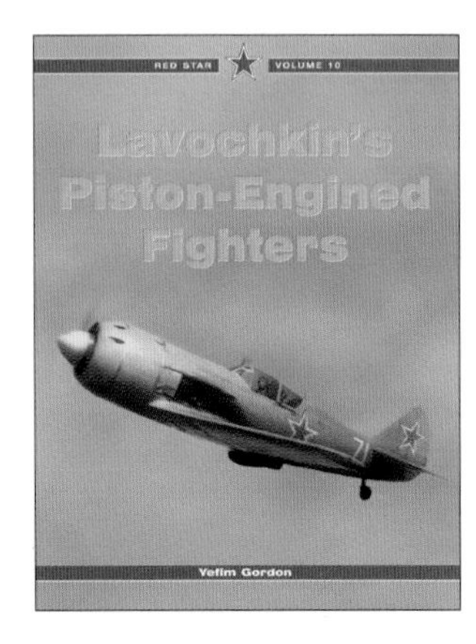

Covers the formation and early years of OKB-301, the design bureau created by Lavochkin, Gorbunov and Goodkov, shortly before the Great Patriotic War.

It describes all of their piston-engined fighters starting with the LaGG-3 and continues with the legendary La-5 and La-7. Concluding chapters deal with the La-9 and La-11, which saw combat in China and Korea in the 1940/50s.

Illustrated with numerous rare and previously unpublished photos drawn from Russian military archives.

Sbk, 280 x 215 mm, 144pp, 274 b/w & 10 col photos, 9pp col views, plus dwgs
1 85780 151 2 **£19.99/US $32.95**

Red Star Volume 11
MYASISHCHEV M-4 and 3M
The First Soviet Strategic Jet Bomber

Yefim Gordon

The story of the Soviet Union's first intercontinental jet bomber, the Soviet answer to the Boeing B-52. The new bomber had many innovative features (including a bicycle landing gear) and was created within an unprecedentedly short period of just one year; observers were stunned when the aircraft was formally unveiled at the 1953 May Day parade. The M-4 and the much-improved 3M remained in service for 40 years.

Softback, 280 x 215 mm, 128 pages, 185 b/w, 14pp of colour photographs, plus line drawings
1 85780 152 0 **£18.99/US $29.95**

Red Star Volume 12
ANTONOV'S TURBOPROP TWINS – An-24/26/30/32

Yefim Gordon

The twin-turboprop An-24 was designed in the late 1950s and was produced by three Soviet aircraft factories; many remain in operation.

The An-24 airliner evolved first into the 'quick fix' An-24T and then into the An-26. This paved the way for the 'hot and high' An-32 and the 'big head' An-30, the latter for aerial photography.

This book lists all known operators of Antonov's twin-turboprop family around the world.

Softback, 280 x 215 mm, 128 pages 175 b/w and 28 colour photographs, plus line drawings
1 85780 153 9 **£18.99/US $29.95**

Red Star Volume 13
MIKOYAN'S PISTON-ENGINED FIGHTERS

Yefim Gordon and Keith Dexter

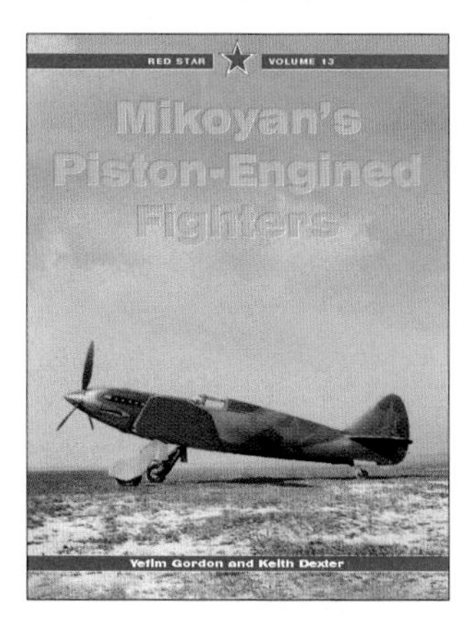

Describes the early history of the famous Mikoyan OKB and the aircraft that were developed. The first was the I-200 of 1940 which entered limited production in 1941 as the MiG-1 and was developed into the MiG-3 high-altitude interceptor. Experimental versions covered include the MiG-9, the I-220/225 series and I-230 series. A separate chapter deals with the I-200 (DIS or MiG-5) long-range heavy escort fighter.

Softback, 280 x 215 mm, 128 pages 195 b/w photos, 6pp of colour artwork, 10pp of line drawings.
1 85780 160 1 **£18.99/US $29.95**